Yale French Studies

NUMBER

Corps My[...]
Sacré: Tex[...]
Transfigurations of the
Body from the Middle
Ages to the Seventeenth
Century

Yale French Studies

Françoise Jaouën and Benjamin Semple, *Special editors for this issue*
Alyson Waters, *Managing editor*
Editorial board: Denis Hollier (Chair), Peter Brooks, David Dean, Shoshana Felman, Françoise Jaouën, Christopher Miller, Charles Porter, Dominic Thomas, Richard Watts
Staff: Noah Guynn
Editorial office: 82-90 Wall Street, Room 308.
Mailing address: P.O. Box 208251, New Haven, Connecticut 06520-8251.
Sales and subscription office:
Yale University Press, P.O. Box 209040
New Haven, Connecticut 06520-9040
Published twice annually by Yale University Press

Designed by James J. Johnson and set in Trump Medieval Roman by The Composing Room of Michigan, Inc. Printed in the United States of America by the Vail Ballou Press, Binghamton, N.Y.

ISSN 044-0078
ISBN for this issue 0-300-06193-5

**FRANÇOISE JAOUËN
AND BENJAMIN SEMPLE**

Editors' Preface: The Body into Text

From time immemorial, the body has been a central focus of reflection on the relationship between the physical and the sacred, between the flesh and the mind, between the literal and the spiritual. It is, above all else, the site of a tension, of a struggle to reconcile the two antagonistic natures of man. As both the locus and the object of sensual and erotic pleasure, as the site of satisfaction of desire and, in the person of the "other," as the goal of desire, the physical body pervades Western literature, from the Song of Songs to the courtly romance, to the lyric poetry of the Renaissance. Yet the body at the same time participates in the sacred and the mystical and houses them. Holiness dwells within the body—"Thy body is the temple of the Holy Ghost"—and the central sacrament of Christianity—the Eucharist—privileges absorption of and fusion with a god through either the symbolic or the effective ingestion of his corporality—"Take, eat, this is my body."Incarnation, as the founding model for the duality inherent in the body, remains, throughout the early modern period, the ultimate referent. Thus the lesser, imperfect image of its creator, the human body, as both the stigma of the fall and the instrument of redemption, opens up a critical space.

Participating in the divine as well as in the mundane, as an object both to be reviled and exalted, its legitimate place must, time and again, be redefined.

As ineradicable as the Pascalian *figmentum malum*, the body is both the stigma of the fall and yet the vehicle of its own transcendance. It is this aporia which must be maintained, preserved; it is the contra-

YFS 86, *Corps Mystique, Corps Sacré: Textual Transfigurations of the Body from the Middle Ages to the Seventeenth Century,* ed. Françoise Jaouën and Benjamin Semple, © 1994 by Yale University.

diction between the aspirations of the spirit and the necessities of corporeal existence which must somehow be represented. Thus the question—and the difficulty—becomes to find an adequate medium for the representation of what essentially lies beyond the limits of representation. The visual arts have struggled to assign a place of equilibrium between *spiritus* and *anima*, between *colore* and *disegno*, between the idea and its figure, between the spiritual meaning and its literal effect; but the inherent power of painting and sculpture—the ability to convey atemporally the figuration of a concept—is also the potential instrument of their undoing. The image of the sacred is constantly threatened by its powers of fascination, by the unholy attraction of the spectacle. The representation of the virtual sacrality of the body is permanently faced with the danger of deviation. The ecstatic figures of Bernini's Saint Theresa or Mantegna's Saint Sebastian carry with them something other than what they are supposed to represent; Grünewald's Christ does not elicit compassion, but the morbid attraction of a decaying body. Painted martyrdom may not be the focal point of awe and admiration for the saints' fortitude and religious zeal, but the ambiguous portrayal of the appeal of a tortured body. Non-Christian lore also reflects misgivings about visual representation. Plato's *Meno* evokes the fate of Daedalus's statues, chained for fear they might escape; and from Pygmalion to Zeuxis, myths and legends tell of the potential for disorder and chaos inherent in the work of art, of the threat of the statue coming to life, of the painting fooling nature and becoming more real than reality itself. Plato's banishment of the painter from his Republic and the Judaic prohibition of representation participate in the same apprehension of the powers of the image.

Textual representation operates in this same dichotomous and ambiguous space, though to a lesser degree. Stripped of the image of the body, the text has the potential to escape the fascination the image compels. In the text, the spectacular manifestations of the body—that of the king, the saint, or the hero—become the sign, symbol, or symptom of a greater significance that the recorded, written testimony of its witnesses can give access to, thereby deflating and deflecting the seductive powers of the image. The spectacular can be tamed, rearranged in its proper narrative order. The troubling antagonism of the body can be elevated to the height of a model. The body politic, the corpus of an author, and the body of the text can function as true, unsullied metaphors. The dangers of ambiguity may be averted, while maintaining the tension between the carnal and the spiritual, between the corporeal existence of a body and the sacredness within. This is not to say that the text is a "safe" medium, permanently removed from the concerns of representation and immune to the risks of fascination; the medieval distrust of ekphrasis, or the image in the word, the Renaissance debates over the Horatian dictum (*Ut pictura poesis*) as well as the seventeenth-century controversies over the proper use of figures (the "colors" of discourse), or again the confrontation between profane and sacred eloquence, attest to similar uncertainties. But at least the danger is not a generic component of textual representation. The multiplicity of meanings with which the body is invested make it a site that is at once threatening and exalted, a place of exile and a promised land. It is a locus of temptation and frailty, yet also the very figure of identity, integrity, harmony, and power.

Yet the power assured by the body as model is not without ambiguities of its own, since the violence that can be wrought through representation does not equally affect all the members of the body politic; the "raison d'Etat" may be fully embodied in the "head" or monarch alone; transcendence often obtains to the exclusion of the female body; as a figure of the community, the body may be but a figure of speech, the *terminus ad quem* in which swift retribution, "coups d'Etat," and political repression find their ultimate justification.

From the Middle Ages to the end of the seventeenth century, in hagiography, epic, spiritual autobiography, political treatises, portrayals of the king and queen in history books and memoirs, the sacred body is emblematized and often functions as a model for writing and reading (as, for instance, in Quintilian's notion of organic textuality, or in patristic exegesis of sacred writings). Beyond the simple metaphorization or allegorization of the text as a body, it is the adoption of the sacred body as a model which appears to be a central notion to both the creative process and theoretical investigations during the premodern period. One model in particular plays a key role—the formula of the Eucharist, which exemplifies the fusion between the sacred and the carnal. Transubstantiation effects a paradoxical union of the body with the evanescence of the sacred. The physical is appropriated along with the sacred even as the letter is ingested along with its "spirit." This covenant of literal and spiritual, of corporeal and mystical, is the source and the substance of a meditation on the relations between *res* and *verba*. The sacred body figures the commingling of the human and the divine, the earthly and the transcendental. The figure of the text in the body (the word made flesh) and the body into text (the flesh as word) is used, reformulated, and operates at many levels, crossing the boundaries between genres, centuries, and practices: the model of the Eucharist provides the necessary, "natural" link between the text and the body, and ensures its legitimacy, from the divine powers of the book and the body to the mystical practice of "manducation" or rumination of sacred texts; from Rabelais's bookish "substantifique moelle" to Port-Royal's use of the Eucharist as semantic principle of the effectuation of meaning; from the incarnation of the sacred in the body of the saint become relic or in the body of the sovereign whose touch works miracles to theories of the body politic; from the prohibition of dissection to writings on the diseased body of the king or the State.

This volume explores the manifold aspects of the invocation, creation, and transformation of the mystical or sacred body in texts from the medieval and early-modern periods. If the sacred empowers the body, is the text that inscribes it granted some of its *potentia*? How may the multiple (or unique) body of the king be preserved in writing? How does the sacred or mystical body curb aggression, purge violence, control sexuality, or summon unity? How is this body turned to the benefit of the community, and at what price? Conversely, how is the notion of the individual and of individuality grounded in the body? Can the textual body of a saint—or the written corpus of an author—be considered a relic? And is the body, as the site of both mystical power and corporeal decay, itself a text to be deciphered? Between eating the book and reading the body lies a space where politics, theology, literature, science, philosophy, and religion come together and conflate into questions on the construction of power, the making of the body politic, the transfiguration of the flesh, and the role of texts.

ALAIN BOUREAU

The Sacrality of One's Own Body in the Middle Ages

Man rediscovered his body and the joy of the body during the Renaissance: thus goes a persistent myth which, conversely, creates an image of the Middle Ages as a period when the body and physical pleasures were censured and mortification of the flesh and denial of the senses were promoted. This myth did not, however, stem from a mere historiographical inadvertence; the men of the Renaissance developed it by design. Consider Rabelais's famous pages on the education of Gargantua, on his abandonment of squalor and physical laziness in favor of hygiene and exercise; or consider the success of the precept "mens sana in sano corpore." We must not let the erosion of the meaning of this saying obscure its intent: it does not celebrate the body so much as reduce the body to the status of instrument, and it announces a concept that will be fully developed in Descartes: intellect, or intelligence, constitutes the motivating force of a body whose coarseness and peculiarities must be effaced to permit the proper transmission of the directives of the intellect.[1] The training of muscle and nerve does not proceed from attention paid to the body for its own sake, but from a concern about controlling it; for this reason, Renaissance hygiene corresponds to its exact opposite, the extreme mortification of the flesh that developed during the sixteenth and seventeenth centuries in the Spanish, Italian, or French currents of mysticism with their extravagant and systematic practices of suffering, filth, and self-abasement (St. Peter of Alcántara, St. John of the Cross, St. Charles Borromeo,

---

1. See Gilbert Ryle's famous analysis of Cartesian instrumentalism in *The Concept of Mind* (London: Hutchinson's University Library, 1949).

YFS 86, *Corps Mystique, Corps Sacré: Textual Transfigurations of the Body from the Middle Ages to the Seventeenth Century,* ed. Françoise Jaouën and Benjamin Semple, © 1994 by Yale University.

Louise du Néant). The implicit precept "anima sana in corpore morbo" is the negative counterpart of the humanist adage; it is in no way medieval.

Neither the contemporary prestige of the Renaissance nor its claim to the Greek heritage can be said to be illegitimate: modern "body-building" does indeed find its roots in Greek plasticism or in the cult of exercise during the Renaissance.[2] Yet this aspiration towards a perfect instrumentality of bodies cannot presume to fully actualize human corporeal reality: the hygienic model rejects the singularity, the instability, and the fragility of corporeal man.

I would therefore like to show that, in contrast to this construction of a functional "common body," the Western Middle Ages elaborated the powerful and sacred image of an existential "one's own body" as the sign of the irreducible singularity of the individual. A few years ago, I believed that I had found the traces of this development at the end of the Middle Ages.[3] I inquired into the reasons for the absence of a specific sacrality of the body of Western monarchs. Indeed, what appeared as a sacralization of the royal body—the famous theory of the king's two bodies according to Kantorowicz—stripped all dignity from the natural body, which was destined to decreptitude and infirmity. The body of royalty merely designated an intellectual principle of continuity of sovereignty; it constituted no more than an ephemeral representation of this principle for which a wax effigy, a pattern of behavior, or a statement could have served just as well. Nowhere in the West did the concrete materiality of the sovereign lead to veneration or active adoration. Thaumaturgy, the most tangible sign of the supposed corporeal sacrality of kings, only served as a provisional and subordinate proxy for the liturgical thaumaturgy of the Church.[4] On the other hand, between 1350 and 1550, I perceived the development of a convergence of different trends (in the domain of war, legal sentencing, surgery, mysticism) which ultimately constituted an exaltation of one's own body, of "corporeal ipse-ity"; it was the equivalent of a collective statement that would have declared: "I have a body, whose use I enjoy

2. See Jean-Pierre Baud, *L'affaire de la main volée: Une histoire juridique du corps* (Paris: Editions du Seuil, 1993).

3. Alain Boureau, *Le simple corps du roi. L'impossible sacralité des souverains français. XVème-XVIIIème siècles* (Paris: Editions de Paris, 1988), 43–63.

4. See the analysis presented by Cristiano Grotanelli, "Unzione del re, miracoli regali," in *Gli Occhi di Alessandro. Potero sovrano e sacralità del corpo, da Alessandro Magno a Ceausescu,* ed. Sergio Bertelli and Cristiano Grotanelli (Florence: Il Ponte alle Graze, 1990), 47–76.

as if it were an inalienable possession, untransferable to anyone except God; this body establishes me as a unique subject." I chose as a starting point for my chronology the terrible holocaust that resulted from the Great Plague of 1350, which made man precious and rare.

At present, although I maintain the idea of the sacrality of one's own body in the Middle Ages, I think that my causality and chronology were a bit too recent. I therefore intend to prove, or at least to suggest, that corporeal ipseity depends closely on elements latent in Christian doctrine and vigorously actualized by thirteenth-century scholasticism.

The first latent element of Christianity obviously resides in the Incarnation: God took on a body to save humanity. He thus instituted the sacrality of the ordinary human body (with the exception of sexuality, a point to which I will return) in its growth, in its fragile physiology. It is well known how medieval exegetes were fascinated by the suffering, the tears, the bodily fatigue of Jesus.[5] In the twelfth century, the time of the greatest sensitivity to the humanity of Christ, the Cistercian Aelred of Rievaulx meditated extensively on the fate of Jesus at the age of twelve when he left his parents' home for three days: "Where were you, good Jesus? Who found food or drink for you? Who made your bed? Who took off your shoes? Who comforted your body by anointing and bathing it?"[6] This sweeping appropriation of the body did not happen automatically as the continuing success of Arian or dualist heresies demonstrates; the success of these heresies needs to be considered more as an ongoing refusal of the Incarnation than in the context of a succession of specific theological systems.

Second, the Incarnation established from the outset a fundamental and clear-cut distinction between the body and the flesh: the night before the violent destruction of his flesh, Christ designates the ontological permanence of his body in its manifestation as the Eucharist: "This is my body." The Eucharistic body and the resurrected body, each of them incorruptible, underwrite both the ontological alliance of body and soul and the exclusion of the flesh, which is understood to fill out the body imprecisely but is often either lacking or in excess as opposed to the abstract precision of the body. The distinction between

5. See Piroska Nagy, "Les larmes du Christ," forthcoming in *Médiévales* (1994).

6. Aelred of Rievaulx, *Quand Jésus eut douze ans*, ed. and trans. Anselme Hoste and Joseph Dubois (Paris: Les Editions du Cerf, 1958). [English translations are based on the French translation.] I also refer the reader to my analysis of this text in *L'événement sans fin. Récit et christianisme au Moyen Age* (Paris: Belles Lettres, 1993), 42–44.

body and flesh can easily be seen in the Christian treatment of nocturnal emissions. It was probably John Cassian, in the fifth century, who
began the reflection on wet dreams; in his twenty-second Conference
(Collatio),[7] he analyzes three types of causes of this phenomenon. The
first type results from the direct moral responsibility of the subject: the
man who has misused food or drink must evacuate this surplus which,
during sleep, is passed into his sperm. Second, the Christian who has
allowed a void to invade his meditation must not be surprised if the
most voluptuous images slip into this space; in this case, the will of the
victim seems less implicated, but the technique of mental asceticism
and of meditation ought to prevail. The third cause comes from an act
which is understood to be satanic in the strict sense, producing a discharge that is not linked to morality or to the will: the flesh gives in
without compromising the body.

This opposition between the body for which the soul is responsible
and the flesh which is exposed to diabolical rays reappears during the
sixth century in an entirely different ethical context: the answers given
by Pope Gregory the Great to Augustine, who evangelized England,
after Augustine had asked him about the recommended steps to be
taken for priests who suffered from nocturnal emissions. Gregory repeated the threefold causality of Cassian in a less ascetic vein; the first
two causes of wet dreams procede from two specific moral failings:
drunkenness or bad thoughts during the day. The third cause is no
longer imputed to Satan, but to an insignificant natural aspect of the
body, namely, the flesh operating without the guidance of the soul:
"When such illusion occurs through excess or lack of bodily vigor, it
need not be feared, because it is to be deplored rather as something the
mind has unwittingly suffered than as something it has done."[8] Gregory's text, cited in its entirety by the Venerable Bede, then revived in
the *Decretum* of Gratian, was dispersed and read widely. A concrete
illustration of the principle of detachment of the flesh from the body
appears in the tenth century in the biography of St. Gerald of Aurillac
written by Odo of Cluny. The pious layman, a victim of wet dreams in

7. John Cassian, *Conférences*, ed. and trans. Dom E. Pichery (Paris: Les Editions du
Cerf, 1959), vol. 3, 117–18.
8. Bede, *A History of the English Church and People*, trans. Leo Sherley-Price,
revised R.E. Latham (Harmondsworth, Middlesex, England: Penguin 1968), 82. Latin
text: *Ecclesiastical History of the English People*, ed. B. Colgrave and R.A.B. Mynors
(Oxford: Clarendon Press, 1969), 100. The text was reinserted into Gratian's *Decretum*
(c. 1140), Pars 1, distinctio 6, cap. 1, in *Patrologia Latina*, vol. 187, ed. J.P. Migne (Paris:
Migne, 1855), cols. 39–40.

spite of his great chastity and strict discipline, suffered them without too many pangs of conscience according to Odo: he had his servant prepare a change of clothing and when a wet dream woke him, he washed and changed without calling his servants. Of course, it is not the techniques of hygiene that are important here, but rather Odo's choice of this episode for the hagiographical portrait: this holy man knows how to react without distress to the impersonal superfluity of his flesh by taking care of his body.[9]

The distinction between body and flesh could easily be traced throughout the entire Middle Ages; it will suffice to skip over the scholastic period to examine a somewhat unexpected occurrence of the distinction between body and flesh which bears the stamp of Thomistic thought. This passage is found in the *Hammer of Witches* published in 1485 by the Dominican inquisitors Institoris and Sprenger. This extremely important text, the first coherent treatise on demonology to prove the real (as opposed to the imagined) existence of sorcery, includes an entire portion devoted to theory. The authors, while respecting the strict constraints of the psychological knowledge of the scholastics, take upon themselves the task of explaining the possibility of demonic possession. The causes of demonic possession can no longer be attributed to the rudimentary complex of "inhabitation" developed by early Christianity. Here is one of the mechanisms used to explain possession: the devil can slip into the superfluity of the flesh but not into the body, which is protected by divine guarantee: "[It happens that] a good or bad angel enters into the body, in the same way that we say that God alone is able to enter into the soul, that is, the essence of the soul. But when we speak of an angel, especially a bad angel, entering the body, as in the case of possession, he does not enter within the limits of the essence of the body; for there only God the Creator can enter, who gives being. . . . But the devil is said to enter the body when he effects something about the body: for where he works, there he is, as St. John Damascene says. Now, there, he operates within the limits of the corporeal quantity and within the limits of the es-

9. See A. Poncelet, "La plus ancienne vie de saint Géraud d'Aurillac," *Analecta Bollandiana* 14 (1895): 100–01. I would like to thank Mathias Grässlin for having indicated this text to me. After having written these lines, I discovered that Vito Fumagalli had assembled the same body of texts on wet dreams in his study *Solitudo carnis. Vicende del corpo nel Medioevo* (Bologna: Il Mulino, 1990). Fumagalli draws completely opposite conclusions from these texts from my own. Below, I try to explain the reason for the diametrically opposed interpretations of the relations between the body and the soul in the Middle Ages.

sence of the body. For it is said that the body has two types of limits, in quantity and in essence."[10] This analysis proceeds directly from Thomas Aquinas and results in the distinction within the body of a pure inalienable essence and an organic materiality susceptible to natural variations that leave the corporeal identity of the subject unaffected (the body of Peter can become thinner or older but it remains the body of Peter).

The third latent element in early Christianity that led to the exaltation of one's own body is to be found in the notion of person: from the time of the earliest tentative formulations of Trinitarian theology, it was the event of the Incarnation, of the historicity of the body assumed by God, that necessitated a theory of the distinction between persons. The existence of a divine body, which violated the basic premise of monotheism, required a diversification in the modes of the divinity's manifestation according to a theory of salvation centered on the mystery of the assumption of the human body.

To be sure, the Gospels had not furnished any Trinitarian doctrine and it was only in the third century that Tertullian invoked the word "persona" to indicate the differentiation among the three persons of the Trinity. But in the course of difficult Trinitarian and Christological debates, in the East as well as in the West, the concept of the Trinitarian person developed and was refined in opposition to the serious challenges posed by anti-Trinitarian heresies (Arianism, Sabellianism).[11] At the beginning of the sixth century, Boethius instituted a formula which, in the West, would henceforth make the divine pattern the reference point for the human totality: the person is defined as "the individual substance of a rational nature."[12] This definition invested the human entity with the dignity of the model of Christ and therefore conferred divine legality on the humble union of the body and the soul. It matters little that this formula, extracted from Boethius's extremely difficult small theological treatises, was not always well understood; after a long period of dormancy, in the twelfth century, it was enthusi-

10. Henry Institoris and Jacques Sprenger, *Malleus Maleficarum*, photographic reproduction of the original edition of 1485 or 1486 published without any indication of the place or date, probably in Strasbourg (Göppingen: Kümmerle Verlag, 1991). [The English translation is based on the author's French translation and on that of Reverend Montague Summers, *Malleus Maleficarum* (London: The Pushkin Press, 1951), 53.]

11. See Andrea Milano, *Persona in teologia. Alle origini del significato di persona nel cristianesimo antico* (Naples: Edizione Dehoniane, 1984).

12. Boethius, *Contra Eutychen*, in *The Theological Tractates*, trans. H.F. Stewart, E.K. Rand, S.J. Tester (Cambridge, Massachusetts: Harvard University Press, 1978), 85.

astically received, not only in the many commentaries on Boethius during this "aetas boethiana"[13] but just about everywhere, even in the commentaries on the grammarian Priscian.[14] Boethius's definition was well-suited to the idea Christian anthropology wanted to promote: the individual body (which was in fact the cause of individuation) was fastened to the perfection of the soul.

The actualization of these latent elements of early Christianity was fully realized in scholasticism for many reasons, of which the principal one probably is linked to the threat of dualism. Historiography has always had a tendency to follow the contours of the Church's characterization of heresy in that it interprets the different heresies or religious disputes as a chronological series composed of units that are arranged both serially (each unit falls under the instigation of perverse, lunatic, or ambitious leaders) and cyclically (each heresy is placed under the accursed patronage of a given heresiarch of the past); there has therefore been a tendency to neglect both sociocultural context and genuine elements of continuity. Within the scope of this study, only the elements of continuity are important: the dualism of the Cathars, stripped of its picturesque attire, is the revival of a very ancient dualism, perhaps Arian, perhaps Manichean. Michel Meslin demonstrated that Western Arianism was in fact much less "political" and "ethnic" than had been thought.[15] Texts and documents reveal that Arianism was established before the Germanic invasions of the fifth century; the fragments of this local Arianism clearly show that this dualism reiterated the condemnation of the body and praised ascetic flight from the world. Now, the map of Arian bishoprics and synods from the fourth century corresponds fairly closely to the zone in which the earliest Catharism spread (the Illyria of the Bogomiles, Northern Italy). There is no need to imagine secret traditions maintained in an occult fashion to explain these continuities: dualism seems much more "natural" or spontaneous than Nicene Christianity, with its incarnate God as the guarantor and support of corporeal man. Dualism does not conceal itself in the folds of history; rather it looms constantly on the horizon of Christianity and establishes its inner tension: this is why

13. This expression provided the title for an article by Father Marie Dominique Chenu, reprinted in his *Théologie au XIIème siècle* (Paris: Librairie Philosophique J. Vrin, 1978), 142–58.

14. See, for example, Petrus Helias, *Summa super Priscianum*, ed. Leo Reilly (Toronto: Pontifical Institute of Medieval Studies, 1993), vol. 2, 551.

15. Michel Meslin, *Les Ariens d'Occident* (Paris: Université de Paris, Faculté des Lettres, 1967), 335–430. The map of the earliest diffusion of Arianism is on page 416.

one can reconstruct equally plausible versions of medieval Christianity, at a certain general level, by invoking the formula of contempt for the body or the formula glorifying man as microcosm. The two tendencies are to be found at all times and are in constant conflict. Perhaps it would be more accurate to say that they complement each other dialectically: the chastity of the clergy as a class (a characteristic of the West, let us not forget), modeled on the chastity of Christ, is the basis of the different status of the ecclesiastical community and grounds the power of a class that in theory is chaste as opposed to the mass of the faithful who are legitimately equipped with a body. The gap between the two categories gives rise to many connecting bridges that make the system functional: institutional bridges (the various semi-ecclesiastical forms of lay existence), pastoral and liturgical bridges (strong encouragement of sexual and dietary abstentions, Tobias nights), or even existential bridges: the figure of the unchaste cleric who, by his lack of chastity approaches lay corporeity, is too widespread to stem from isolated instances of weakness. Caroline Bynum has conducted an impressive analysis of this functional complementarity in the realm of the roles of the sexes by showing how the theme of the body in feminine spirituality serves as a foil to priestly acorporeal masculinity although, of course, this distribution of roles does not correspond to any natural predisposition or even to the way in which functions were actually shared.[16] This mechanism probably indicates that the most concrete danger for the Church was much more to be found in the escalation of asceticism and in the spread of dualism than in fleshly excesses, which were quite easily integrated into the pastoral system.

Faced with the vigorous dualism of the twelfth century, the Church found a firm support in the scholastic anthropology of the thirteenth century which actualized the earliest latent elements of Christianity by basing them on a new interpretive system. As Aristotle's works were translated, scholastic psychology developed out of the discovery of hylomorphism, a general theory of the composition of natural creatures, made from a form imposing a structure on matter. Aristotle's treatise *De Anima* applied this principle to the structure of man by positing that "the soul is the substantial form of the body." In fact, this was an enormous but productive misunderstanding, for Aristotle's treatise did not consider the soul to be an eternal principle divinely

16. Caroline Walker Bynum, *Fragmentation and Redemption: Essays on Gender and the Human Body in Medieval Religion* (New York: Zone Books, 1991).

infused with the human substance, but, rather, it was the "psyche" that was a unifying and regulating principle of animate beings. This misunderstanding enjoyed considerable success because, through this play on the word "soul," it provided a firm basis for the fundamental monism of Christianity, which was secured by the doctrine of the Incarnation, but constantly threatened from within by Platonizing interpretations of Augustine and from without by heterodox dualisms. The new doctrine, which reached its full development in Thomas Aquinas, confined the unity of the subject within strict parameters: man does not deviate from the general law of hylomorphic composition, for he exists as a composite of form and matter. This composite is inseparable, for the form is the act of composition; but the case of man presents a major difficulty: the soul, a substantial form, is not produced from any potential inherent in matter but is infused by God. In other words, man would in theory receive being simultaneously from the composite and the soul construed as a spiritual reality antedating the body and surviving it. Thomas must therefore say that the being of the composite participates in the being of the soul. This is not a mere quodlibet, but a strong humanist conviction that animates the anthropology and noetics of Thomism: the intellective soul, the unique substantial form of the human body, proceeds from the divine and participates in it, thus guaranteeing the infallibility of knowledge.[17]

Far from creating a logical obstacle, the double ontological grounding of man (in his soul and in his composite) provides a basis for the principle of cooperation between God and man by means of the operative agencies (intellect, will, and memory). All the intellectual and organic functions of man collaborate in this unity. Error and sin originate in simple accidents, in weaknesses in this anthropological mechanism.

The triumph of Thomism at the beginning of the fourteenth century, after a period of hesitation and criticism at the end of the thirteenth century, guaranteed the widespread transmission of this tribute to the corporeal totality of man. At this point, I could claim to reconcile my first hypothesis concerning the emergence of one's own body in the second half of the fourteenth century with this new hypothesis of a previous doctrinal implantation of the ontological corporeity of man. It would follow that the lay version of corporeal ipseity, which was

17. See E.H. Weber, *La personne humaine au XIIIème siècle* (Paris: Librairie Philosophique J. Vrin, 1991) and A. Boureau, "Droit et théologie au XIIème siècle," *Annales E.S.C.* 6 (1992): 1113–25.

aggressive and insistent, had been integrated into the calmer legacy of Thomas Aquinas.

However, this facile reconciliation is unsatisfactory, for the spheres of reality involved reveal themselves to be too different. Furthermore, it leaves unexplained the disintegration of corporeity during the Renaissance even as Thomism, in spite of the Reformation, maintained for centuries a dominant position in the domain of ecclesiastical Catholicism.

In fact, in spite of the power of the Aristotelo-Thomist model, the unified conception of the person, of the single substantial form, had not completely prevailed in scholastic thought. In the path of this conception appeared new avatars of dualism within the church, among those called the "neo-Augustinians," who were found in large numbers among the Franciscan masters of the University of Paris. They set the radical unity of the soul and the body in opposition to the plurality of substantial forms in man, a composite of diverse levels of organization and animation: thus the composite of soul and body was presented at a higher level as the principle of organization of the level immediately below, which gives matter form, and so on; in man, a rational soul, a sensible soul, and a vegetative soul can therefore coexist. Numerous other hierarchical systems, more or less based on the science of Aristotle, arose in the thirteenth century, from William of Auvergne to Peter John Olivi; all these systems tended to invest the old duality of soul and body with a new rationality. Their success, which guaranteed their triumph over Thomism in the years 1270–1300 and which, later, contaminated the Thomist heritage by injecting it with a dose of duality, can be explained in part by the strength of their objections: the Thomistic system of the person worked admirably well in its application to living, adult, healthy man. On the other hand, it accounted poorly for thresholds, excesses or lackings of the soul with respect to the body. Now, scholasticism, which based itself on the empirical data of the new science, privileged threshold situations: how does one explain the sleepwalker, the crazy person, the child, the body of Christ during the three days separating his death from his resurrection, the soul before the Last Judgement?[18]

The equal power of the two systems of the scholastic person, in

18. See A. Boureau, "Satan et le dormeur: une construction médiévale de l'inconscient," *Chimères* 14 (1991–1992): 41–61 and "Pierre de Jean Olivi et le semi-dormeur. Une élaboration médiévale de l'activité inconsciente," *Nouvelle Revue de Psychanalyse* 48 (1993): 143–50.

which the old struggle between monism and dualism was played out again, could only be resolved by a disastrous compromise, of which one result was the terrible invention of the reality of witchcraft during the fifteenth century. Indeed, the history of scholastic science during its second period (fourteenth and fifteenth centuries) seems to reveal that this science had to confront two conflicting statements:

1. Each man possesses a unique personal identity, ensured by God.
2. Each man possesses two or several personal identities.

The compromise would be stated as follows, by manipulating the quantification:

3. Certain men, in exceptional, supernatural cases, have a double or multiple personal identity.

Henceforth, the Church which, in the late fifteenth century, adhered massively to the idea of sorcery, could integrate the extreme case of a sorceress who, on one hand, had a normal personhood which was therefore, in Thomistic terms, beyond the reach of corporeal possession by the devil; and who, on the other hand, had a satanic personhood. The compromise formula also made it possible to account for the exceptional cases of mysticism or prophecy, two vital activities in these last centuries of the Middle Ages.

The sociopolitical context had prepared for the appearance of this compromise and for these exceptions to the equal ontological dignity of single persons. Indeed, a lot was at stake in the definition of person in regard to the way subjects would be regulated. By dissociating the person from the empirical individual, the "dualist" current of the scholastic episteme allowed for the definition and construction of conditions of access to personhood and, therefore, for the exclusion of nonpersons. On the boundary between theology and law, the notion of irresponsibility and of capacity moved, in the thirteenth and fourteenth centuries, from sacramental theology to canon law and, implicitly, to penal law. The nascent State thus began to describe the conditions which designate the legal subject by excluding the nonlegal subject and then the legal nonsubject. At this juncture, the Roman legacy and the new requirements to possess a given status (as a member of a church, as a citizen) merge. In Roman imperial law, which was subsequently extended into the Civil Code of France, the true subject, the person, is defined patrimonially and agnatically: he is the being who inherits from his father. Now, it is during the scholastic period that certain great transformations took place, arising from complex causes, and linked notably to the status of landed property in the sphere of the great feudal lords. Thus Robert Jacob, through extremely precise research on matrimonial law in northern France, has been able to hypothesize that in the thirteenth century a profound transformation in the mores of commoners occurred; it led to the destruction of the principle of the "conjugal couple" [*ménage*], of the transmission of property between spouses, in favor of agnatic transmission.[19]

I seem to have moved away from the question of one's own body; however, by a surprising paradox, whose steps I have tried to retrace somewhat schematically, it is in fact the notion of person, this ambivalent instrument that could pass from Trinitarian speculation to the domain of the management of collectivities, which ultimately furnished the most decisive support of one's own body against Christian corporeity.

Henceforth, the demand for corporeal ipseity, from the mid-fourteenth century on, seems to be less the natural fulfillment of the Christian tradition of one's own body than a defensive reaction against the encroachments of the Body of the state and, more generally, of the bodies constituted (moral persons, or fictive persons as defined by Pope Innocent IV in the mid-thirteenth century) in opposition to the unique body of the individual. Perhaps it is against this background of conflicts between the two principles that one ought to understand the extreme violence against the other's body seen both in the persecution of witches and in the unthinkable atrocities of the religious wars on both the Catholic and Protestant sides. The impressive documentation assembled by Denis Crouzet testifies to the fury with which the Reformers attacked the bodies of priests, especially their genitals, as if to demonstrate the falsehood of the notion that the clergy were excepted from the sacral principle of the individual body.[20] The act of burning churches after having first removed the relics and the host was also a reduction of true sacrality to the one resurrected body, before Calvinist theology effected the ultimate reduction of the Eucharist to the status of symbol. During this period that saw the coexistence of wartime mutilations and humanist gymnastics, the last struggles were waged between the flesh and the body, between the multiplicity of small

19. Robert Jacob, *Les époux, le seigneur et la cité. Coutume et pratiques des bourgeois et paysans de France du Nord au Moyen Age* (Brussels: Facultés Universitaires Saint Louis, 1990).

20. Denis Crouzet, *Les guerriers de Dieu. La violence au temps des troubles de religion (vers 1525–vers 1610)* (Seyssel: Champ Vallon, 1990).

portable sacralities and the centrality of reverence for the great regular body of the Institution.

Reinhart Koselleck has succeeded in showing how the great fatigue caused by the religious wars led people to keep their religious convictions more to themselves. This in turn was favorable to absolutism.[21] Shortly after people's religious consciousnesses were made uniform in this manner, excessively singular bodies were subjected to discipline, a trend which had already begun during the sixteenth century: the age of French classicism, which rejected the hypothesis of sorcery, also put an end to another religious war, an older and more secret one, which was concerned with the eminent dignity of the unique body. The doubts of judges and inquisitors in the 1620s and 1630s occur during the foundational moment of modern anthropology, the Cartesian *cogito*: a clear consciousness, the hard taskmaster of the instrument of the body, dispelled for a considerable time the idea of a multiple and polyphonic structure of human innerness, rooted in one's own body and in its fantasy of divinity.

—Translated by Benjamin Semple

---

21. Reinhart Koselleck, *Kritik und Krise. Ein Beitrag der Bürgerlichen Welt* (Freiburg: K. Alber, 1959).

KEVIN BROWNLEE

Mélusine's Hybrid Body
and the Poetics of Metamorphosis*

Jean d'Arras's *Roman de Mélusine* (1393) is centered on the identity of
its eponymous heroine, presented as the founding mother of the House
of Lusignan.[1] It is her hybrid status—both inside and outside
history[2]—that allows the figure of Mélusine to lend prestige and authority to the Lusignan lineage, while at the same time legitimizing
the appropriation (by military conquest in 1374) of the fortress of
Lusignan by Jean de Berry, Jean d'Arras's patron, and, along with his
sister, Marie de Bar, the romance's explicitly named dedicatee.[3] This
privileged political status is represented in the text by Mélusine's hybrid body.

* Earlier versions of this essay were presented at the conference "Mélusine at 600"
(University of Massachusetts, Amherst, November 1993) and at the MLA convention
(Toronto, December 1993). I would like to thank Emmanuèle Baumgartner, Don Mad-
dox, and Michèle Perret for stimulating discussions and helpful comments.
    1. For Mélusine's identity as founding mother in anthropological (and comparative
folkloric) terms, see the seminal article by Jacques Le Goff and Emmanuel Le Roy
Ladurie, "Mélusine maternelle et défricheuse," *Annales E.S.C.*, special issue (1973):
587–622.
    2. For Jean d'Arras's manipulation of "historiographic" discourse, see Michèle Per-
ret, "L'invraisemblable vérité. Témoignage fantastique dans deux romans des 14e et 15e
siècles," *Europe* 654 (1983): 25–35.
    3. For the historico-political dimension of Jean's Mélusine and its links to Jean de
Berry, see Laurence Harf-Lancner's magisterial study, *Les fées au moyen âge. Morgane et
Mélusine. La naissance des fées* (Genève: Slatkine, 1984), 170, 176–78, as well as the
"Introduction" to her translation of Coudrette, *Le Roman de Mélusine*, (Paris: GF-
Flammarion, 1993), esp. 30; and Louis Stouff, *Essai sur «Mélusine. Roman du XIVe
siècle par Jean d'Arras»* (Dijon: Auguste Picard, 1930), esp. 89–118. See also Emmanuèle
Baumgartner, "Fiction et histoire: l'épisode chypriote dans la *Mélusine* de Jean d'Arras,"
paper given at the conference "Mélusine at 600."

YFS 86, *Corps Mystique, Corps Sacré: Textual Transfigurations of the Body from the
Middle Ages to the Seventeenth Century,* ed. Françoise Jaouën and Benjamin Semple,
© 1994 by Yale University.

18

In this essay I explore the implication of Mélusine's corporeal hybridity by focusing on the two key narrative moments which stage her metamorphoses. On the one hand, I analyze how these densely patterned and carefully structured sequences function as such, and on the other hand, on how (in effect) they read each other, on how they are linked. These close readings strive to reveal the various discursive components of the composite figure of Mélusine in their dynamic (and unstable) juxtapositions and interrelations. I am particularly concerned with the potent female-gendered categories of the erotic and the "natural"; the courtly and the Christian; the human and the monstrous—and how the text purposefully stages their ultimately unresolvable contradictions. In terms of the topic of the present volume, the figure of Mélusine may be seen as a striking treatment of the problematic relations between the female body and power.

At the same time, it is important to stress at the outset certain broader literary and cultural implications of the notions of hybrid and metamorphosis utilized by Jean d'Arras. For Mélusine functions as a kind of master figure for his discursively and generically hybrid text as a whole. And in this capacity, she also can be seen as a figure for the overtly and problematically hybrid poetics of the late Middle Ages. Both Mélusine the female subject in Jean d'Arras's romance, and that romance as a whole are constructed from—built up out of—radically divergent generic, rhetorical, and narrative components. The final textual result is paradigmatic with regard to fourteenth- and fifteenth-century vernacular poetics in France.[4]

Mélusine is a genealogical hybrid, born of a fairy mother and a human father. And Jean d'Arras's text represents this hybridity as a tension. In corporeal terms, this tension is figured by means of Mélusine's three bodies: 1) a woman's body; 2) a mixed body, half-woman and half-snake; and 3) the body of a flying snake. Mélusine's polycorporality is carefully structured in terms of the romance's plot. Indeed, it may be said to constitute the very basis of the plot. At issue are two different kinds of metamorphosis, each resulting from a different sort of trans-

---

4. See Kevin Brownlee, "Generic Hybrids. 1225: Guillaume de Lorris Writes the First *Roman de la Rose*" in Denis Hollier *et al.*, eds., *A New History of French Literature* (Cambridge, Massachusetts: Harvard University Press, 1989), 88–93; and "The Ideology of Periodization: Auerbach's *Mimesis* (Ch. 10) and the Late Medieval Aesthetic" in Seth Lerer, ed., *Literary History and the Challenge of Philology* (Stanford: Stanford University Press, forthcoming).

gression. At the level of plot, we thus have a kind of transgressive causality, with female corporeal consequences.[5]

First there is the transgression that the human-bodied Mélusine commits against her human father, Elinas: imprisoning him for life in Mt. Brumbloremllion in Northumberland (11–12).[6] The punishment visited upon her by her fairy mother involves Mélusine's first metamorphosis, into a periodic double corporality.[7] This is initially presented indirectly as Presine explains the transformation that her daughter will undergo beginning in the diegetic present and extending for an (as yet) indeterminate time into the diegetic future. The defining terms of this transformation are those of Mélusine's hybridity, whose two constitutive parts are henceforth to be set in a fundamentally unstable, tension-laden relation, which replaces the (now irrevocably lost) progressive resolution of hybridity into unity that would have been Mélusine's fate:

> La vertu du germe de ton pere toy et les autres eust attrait a sa nature humaine, et eussiés esté briefment hors des meurs, nimphes et faees, sans y retourner. Mais desormais je te donne le don que tu seras tous les samedis serpente du nombril en aval. Mais, se tu treuves homme qui te veuille prendre a espouse, que il te convenance que jamais le samedy ne te verra, non qu'il te descuevre, ne ne le die a personne, tu vivras cours naturel comme femme naturelle, et mourras naturelment. . . . Et se tu es dessevree de ton mary, saiches que tu retourneras ou tourment de devant, sans fin, tant que le Hault Juge tendra son siege. [12-13]

> The power of your father's seed would have attracted you and your sisters to its human nature, and you would have been, before too long, definitively detached from the world of nymphs and fairies. Now, how-

5. For the basic structure of Jean's *Mélusine* in terms of the tripartite pattern "rencontre-pacte-transgression," see Harf-Lancner, *Fées*, 156–78. Cf. also Claude Lecouteux, "La structure des légendes mélusiniennes," *Annales E.S.C.* 33 (1978): 294–306; and Guillaume Pillard, "Les thèmes initiatiques dans les romans de Mélusine" in *Mélanges . . . Dontenville* (Paris: Maisonneuve et Larose, 1980), 218–45.

6. All references and citations are from the edition of Louis Stouff, *Mélusine. Roman du XIVe siècle* (Dijon: Imprimerie Bernigaud et Privat, 1932; reprinted, Geneva: Slatkine, 1974). I have consulted with profit the modern French translation by Michèle Perret, *Le Roman de Mélusine ou l'Histoire des Lusignan* (Paris: Stock, 1979). English translations are mine.

7. For metamorphosis as a figure in Jean d'Arras, cf. Sylvie Roblin, "Le sanglier et la serpente: Geoffroy La Grant' Dent dans l'histoire des Lusignan" in Laurence Harf-Lancner, ed., *Métamorphose et bestiaire fantastique au moyen âge* (Paris: Ecole normale supérieure de jeunes filles, 1985), 247–85. Cf. also, in the same collection, Francine Mora-Lebrun, "Métamorphoses dans *Le Paradis de la Reine Sibille*: Des archétypes mythiques aux jeux d'une écriture," 287–315.

ever, I give you the gift that you will become a serpent from your navel down every Saturday. But if you find a man who will marry you with the proviso that he will never look upon you on Saturday, nor reveal your secret, nor tell it to anyone, then you will live out your natural life as a natural woman, and you will die naturally. . . . And if you are betrayed by your husband, know that you will return to your previous torment until the Last Judgement.

The second sequence of transgression and metamorphosis grows directly out of the conditions of the first, which, however, it both reverses and elaborates. Here, it is Mélusine's husband Raimondin who transgresses against her by violating his oath (26; 42) not to see her on Saturday, the oath that had enabled their marriage to occur in accord with the requirements of Mélusine's first metamorphosis.

This transgression takes place in two stages: first visual, and then verbal. In each case the initial impetus comes from outside, rather than originating within Raimondin's own psyche. In each case also, it is a question of a fraternal crime. The two scenes are thus linked by various parallels, at the same time as a dramatic telescoping obtains: the second elaborates and intensifies the first.

The first stage of Raimondin's transgression against Mélusine is introduced by the narrator's intervention: "Alas! Now begins a part of Raimondin's painful sadness" (241). It takes place during a Saturday night visit by his brother, the Count of Forez, who recounts two rumors concerning his sister-in-law's (necessary) absence, one, in fact, false; the other, true: people are saying that Mélusine's hidden Saturday activities involve either illicit sex or an illicit nonhuman identity.

Raimondin reacts to the first (false) rumor: instantly "overcome by rage and jealousy " (241), he uses his phallic sword to penetrate the door behind which Mélusine is concealed. This metaphoric scene of aggressive sexual penetration has a purely visual climax. Furthermore, suspense is built up by a careful deferment of this climax, titillating the reader by withholding the image of Mélusine:

Quant il appercoit l'uis, si tire l'espee et mist la pointe a l'encontre, qui moult estoit dure, et tourne et vire tant qu'il y fist un pertuis; et regarde dedens, et voit Melusigne qui estoit en une grant cuve de marbre, ou il avoit degrez jusques au fons. . . . Et la se baignoit Melusigne en l'estat que vous orrez cy aprez en la vray histoire. [241]

As soon as he saw the door he drew his sword and placed its point against the door's surface, which was very hard, and turned and twisted it until he made a hole; then he looked inside and saw Mélusine who was in a large marble tub with steps down to the bottom. . . . And Mélusine was bathing there in the condition which you will hear recounted hereafter in this true story.

Into this sequence of scopic eroticism at the level of plot is interposed a series of recalls of the basic textual situation which work to break the mimetic illusion: the distancing writerly perspective of the locutionary relationship between narrator and reader; the evocation of "time of reading" ("hereafter") in contradistinction to "time of narrative event"; the explicit recall of the reader's status as reader, whose "metaphoric" gaze is both mediated by and detached from the "literal" gaze of the character Raimondin. This textual self-consciousness is heightened by representing the reader's experience of the text (i.e., the naked body of Mélusine) in an auditory mode ("in the condition which you will hear") which involves a further "disruptive" contrast with the visual erotic mode of the story-line at this climactic moment.

This "disruption" is compounded by an additional—and strategic—double intrusion of textual materiality between the transgressive gaze of the male subject and the visual image of the female object. First there is interposed an authorial rubric, graphically marked and functioning to establish material and interpretive divisions within the body of the text *qua* book. On fol. 130, r°, col. 2 (of Paris, Arsenal BL 234 [3353]) we find "How Raimondin saw Mélusine bathing, through the prodding of his brother the Count of Forez, and how he broke the oath he had sworn to her" (242). In addition, the return to the plot line is introduced by yet another evocation of the extradiegetic literary speech situation, followed by a deliberately repetitive second description of the special physical activities that enable Raimondin to arrive at the (still for the moment deferred) spectacle of Mélusine's naked body: "Here the story says that Raimondin turned and twisted his sword until he had made a hole in the door through which he could see everything inside the room" (242).

It is only at this point that the reader's gaze (following that of Raimondin, but carefully distanced from it) is allowed to see Mélusine's transformed body "directly," i.e., to observe both the body and Raimondin's transgression in gazing upon it:

Et voit Melusigne en la cuve, qui estoit jusques au nombril en figure de femme et pignoit ses cheveulx, et du nombril en aval estoit en forme de la queue d'un serpent, aussi grosse comme une tonne ou on met harenc, et longue durement, et debatoit de sa coue l'eaue tellement qu'elle la faisoit saillir jusques a la voulte de la chambre. [242]

And he saw Mélusine in the tub: from her head to her navel she had the form of a woman and was combing her hair; and from her navel down she had the form of a serpent's tail, as thick as a herring barrel, and very long, and she was splashing her tail in the water so much that she made it shoot up to the ceiling.

The careful preparation for this vision of Mélusine's meta-morphized, hybrid body has created in the reader the anticipation of an erotic spectacle. The scene of the voyeur gazing through a secret per-foration in the door leading to a lady's bath is a stylized generic conven-tion within the context of late fourteenth-century French romance narrative.[8] Perhaps the most significant anterior example from the point of view of Jean d'Arras's *Mélusine* occurs in the key scene of Gerbert de Montreuil's *Roman de la Violette* (ca. 1227–29),[9] in which Gondree, the old serving woman of the heroine Euriaut, plots to pro-vide Lisïart with evidence that the latter can use to demonstrate—falsely—Euriaut's sexual infidelity to Gerart, the romance's hero. Ger-art has foolishly agreed to wager his lands against those of Lisïart depending on the latter's success in seducing Euriaut within a week. In the scene in question, Gondree, after discovering (vv. 574–605) that Euriaut bears a sign (*saing*, 598) on her body whose concealment is the guarantee of her sexual fidelity to Gerart (in a *couvens* ["agreement," 601] between the lovers), proceeds to spy upon her mistress in her bath. The old servant first pierces a hole in the door, then gazes through it:

L'aisié . . .
a lués perchié d'un percheoir;
par la fera son mireoir
a sa damoisiele esgarder . . .
A lués mis son oel au pertruis;
Sa demoisiele esgarde el baing,
Et tantost a coisi le saing,
Et voit sor sa destre mamiele
Une violete nouviele

8. Also see the famous case of Ginevre in Boccaccio's *Decameron* 2.9.
9. See especially the luxury ms. C. (St. Petersburg, Bibl. publ., fr. F.r. XIV, n°3; in which the *Violette* is followed by the *Dit de la Panthere*), written 1400–20. Citations from the *Violette* are from the edition of D.L. Buffum, *Le roman de la violette ou de Gerart de Nevers par Gerbert de Montreuil* (Paris: Champion, 1928). Translations are mine.

Inde paroir sor la car blanke.
La vielle vit cele samblanche,
Molt par li vint a grant merveille. [vv. 637–40, 645–52]

She immediately pierced the door with an awl to make the peephole through which to see her lady . . . then she put her eye to the peephole; she looked at her lady bathing and immediately recognized the sign as she saw on her right breast a fresh violet whose purple was set off against the white flesh. The old woman marveled greatly at this image.

Finally, Gondree has Lisïart repeat her voyeuristic procedure:

La vielle le prent, si l'adreche
Au pertruis qu'elle fait avoit.
Li quens i met son oel et voit
Desor sa destre mamelete
Indoier cele vïolete. [vv. 663–67]

The old woman took him and placed him before the peephole that she had made. The count looked through and saw upon her little right breast the purple hue of the violet.

It is also suggestive, in terms of *Mélusine,* that the treacherous Lisïart in the *Violette*—who causes the betrayal of the heroine's corporeal secret which leads to her separation from her beloved—is the Count of Forez, just like Raimondin's brother in *Mélusine.*

The visual climax of this classic version of the voyeuristic scene in the *Violette* is doubly erotic: Euriaut's semantically overdetermined naked breast, marked by the metonymic sign of her sexual identity.[10] In addition, this intensive, fetichistic, reductive focus on a single ana-tomical detail signifying female sexuality incorporates the conven-tional erotic detail of Euriaut's "white flesh" (650), whose force is heightened by the sensual contrast with the violet birthmark.[11]

By contrast, the transgressive spectacle of Mélusine's body voy-euristically viewed is deeroticized in a way which receives special emphasis because of the generic *horizon d'attente* with which it is introduced. First, her hybrid quality is carefully stressed: she appears

10. Cf. the rose-shaped birthmark on Lïenor's thigh in Jean Renart's *Roman de la Rose.* See Michel Zink, *Roman rose et rose rouge: le Roman de la Rose ou de Guillaume de Dole de Jean Renart* (Paris: Nizet, 1979).

11. Also significant in this regard is the erotic diminutive "mamelete," v. 666. Cf. *Aucassin et Nicolette* 12, where the "mameletes dures" [firm little breasts] of Nicolette function as part of the eroticized description of her body.

as a rhetorical figure, analogous to Dante's Geryon in *Inferno* 17.[12]
Thus the "secondary" nature of the physical manifestation of her composite identity is emphasized: she is not simply half woman and half
serpent, but rather half "in the form of a woman" and half "in the form
of a serpent's tail." Of particular importance in this context is the
comparison of her tail to "a herring barrel." Not only does this metaphor deeroticize Mélusine's composite body, it also transposes that
body abruptly and comically out of the courtly register.[13] She is portrayed not only as a monster, but as a somewhat comical monster. The
playful splashing of the tail heightens this effect.

Within the context of Jean d'Arras's story line, however, the deeroticized revelation of Mélusine's hybrid body to her husband is immediately recuperated in the courtly erotic context. Not only does the
physical spectacle of his wife's half-human, half-fairy identity instan-
taneously convince Raimondin of her innocence of the charges of sexual transgression hypothetically adduced against her by his treacherous brother, the Count of Forez, but this same spectacle gives rise to a
courtly erotic lament by Raimondin for what he believes to be the
irrevocable loss of his lady. His reaction to the sight of Mélusine *qua*
female monster is to bemoan his loss of Mélusine as courtly lady.

At this point in the plot, there is no overt reaction in Raimondin to
Mélusine's corporeal status as hybrid monster, nor to her "existential"
status as fairy. It is as if the text temporarily suppressed any reaction to
this identity as such, deferring its full implications until later.[14]
Rather, Raimondin's extended lament here presents his transgressive
violation of his fairy pact with Mélusine as a courtly *mesfait* against a
courtly *dame*. Particularly important in this construction of Mélusine
are the standard courtly epithets Raimondin uses to refer to her. He
begins by exclaiming: "Hay . . . m'amour, or vous ay je trahie" (242)
[Alas . . . my love, now I have betrayed you]. He goes on to characterize
her to his brother as "la meilleur et la plus loyal dame qui oncques

12. See Teodolinda Barolini, *The Undivine "Comedy": Detheologizing Dante*
(Princeton: Princeton University Press, 1992), 58–79.
13. Cf. the function of herring in the non-courtly food code in Adam de la Halle's *Jeu
de Robin et Marion*. See Kevin Brownlee, "Transformations of the Couple: Genre and
Language in Adam de la Halle's *Jeu de Robin et Marion*," *French Forum* 14 (1989): 419–
33; and Jean Dufournet, "Complexité et ambiguïté du *Jeu de Robin et Marion*: L'ouver-
ture de la pièce et le portrait des paysans" in *Etudes de philologie romane et d'histoire
littéraire offertes à Jules Horrent* (Liège: J.M. d'Heur, N. Cherubini, 1980).
14. Cf. Harf-Lancer, *Fées*, 172–74.

nasquist" (242) [the best and most loyal lady ever born].[15] The "piteous regrets" (243) with which the now bed-ridden Raimondin concludes are dense with courtly constructs, and are rhetorically structured around three standard courtly vocatives: 1) "Haa, Melusigne . . . *dame de qui tout le monde disoit bien*" [Ah, Mélusine . . . lady about whom everyone spoke well]; 2) "Aveugle *Fortune*, dure, sure et amere" [blind Fortune, harsh, certain, bitter]; 3) "Las, ma tres doulce *amie*" [Alas, my very sweet friend]. Both the language and the structure of Raimondin's *complainte* belong to the system of fourteenth-century courtly discourse embodied most authoritatively in Guillaume de Machaut, especially in his *Remede de Fortune*.[16]

The most strikingly characteristic feature of this highly distinctive and highly conventional discourse (clearly perceptible as such to Jean's audience of the 1390s) is the catalogue of courtly and ethical virtues attributed by Raimondin *qua* courtly *amant* to Mélusine *qua* courtly *dame*, lost through his *mesfait:*

> Or ay je perdu beauté, bonté, doulcour, amistié, sens, courtoisie, charité, humilité, toute ma joye, tout mon confort, toute m'esperance, tout mon eur, mon bien, mon pris, ma vaillance, car tant pou d'onneur que Dieu m'avoit prestee me venoit de vous, *ma doulce amour.* [243][17]

> Now I have lost beauty, goodness, sweetness, friendship, judgment, courtliness, charity, humility, all my joy, all my comfort, all my hope, all my happiness, my fortune, my worth, my courage, for the little honor that God had lent to me came from you, my sweet love.

The net effect of Raimondin's reaction is to intensify Mélusine's human side at the very moment that her hybrid corporeal identity has

---

15. This epithet ends with a suggestive comparative evocation of the Virgin Mother, thus activating both Mélusine's maternal and her Christian sides: "après celle qui porta Nostre Createur" (242) [aside from the lady who bore Our Creator].

16. See Kevin Brownlee, *Poetic Identity in Guillaume de Machaut* (Madison: University of Wisconsin Press, 1984), 37–62.

17. It is interesting that this catalogue ends with the statement "J'ay fait le borgne" (243) ["I acted blindly," lit. "I acted like a one-eyed man"], which both evokes the figure of Machaut in the *Voir-Dit,* and suggestively elaborates the thematic network of spying and visual perception/misperception/transgression that looms large in this entire sequence. See Jacqueline Cerquiglini, "Le clerc et le louche: Sociology of an Esthetic," *Poetics Today* 5 (1984): 479–91. See also the subsequent characterization of Fortune in *Mélusine* as "faulse borgne" [false one-eyed woman], as well as Raimondin's earlier attempt to undo his visual violation by closing up the peephole (metaphorically equivalent to attempting to restore virginity): "Il court en sa chambre, et prend la cire d'une vieille lettre qu'il trouva, et en estouppa le pertuis" (242) [he ran to his bedroom, took the wax seal of an old letter that he found there and stopped up the hole with it].

been most graphically presented in the text up until now. The spectacle of Mélusine's monstrous body is juxtaposed to Raimondin's construction of her in poignantly human terms, by means of courtly discursive conventions. At the same time, Mélusine as female fairy monster is deeroticized, while Mélusine as courtly human lady is reeroticized. The culmination of this program occurs after Raimondin's despairing lament, at dawn on Sunday. The retransformed Mélusine enters the couple's bedroom "and she undressed and lay down completely naked next to him" (243).

Within the context of the plot, the naked human female body of Mélusine signals that her second and definitive metamorphosis has not yet taken place, that Raimondin's transgression does not constitute an effective violation of the pact. This is explained by the narrator by way of contrasting Raimondin's incorrect assumption of Mélusine's ignorance of his deed with the reality of her full and complete knowledge: "She knew everything. But because he had not revealed it to anyone, she tolerated his transgression, and gave no sign that she knew" (244). Raimondin's final expression of happy relief is couched in the same conventional courtly terms as his earlier lament: "Par ma foy, m'amie et ma dame, je me sens tous assouagiez de vostre venue" (244) [By my faith, my friend and my lady, I feel entirely healed by your arrival].

The passage as a whole works to heighten the contrast (and the tension) between Mélusine's two bodies. The first direct presentation of her hybrid body calls forth contrastively (by way of "response") a more elaborate and intensive presentation of her human (courtly erotic) body (and identity) than virtually anywhere else in the text before this point. What is given particular emphasis is the bivalent (bidirectional) character of her first metamorphosis.

To sum up: the first—visual—betrayal of Mélusine by Raimondin involves questioning her status as wife. Raimondin's second—verbal—betrayal of Mélusine will involve questioning her status as mother. The first stage of Raimondin's transgression is against the uxorial Mélusine in terms of her sexual conduct. The second will be against the maternal Mélusine in terms of her offspring. Together, they constitute a "full" questioning of her status as *woman*.

Furthermore, the first time, Mélusine's monstrous hybrid body constitutes absolute proof of her sexual, uxorial fidelity, which is, as it were, guaranteed by her (part-)fairy identity and its corporeal manifestation—neither of which are mentioned at all in Raimondin's reaction. The second time, this same hybrid body (remembered by Raimondin in a kind of delayed reaction) will provoke his reproach against Mélusine's maternity, as a function, precisely, of his now explicit articulation of her status as fairy, as monster, as serpent.

The fraternal crime that motivates the second stage of Raimondin's betrayal of Mélusine—the second stage of his violation of his oath to her, which causes her second metamorphosis—is Gieffroy's murder of his brother Fromont. This narrative sequence is initiated by Raimondin's letter to Gieffroy recounting Fromont's decision to enter a monastery, introduced—as was Raimondin's first transgression—by the narrator's intervention, this time more explicit, more elaborate, and more intensely affective: "Alas! He did it in an evil hour. For this was the cause of his very cruel suffering and of the loss of his wife, because of which he never felt joy again, as you will hear" (248).

It is his definitive discovery of Gieffroy's crime that causes Raimondin to condemn and reject Mélusine's identity as a mother, as a fairy, and as a woman. His first articulation of this is private:

> Par la foy que je doy a Dieu, je croy que ce ne soit que fantosme de ceste femme, ne ne croy pas que ja fruit qu'elle ait porté viengne a perfection de bien; elle n'a porté enfant qui n'ait apporté quelque estrange signe sur terre. . . . Et ne vy je leur mere, le samedy que mon frere de Forests m'acointa les males nouvelles, en forme de serpente du nombril en aval? Si fiz, par Dieu. C'est aucune esperite ou c'est toute fantosme ou illusion qui m'a ainsi abusé. [253]

> By the faith I owe God, I think that this woman is nothing but a phantom, and I do not believe that any fruit she has born can grow to perfection. . . . And did I not see their mother, on the Saturday when my brother of Forez brought me the evil tidings, in the form of a serpent from the navel down? Indeed I did, by God. She is some kind of spirit, or else a total phantom or illusion who has thus deceived me.

The immediate narrative cause of the ensuing public articulation of Raimondin's condemnation of Mélusine is the message his barons send to her to come from Nyort to Meurvent in order to comfort her husband. This provokes the third and most elaborate commentary by the narrator:

> Las! Tant mal le firent, car ilz les mirent tous deux en grief tourment et en grief misere. Or commence leur dure departie. Or commence la doulour qui durra a Remond tout son vivant. Or commence la penitence qui durra a Melusigne jusques a la fin du monde. [254]

> Alas! They acted badly, for they plunged both of them into painful

suffering and bitter affliction. Now begins their harsh separation. Now begins Raimondin's pain which will last all his life. Now begins Mélusine's penitance which will last until the end of the world.

Mélusine's opening words to her husband involve a Christian explanation of Gieffroy's crime (and its possible expiation) which echoes Jean d'Arras's prologue in terms of the topos of the inscrutability of God's judgments. Raimondin's fatal response is thus implicitly set up as constituting a sin. This becomes explicit in the careful presentation of Raimondin's reaction, both internally (in psychological-moral terms) and externally (in affective-descriptive terms). He knows that his wife speaks the truth (*voir*) and "according to reason," but he is completely possessed by the sinful emotion of "anger" (*yre*), and rejects his own "natural reason": his actual words are presented by the narrator as spoken in "a very cruel voice" (255).

The final and definitive stage of Raimondin's transgression against Mélusine is his explicit, public, condemnatory articulation of her fairy identity which proceeds in a pseudological chain: 1) her serpentine corporeal status; 2) her illusory, mendacious metaphysical status; 3) her necessarily flawed offspring; 4) the generally diabolical context in which both she and her children operate:

> Hee, tres faulse serpente, par Dieu, ne toy ne tes fais ne sont que fantosme, ne ja hoir que tu ayes porté ne vendra a bon chief en la fin. Comment raront les vies ceulx qui sont ars en grief misere, ne ton filz qui s'estoit renduz au crucefix? Il n'avoit yssu de toy plus de bien que Fromont. Or est destruit par l'art demoniacle, car tous ceulx qui sont forcennez de yre sont ou commandement des princes d'enfer; et par ce fist Gieffroy le grant et horrible et hideux forfait d'ardoir son frere et les moines qui mort ne avoient point desservie. [255]

> Ah, most false serpent, by God, you and your deeds are nothing but phantoms, and no heir whom you have born will come to a good end. How can those who were cruelly burned come back to life, including your son who took holy orders? You bore no child more worthy than Fromont. Now he is dead through demonic art, for all those who are mad with rage are under the power of the princes of hell; and it was in this way the Gieffroy committed the enormous, horrible, and hideous crime of burning his brother and the monks who did not deserve to die.

Even as he speaks these words, however, Raimondin undercuts the judgmental (as opposed to the merely descriptive) aspects of his (thus overtly limited and inadequate) characterization of Mélusine. Two ironic contradictions are built into his condemnation: the assertion of Fromont's goodness undermines the global condemnation of

Mélusine's offspring; the condemnation of Gieffroy's "rage" (*yre*) undermines the validity of Raimondin's own words, since this is the essence of his affective state as he speaks.

This verbal transgression of Raimondin, a literally correct but spiritually inadequate description of Mélusine, will, within the context of the romance's plot, cause her second, and putatively definitive, metamorphosis.

The scene (256–60) that immediately precedes Mélusine's actual physical transformation (260) is perhaps the most dense in the entire book. From a narratological point of view, it both parallels and elaborates Raimondin's monologic reaction to the first (visual) stage of his betrayal of Mélusine, with a significantly more complex dialogic reaction to the second (verbal) stage of this same transgression. At the same time, the discursive situation at his second stage is compounded by the intradiegetic presence of a courtly public audience, as well as by Mélusine's own explicit articulation of the public (and political) consequence of Raimondin's second-stage transgression against her. Mimetically, this scene constitutes the high point of Mélusine's self-representation as a desiring female subject in courtly erotic terms, in other words, as a human female body. Of particular importance to my present reading is the fact that this extreme intensification of Mélusine's human female corporeal identity immediately precedes and thus is strategically juxtaposed with the diegetic moment that most dramatically emphasizes the opposite extreme with regard to her corporeal identity: her metamorphosis into a nonhuman, nonfemale, nonerotic monster—a flying snake.

The scene is structured by a repeated pattern of courtly behavioral and linguistic constructs, in particular, the faint, the embrace, and the stylized amorous vocative. In each case, repetition works to heighten the rhetorical (and the erotic) effect. The initial reactions are paradigmatic: Mélusine faints; Raimondin repents, but this time it is too late, as the narrator explicitly tells us, and as Mélusine's corporeal reaction *qua* courtly lady guarantees intradiegetically. Her ensuing *complainte*—the first direct discourse of the scene—makes explicit her *retrospective* status as desiring subject:

> Haa, Remond. . . . Mal vy oncques ton gent corps, ta facon, ne ta belle figure, mal convoitay ta beauté. . . . Las! Mon amy, or sont noz amours tournees en hayne, noz doulceurs en durté, noz soulaz et noz joyes en larmes et en plours, nostre bon eur en tres dure et infortuneuse pestillence. [256]

Ah, Raimondin. . . . Alas that I ever saw your noble body, your manner, your beautiful face, alas that I desired your beauty. . . . Alas! My friend, now our love has turned to hate, our sweetness to bitterness, our pleasures and our joys to tears and sobs, our happiness to most harsh and luckless pestilence.

Her speech of regret now proceeds to rearticulate the two conflicting components of her hybrid identity from what appears to be the temporal perspective of a definitive—though negative—resolution: first, the human, i.e., her now-lost hypothetical status as "femme naturelle" [natural woman] in an explicitly Christian context; and second, the fairy, presented as a "penance obscure" (256) [dark penance] that is about to be fully and definitively revealed in terms of her body. The scene's first segment closes as Raimondin faints, his corporeal reaction to Mélusine's words concerning the full implications of her hybrid body thus paralleling her initial reaction to his transgressive condemnation of the temporary metamorphosis of her body, whose full significance he had misunderstood.

What ensues is a symmetrical exchange in courtly terms. First, Raimondin asks his wife's pardon, addressing her as "Ma chiere amie, mon bien, mon esperance, mon honneur" (257) [my dear friend, my treasure, my hope, my honor]. Next, Mélusine responds by explaining that her freely granted pardon is subordinate to the divine necessity that ordains her departure, addressing him as "Mon doulz amy" (257) [my sweet friend]. There follows one of the most explicit corporeal erotic moments between the two protagonists in the romance up until now, initiated, significantly, by Mélusine: "Le lieve, et l'embrace et l'acole de ses bras, et s'entrebaisent" (257) [she raised him up, and embraced him and hugged him in her arms and they kissed each other].[18] This erotic reciprocity is now refigured in the courtly gestural register as the third instance of the "faint motif": the two lovers—having each fainted alone in sequence—now faint together, their bodies commingled.

18. The first of these (quite rare) erotic moments had been (at least superficially) initiated by Raimondin as he took leave of Mélusine after their first meeting "en la acoulant moult doulcement, et la baisa tres amoureusement . . . car il estoit ja si sousprins de s'amour que quant qu'elle lui disoit, il lui affermoit toute verité; et il avoit raison, si comme vous orrez ca avant en la vrays histoire" (27) [embracing her most sweetly, and he kissed her lovingly . . . for he was already so smitten by love of her that whatever she said to him he held to be true; and he was right, as you will hear further on in this true story]. Cf. also the nonerotic presentation of their wedding night (42), with the single—but significant—final indirect presentation of the couple in courtly erotic terms: "Tant furent et demourerent les deux amans ou lit que ly soulaux fu levez" [The two lovers remained in bed until the sun rose].

The inscribed courtly audience reacts to this spectacle with an affirmative articulation of the couple's courtly erotic identity, designating them as "ces deux loyaulx amans" [these two faithful lovers]. A discursive shift begins, however, in their ensuing proleptic lament for the loss of Mélusine *qua* political ruler: "La plus vaillant dame qui oncques gouvernast terre" (257) [the bravest lady who ever ruled a state].[19]

Her next speech involves the locutionary stance of ruler—of founding mother—as she sets out a set of prophecies and instructions, initiated by the courtly vocative "Mon doulz amy" (257). Significantly, this speech is preceded by a careful "undoing" of the "lovers' faint motif" which emphasizes Mélusine's dominance as acting subject: it is she who first awakens from the swoon and then both revives and physically raises up her lover. Her prophetic instructions involve a chiastic structure: two positive (maternal) components are framed by two negative ones: first, the House of Lusignan after Raimondin will not hold together; second, the postmetamorphosis Mélusine will continue—indirectly—to take care of Raimondin himself during his lifetime; third, this same postmetamorphosis Mélusine will intervene directly—i.e., "en forme femmenine" (258) [in the form of a woman]—to take care of her two youngest children; fourth, her eighth child, Eudes/Horrible, must be put to death in order to preserve her geopolitical heritage.

There follows the final direct exchange of words between the couple, and the culmination of the courtly erotic status of Mélusine's human body. Raimondin, addressing her as "ma doulce amour" [my sweet love], one last time begs her to remain; Mélusine, addressing him as "mon doulz amy," again explains the necessary subordination of her own desire to stay with him to the will of God. Her rearticulation of this divine necessity leads—as it had the first time—to the second and final erotic embrace between the lovers, again initiated by Mélusine: "And then, having said these words, Mélusine went to embrace and kiss him most tenderly" (258).

Her ensuing definitive farewell rewrites in a positive future mode the negative past evocation of Mélusine's erotic appreciation of Raimondin's body that had opened the scene (256, ¶2): "Adieu, mon tres doulz amy, mon bien, mon cuer et toute ma joye. Et saches encore que,

19. Cf. Harf-Lancner's discussion of this scene in *Fées*, and in particular, of how Jean d'Arras here inflects "the folkloric model yet again in a way favorable to Mélusine. The same concern to give a pure and reassuring image to the Lusignans' ancestor, in spite of her serpentine metamorphosis, may be seen in Mélusine's final speech" (175).

tant comme tu vivras, j'auray toujours recreacion en toy veoir" (258–59) [Farewell, my most sweet friend, my treasure, my heart and my entire joy. And know that for as long as you live I will always take pleasure in seeing you]. Mélusine as female (courtly) desiring subject is thus definitively established in the text at the very moment of her disappearance in this capacity. All of this functions, of course, as part of the romance's larger program of valorizing Mélusine by "neutralizing" the threat of her female erotic desire; and, most particularly, within the context of her fairy identity. She is thus consistently presented as neither a succubus, nor an undine.[20] Mélusine's final words to Raimondin in this context reaffirm her "safely" double erotic status. While she will continue to gaze upon him with the eyes of female desire, he will be protected by virtue of not being able to reciprocate, due to her impending metamorphosis: "But once I have departed from here you will never see me in the form of a woman" (259).

The end of the reciprocal farewell scene between Mélusine and Raimondin is signaled as she changes her physical location, moving to a window sill—an intermediate space which isolates her both from Raimondin and the assembled courtly multitude. It is from this liminal space that Mélusine will deliver the last (and qualitatively different) part of her final speech, already, as it were, half-way between her human and her serpentine form, as she is (within the stylized spatial configuration of the scene) half-way between the floor and the sky. Significantly, Mélusine's jump onto the window sill already involves a proleptic metaphoric corporeal transformation that anticipates (and prepares) the literal metamorphosis that Mélusine is about to undergo: she "jumped up onto one of the windows of the room . . . as lightly as if she were flying and had wings" (259).

Mélusine's final speech in her human body—from the liminal space of the window sill—involves a series of increasingly intense and explicit affirmations of the different aspects of her human identity. First, she speaks as courtly erotic desiring subject, addressing Raimondin (for the penultimate time) as "mon doulz amy," as she gives him a pair of magic, protective rings, in a gesture that is at once amorous and maternal (at once human, as love token, and merveilleux, as magic fairy power). This is, of course, a stylized recall of her first lover's gift to him at the time of their first meeting (27), which simultaneously recalls the various protecting gifts to her children made in the interim.

20. See the typology of female fairies in Jean d'Arras's prologue (3–4).

Next, she speaks as founding mother in geopolitical terms, regretting Lusignan, the domain she has created, in the same erotic terms she had used to characterize her (soon-to-be lost) pleasure in Raimondin's body: "Ah, sweet land, I have had such pleasure and delight in you, and my happiness has been here. . . . Alas! I used to be called its lady" (259). This lament for her positive past political status quickly turns into an anticipatory lament for her contrastively negative future political status, imagined from the perspective of her former subjects reacting to her postmetamorphosis monstrous body: "Those who used to make merry when they saw me will flee from me and will be afraid and terrified when they see me" (259).

At this point, Mélusine addresses these very subjects ("vous . . . tous et toutes") in terms of the two complementary aspects of her human identity: her Christian soul and her human lineage. First, she asks them to pray for her. Then she proceeds to explain her identity in terms of her human genealogy:

> Je vueil bien que vous sachiez qui je sui ne qui fu mon pere, afin que vous ne reprouvez pas a mes enfans qu'ilz soient filz de mauvaise mere, ne de serpente, ne de faee, car je suiz fille au roy Elinas d'Albanie et a la royne Presine, sa femme. [259–60]

> I want you to know who I am and who my father was, so that you will not reproach my children with being the sons of a bad mother or of a serpent or of a fairy, for I am the daughter of King Elinas of Albanie and of Queen Presine, his wife.

Even as her metamorphosis is about to take place, therefore, Mélusine reinscribes herself into her human lineage, between her parents and her children. At the same time, she speaks as a political mother, attempting to protect her heirs. And her verbal strategy here constitutes a specific response to Raimondin's reproaches against her maternal identity, the reproaches that had motivated the verbal transgression of his pact with her (253; 255), which is about to lead to the very metamorphosis she is here preparing for. But this affirmation of Mélusine's human status is simultaneously (for the reader) a reminder of her fundamentally hybrid nature: the daughter of a human father and a fairy mother, both of whom are explicitly named in her genealogical self-description. In addition, her explicit rejection of a maternal identity contaminated by "fairy" and "serpent" components is of course about to be dramatically contradicted by the physical transformation she is on the verge of undergoing.

The final words of farewell from her human body, the discursive

signs of closure for this stage of her polycorporeal life, are addressed to
Raimondin. Her final vocative, "Adieu, mon amy" (260) [farewell, my
friend] constitutes a discursive frame with the opening vocative of the
concluding section of her speech ("mon doulz amy," 259), at the same
time establishing a parallel with the opening and closing vocatives of
the first part of that speech ("Haa, Remond. . . . Adieu, mon tres doulz
amy," 256, 258 [farewell, my most sweet friend]). In addition, this final
vocative definitively reemphasizes her status as courtly lady, as wife;
while the final instructions that follow reemphasize her status as political mother.

The elaborate and "extreme" establishment of Mélusine's identity
as courtly-erotic, human-maternal in the farewell scene sets up a striking contrast vis-à-vis the ensuing description of her metamorphosis
into a monster. This contrast functions, I suggest, to present Mélusine
even at the moment of her transformation as still fundamentally hybrid. A series of other rhetorical, mimetic, and structural devices work
to elaborate this presentation. The point of departure is the brilliantly
Ovidian touch in which the physical sign marking the place of
Mélusine's metamorphosis into a flying snake is the last mark of her
corporeal identity as a walking woman:

> Et lors fist un moult douloureux plaint et un moult grief souspir, puis
> sault en l'air, et laisse la fenestre, et trespasse le vergier. Et lors se mue
> en une serpente grant et grosse et longue de la longueur de XV. piez. Et
> sachiez que la pierre sur quoy elle passa a la fenestre y est encores, et y
> est la fourme du pié toute escripte. [260]

> And then she groaned most mournfully and sighed most painfully, then
> she jumped into the air, and left the window and crossed the orchard.
> And then she was transformed into a great serpent, fifteen feet long.
> And know that the stone window sill from which she left is still there,
> with her footprint inscribed upon it.[21]

The process of metamorphosis is thus contrastively linked with
(and guaranteed by, in pseudohistorical terms) the stasis of the foot-
print. The empty trace of the now absent human body points toward
the monstrous presence of the serpentine body, and vice versa.

But in the text of Jean d'Arras, this metamorphosis is not definitive.
First of all, the narrator immediately characterizes the snake as itself a
hybrid by the use of phrases such as "the lady, in the form of a serpent"

21. See Harf-Lancner, *Fées*, on the suggestively unstable iconography of Mélusine's
metamorphosis found in different mss: "since from one manuscript to another the form
of the fairy as she flies away can be that of a serpent, a dragon, or a siren" (166–67).

and "Mélusine in the form of a serpent" (260).[22] Secondly, there is the overtly hybrid combination of Mélusine's serpentine body with her still-human voice.[23] As she flies around the towers of Lusignan she "se lamentoit de voix femmenine" (260) [laments with a woman's voice], to the consternation of the local inhabitants who "voient la figure d'une serpente et oyent la voix d'une dame qui yssoit de lui" (260–61) [saw the form of a serpent and heard the voice of a lady issuing from it]. Finally, Mélusine's metamorphosis is quickly revealed to be bivalent, i.e., she is able to turn back into a woman, to reattain her human body, under various sets of circumstances.

The first of these involves her maternal obligations to her two youngest children, Remonnet and Thierry, while explicitly excluding her husband:

> Melusigne venoit tous les soirs visiter ses enfans, et les tenoit au feu, et les aisoit de tout son povoir; et la veoient bien les nourices, qui mot n'osoient dire. . . . Mais quant Remond scot par les norrices que Melusigne venoit visiter ses enfans tous les soirs, si lui alega moult sa doulour pour l'esperance qu'il ot d'encore recouvrer et ravoir Melusigne. Mais pour neant y pense, car jamais il ne la rara, ne ne la verra en figure femmenine, combien que pluseurs lui ayent depuis veue. [261–62]

> Mélusine came every evening to visit her children, holding them by the fire and taking care of them as well as she could. . . . But when Raimondin learned from the wet nurse that Mélusine came to visit her children every evening, his pain was much assuaged by the hope that he could recover her. But his thoughts were in vain, nor would he ever recover her, nor see her in the form of a woman, although others have since seen her like this.[24]

22. This recalls the overtly "figurative" language used to describe Mélusine's explicitly hybrid body in the bath as viewed transgressively by Raimondin (242).
23. Cf. the initial female voice/body dichotomy, positively—and erotically— deployed in Elinas's first encounter with Presine (5–7).
24. Mélusine's serpentine body is again presented in contrastive combination with her human voice when she reappears at Lusignan to announce Raimondin's death: "La serpente se monstra sur les murs, si que tous la povoient veoir, et ala tout autour par trois foiz. Et puis se mist sur la Tour Poictevine, et la faisoit si griefz plains et si griefs souspirs qu'il sembloit proprement a ceulx qui la estoient que ce feust la voix de une dame, et si estoit ce, si comme dist l'ystoire" (288) [the serpent appeared on the walls, so that everyone could see her, and she flew around them three times. Then she alighted on the Poitevin Tower where she lamented and sighed so piteously that it seemed to those present that it was a lady's voice, and indeed it was, as the story recounts]. In addition, the narrator again utilizes "figurative" language which stresses Mélusine's continuing hybrid status: "Fut Melusigne grant espace sur la Tour Poittevine, en guise de serpente" [Mélusine stayed quite some time on the Poitevin Tower, in the form of a serpent]. Mélusine's postmetamorphosis appearances to indicate that the lordship of the chateau is about to change also suggest a sequence that sets up and valorizes Jean de Berry as the final legitimate Lusignan "heir equivalent." See 13, 289, 307–10.

The final key instance of the bivalence of Mélusine's metamorphosis is even more explicit—and serves to link Jean d'Arras's patron to Lusignan, i.e., to Mélusine as history, as subject matter, and as text. Mélusine's hybrid body—with a direct description of her bivalent metamorphosis—reveals itself to announce Jean de Berry's imminent capture of the fortress of Lusignan, in the first, most elaborate, and most spectacular of the sightings of Mélusine adduced by Jean d'Arras as "proof" of her historicity: at the moment of Jean de Berry's siege of Lusignan (1373–74; i.e., approximately 20 years before the writing of the text). Cersuelle (i.e., Creswell), who holds the fortress for the English, is in bed with his mistress Alixandre de Sancerre. There is thus an eyewitness guarantee for the following:

> Il vit, ce disoit il, apparoir, presentement et visiblement, devant son lit une serpente, grande et grosse merveilleusement, et estoit la queue longue de vii. a viii. piez, burlee d'azur et d'argent. . . . Et aloit la serpente, debatant de sa queue sur le lit, sans eulx mal faire. [308]

> He said that he saw appear clearly and visibly before his bed a marvelously large serpent with a tail seven or eight feet long,[25] striped with azure and silver. . . . And the serpent went beating its tail on the bed without causing them any harm.[26]

Alixandre identifies the snake as "the lady of this fortress, she who founded it" (309). What follows is a set of bivalent metamorphoses, marked for historical specificity, as Cersuelle states that:

> Elle se mua en figure de femme aulte et droicte, et estoit vestue d'un gros burel, et ceinte dessoubz les mamelles, et estoit affublee de blans cuevrechiez a la guise du viel temps. En cel estat . . . elle s'en ala asseoir sur le banc au feu, l'une heure le viaire devers le lit et le doz au feu, si que ilz povoient tout a plain veoir sa face, et bien leur sembloit qu'elle avoit esté mout belle, et l'autre heure retournoit le visaige devers le feu, et gueres de temps ne se tenoit en un moment. . . . Lors se transfigura en guise de serpente comme devant, et s'en ala debatant de sa queue autour du lit et sur leurs piez, sans nul mal faire, et puis dist qu'elle se party, et la perdy si soubdainement qu'il ne scot oncques par ou. [309]

> She transformed herself into the shape of a woman, tall and well-carried, dressed in coarse freize, belted under the breasts, and she wore

---

25. Worth noting is the variable length of Mélusine's tail ("15 feet" [280]), as well as the tail's status as coat of arms (289).

26. Cf. the serpentine metamorphosis of Cadmus and Harmonia in *Ovide moralisé. Poème du quatorzième siècle*, ed. C. de Boer (Weisbaden: Martin Sändig, 1966), 4.5116–5381 (*Met.* 4.563–606), especially v. 5192, "ne n'orent talent de mal faire" [they had no desire to do any harm].

white head gear in the style of days gone by. In this condition . . . she took a seat in front of the fire. Sometimes she turned her head toward the bed with her back to the fire, so that they could plainly see her face, and it seemed to them that she had been very beautiful; sometimes she turned her face back towards the fire; and she did not long remain in the same position. . . . Then she transformed herself into the shape of a serpent as before, and started beating her tail about the bed and upon their feet, without doing them any harm. Then Creswell said that she left, disappearing from his sight so suddenly that he had no idea where she had gone.

Our final image of Mélusine's body thus spectacularly recapitulates the double nature that has been her defining feature from the beginning of Jean d'Arras's narrative. She is first two natures in one body, then a hybrid body, and finally, two alternating bodies. What remains problematically constant is her hybridity as a female figure of power. It is, I think, no exaggeration to speak of her body as a kind of secularized female version of metamorphosis that evokes—contrastively but powerfully—the Incarnation. Both the spiritual glosses of the *Ovide moralisé* and the Dantean use of the Griffin as hybrid animal body to represent Christ's double nature in *Purgatorio* 31 are highly relevant here in terms of how Mélusine must be read in a fourteenth-century literary and political context.

Jean d'Arras's Mélusine is a discursive composite—a figure constructed out of a set of discourses in unstable contrast with each other: fairy-monstrous, courtly-erotic, maternal, political-foundational, Christian. This discursive hybridity, of course, makes Mélusine a figure for Jean d'Arras's text as a whole: a hybrid mixture of the discourses of *conte de fée*, courtly romance, crusade-epic, political historiography, travelogue/pilgrimage, popular theology, Hundred-Years-War propaganda. And in Jean's text, as in the figure of Mélusine, this hybridity remains polymorphic to the end. Her final metamorphosis is not definitive, but open-ended. And as such, it serves to illustrate (to "embody") a particularly fourteenth-century poetics—and politics—of hybridization.

ALAIN CANTILLON

Corpus Pascalis

Le fragment pascalien est une eucharistie textuelle

—LOUIS MARIN[1]

Linked to countless editorial undertakings, scholarly studies have, since the beginning (that is, since 1669–70), established inextricable relations between Pascal's sickness and his ways of writing and composing his apology of the Christian religion, and, more broadly, between his body and the traces of writing found after his death. Before going any further, I will give a single example of this intricate network, an excerpt from the preface, written by Jean Guitton, to the commemorative *Manuscrit des Pensées de Pascal*, a facsimile of the autographic fragments of the *Pensées*, published in 1962 "under the auspices . . . of the National Committee for the celebration of the third centennial of Pascal's death."[2] Guitton first goes back to a time he visibly contemplates as that of the origins:

> In the old days, the faint tremor of the quill or the nib on the parchment was held as a sort of nakedness: it was not preserved. Yet Pascal's family had not consigned to the flames Blaise's papers: . . . the tremor, therefore, had been preserved, as one preserves the bone, the blood, the lock of hair of a martyr.

But he concludes his presentation with a little story which shows how the exchanges between a body and writings can retain their vitality and effectiveness even today:

1. "L'écriture fragmentaire et l'ordre des *Pensées* de Pascal," in *Penser, parler, écrire de Pascal à Perec*, ed. Béatrice Didier and Jacques Neefs (Saint-Denis: P.U.V., Coll. Manuscrits modernes, 1990), 23.
2. *Le manuscrit des Pensées de Pascal* (Paris: Les libraires associés, 1962).

YFS 86, *Corps Mystique, Corps Sacré: Textual Transfigurations of the Body from the Middle Ages to the Seventeenth Century,* ed. Françoise Jaouën and Benjamin Semple, © 1994 by Yale University.

A graphologist, to whom I had shown several pages of this book, made these astute remarks: "The passionate pressure of the bold downstroke and the swift glimpse of the upstroke follow in succession so quickly in these texts that this vibration gives access to Pascal's comportment. His passion, in short, gives impetus to his intelligence; it is the same in his face, where (look closely) the lips and the nostrils draw from the surrounding world impressions which become idealized in the arch of the eyebrows." [*Manuscrit*, 12–15][3]

The *Pensées*, therefore, as long as they are apprehended within their tradition—that is, from the first edition in 1669–70, up until today—, could form a powerful historiographical object for a critique of the notion of *corpus*. What is meant by the *corpus* of an author? What is a body of writings? Is there a link between the author's body and his *corpus*?

Of prime importance for establishing the tradition of Pascal's *Pensées* is the series of editions known as the "Port-Royal editions." The book is indeed a series of books (new editions, reprints, editions, counterfeits)—reflecting various states of rewriting of the papers found after Pascal's death, opening with a *Preface*, and with numerous "approbations," followed by a *Life of Monsieur Pascal written by Madame Périer his sister* after 1684, and to which were thereafter appended several discourses which I will not discuss here. This is the only book which was available until 1776; it could still be found in numerous private libraries in 1842, when Victor Cousin successfully argued that a new book was needed. Pascal's writings and the narrative of his life are so entwined that the renewal of Pascal's *Pensées* at the end of the eighteenth century was done jointly with a reworking of the biographical presentation.[4] Today, most editions available in bookstores still include the original *Preface*, and sometimes even the *Life* which, moreover, continues to be considered a reliable source of biographical information.

HERE LIES BLAISE PASCAL

The most famous of Pascal's epitaphs, attributed to one Aimé Proust de Chambourg, was never engraved on his tombstone; it first appeared in

3. I have tried elsewhere to capture the evocative power of a face (Pascal's death mask) for Pascalian piety today. See A. Cantillon, "Un rêve de plâtre," *Poétique* 90 (1992): 187–201.

4. In 1776, *Eloge et Pensées de Pascal*, anonymous [Condorcet]; in 1779, in the first edition of Pascal's *Oeuvres*, anonymous [Bossut], the *Pensées* are preceded by a *Discours sur la vie et les oeuvres de Blaise Pascal*.

1662 as a separate pamphlet, and was later included in the book of
Pensées, not in 1669–70, but only from 1684 on, along with the *Life*;[5]
in these editions, it is followed by an ambiguous passage:

> Monsieur Pascall is bury'd at Paris in St Stephen's of The Mount, being
> the Parish wherein he lived, behind the great Altar, [near the Chapel of
> the Virgin], on the right Hand, near the Corner of the Pillar of the same
> Chapel; The Epitaph is on the Ground, but obliterated.[6]

There is a subtle equivocation at play here, in the qualities of an article: "*the* great altar," "*the* chapel of the Virgin," "*the* epitaph." This
epitaph is unlike any other, it is determined with precision, not in
relation to a specific location (as the great altar and the chapel of the
Virgin are determined by St Etienne du Mont) but as belonging to the
person it commemorates. However, the position of this paragraph in
the book, immediately following an epitaph, leads to a confusion between typographical and epigraphical epitaphs: the epitaph is that of
Pascal in the church and that of Pascal in the book. And it is the
obliteration of one by the other that allows the substitution, since the
former can no longer be verified. The obliteration of the epigraphical
epitaph allows it to be replaced, superseded, by the typographical epitaph. There is an epitaph which cannot be obliterated, which is multi-
plied and disseminated, and reproduced from one book to the next; as a
book which cannot disappear from the earth, it is a tomb, another
grave, the true one. If we take the words at face value, it is clearly the
book which is called *tumulus*, and which is designated by *hic*:

Nobilissimi Scutarii Blasii Pascalis Tumulus

D.O.M.

Blasius Pascalis Scutarius Nobilis

Hic jacet

5. For the circumstances surrounding the writing and publication of the epitaph, see
Blaise Pascal, *Oeuvres complètes*, ed. Jean Mesnard (Paris: Desclée de Brouwer,
1962-(1992)), vol. 1, 520–531. Hereafter cited as Mesnard.

6. *Monsieur Pascall's Thoughts, Meditations and Prayers, done into English by
Joseph Walker* (London: Jacob Tonson, 1688), 38. The English edition is based on the Port-
Royal edition of 1684, and includes the original "Preface" by Pascal's nephew, Etienne
Périer, and Pascal's "Life" written by his sister, Gilberte Périer. Further references to the
text will be made accordingly, i.e., *Preface, Life,* or *Thoughts*. The English editors, however, have omitted or altered certain passages. When appropriate, corrections have been
made based on the original (French) edition, in this case the *Pensées de Pascal sur la
religion et sur quelques autres sujets* (Edition de Port-Royal), ed. A. Gazier (Paris: Société
française d'imprimerie et de librairie, 1907), hereafter referred to as *Port-Royal*. Modifications will be indicated in brackets. As for the passages initially modified or "censored"
by Port-Royal, they have been translated from Louis Lafuma's edition of the *Pensées*
(Paris: Seuil, Coll. Points, 1962), and appear in italics.—Translator's note

The grave of Blaise Pascal, a splendid gentleman/to God who is very
good, very great/Blaise Pascal, a noble gentleman/Here lies

Let us understand this epitaph literally, let us take this *hic jacet* at its
word—while resisting the easy temptation of the corporeal metaphor.
What is lying there? What is Pascal's body, what is a body whose only
true tomb is a book?

THE DWINDLING BODY

He proved by his Arguments that the Body of Jesus Christ was not made
of the Blood of the Virgin Mary, but of some other matter made on
purpose. [*Life*, 10]

This is the only occurrence of the term "body" [*corps*] in the *Life* as it
was published from 1684 on. Such was the heretical pronouncement of
the poor Sieur de Saint Ange, the first victim of Pascal's zeal. The *Life*
seems to need to say clearly that the body exists, the body whose
matter is blood, and that it existed authentically, once, and that it was
even sanctified by the one who came to incarnate himself in it; thus,
there is a good body, a good usage of the body, the one which Christ
showed us. There are two versions of the *Life*, each distinguished by
significant particularities, although they are both attributed to Gilberte Périer and are judged to be roughly contemporary. The version
published in 1684 is rivaled by another, substantially longer, which
includes a more complete presentation of the *Pensées*, and remained
unpublished until 1908.[7] Whatever story lies behind the relations between these two versions and the reasons for choosing one over the
other, there remains an essential difference, crucial to my argument: in
the version given to the public, the body fades away. In the other, called
here the "second version," following Jean Mesnard, the word "body"
appears twice, referring to Pascal's physical body; these two references
are lacking in the published version. The first occurs in the famous
story of the iron girdle alledgedly worn by Pascal against his bare skin
in order to mortify his flesh with a simple nudge:

And in order to be on guard at all times, he had so to speak voluntarily
incorporated this enemy, which, in pricking his body, kept his mind
alert. [Mesnard, 1, 616]

7. This "second version" may be found in vol. 1 of the Mesnard edition of the
Oeuvres complètes, 603–42.

Then, elsewhere, the word "body" is used again in reference to the frenetic pace of his activities:

> This was not too much for his mind; but his body was unable to with-
> stand it, and so it became the final hardship which ultimately ruined
> his health. [Mesnard, 1, 623]

And yet, we will see that in the *Life of Pascal*, as it became known to the public in 1684, the body is present throughout. But what is this body without a name, what is a body which is not named as such? What vanishes along with the disappearance of the "body" is the dualism created by the division between a body and a spirit hostile to each other. Pascal is, quite simply, a spirit:

> His Genius could not be confin'd quite within those limits . . . and [he]
> told him that he thought 'twas pity to captivate such a Genius any
> longer . . . which is most to be admir'd, that notwithstanding his great
> wit and the Reputation he had gain'd, yet he never was given to any
> Extravagancy . . . and so this Soul, so Great, so Vast. . . . [*Life*, 4, 6, 9]

In its published version, the *Life* leaves no room for utterances which could necessitate a questioning of Pascal and dualism. The second version contains, on the contrary, a passage quite literally borrowed from the famous *Letter writ by Monsieur Pascall upon the Death of this Father* which appeared with the book of *Pensées* as early as 1669–70 with slight variations in chapter 30, "Meditations of Death":

> He would tell us that . . . it would be just to hate [death] then [if we were
> innocent], as it would separate a holy soul from a holy body; but now it
> was just to love it, as it separates a holy soul from an impure body; that
> it would have been just to hate it if it broke the peace between body and
> soul, but not now that it calms the irreconcilable dissension; now that
> it takes from the body the unfortunate liberty of sinning, that it forces
> upon the soul the beatific necessity of only being able to praise God and
> to be with Him in a state of eternal union. [Mesnard, 1, 624–25]

For the true Christian, death is the measure of dualism; it gives dualism its form, for it separates elements which, united, become monstrous—a sainted spirit and an impure body—now that we are no longer innocent, that nature is corrupted, and that the dissension between body and soul is irreconcilable. Only then would the saint's death be just and good, since it appears here that even saints' bodies remain impure till their deaths. Thus circumscribed, this passage opens up an abyss carefully skirted by the published version (which relegates it to the end of the book) in the problematic ensemble of the "Letter"[8]: what about the soul's survival without the body and the nature of bodies after the resurrection? And what then, a few lines down, about the value of the Incarnation, if the body of Christ, the model of the true body, appears so remote from our own?

> He [Pascal] would say that Jesus Christ had loved his life because it was innocent, that he had feared death because, through him, it was striking a body agreeable to God, but that, since it was different in our life, which is a life of sin, we had to strive to hate a life which was contrary to Jesus' own. [Mesnard, 1, 625]

In the *Pensées*, the commingling of body and soul does not adopt the comforting guise of a doctrinal argument; it constitutes a tragic problem, coterminous with the inconceivable nature of man:

> Man is to himself the most prodigious object in nature, for he cannot conceive what a body is, still less what a mind is, and least of all how a body can be united with a spirit. [*Port-Royal* XXII, "Connaissance générale de l'homme," 305]

Among all these inconceivable things, the body itself appears the least mysterious; but the existence of man's body is only possible through its link with the spirit; a body which would be in itself a thinking substance figures as the most inconceivable of all:

> Should anyone maintain that we are simply corporeal, we would be excluded from knowing things even more, since there is nothing so inconceivable as to say that matter knows itself. [*Port-Royal* XXII, "Connaissance générale de l'homme," 304]

There is no separate body, but there is scarcely any union between body and spirit either; as inconceivable as the lack of composition may be, composition in turn is equally inconceivable.

The published *Life* conforms to this critical dualism which begins by pronouncing its judgment against the body. Only the organic functions and the organs of these functions remain of the body:

> And when any would admire the goodness of this Meat, or that, in his presence, he could not bear it, he esteemed it to be sensual, . . . for he

8. Elsewhere in the same chapter of the Port-Royal editions, a passage develops the possibility, in this world and in the present moment, of the sanctity of the body, which is no longer to be considered a "filthy carrion," since "the Holy Spirit dwells in it."

said 'twas a mark of satisfying the Pallate, which was not well. . . . He took care from the time of his Retirement, of what should suffice for his Stomach, after which he appointed how much he would eat, so that whatever Appetite he had, he would not exceed what he had limited; and what aversion soever he had, he would constrain himself to eat his allowance: And being asked the Reason wherefore he would so force himself, he would answer, it was the necessity of his Stomach that he was to satisfie, and not his Appetite. [*Life*, 19]

This dualism—doubly critical since the link it establishes between an impure body and a sainted spirit remains problematic, and since it criticizes dualism as an attempt to unify that which cannot, in larger terms, be unified (the body and the spirit)—manifests itself as a dwindling of the body into organic fragments, which does not dissolve the strange union of body and spirit, but places it in a half-light, thus shading it in a desirable mysteriousness:

God that had put this as well as all other Thoughts in His Mind, was not pleas'd to permit him to finish them, for Reasons unknown to us. [*Life*, 16]

The second version proposes a dualistic explanation of this mystery:

God, who had given him all the genius necessary for such a grand design, did not give him enough health to carry it to its perfection. [Mesnard, 1, 619]

This antagonism between spirit and health deepens the mystery, though it may appear to reveal it. It removes it into the generality of the most incomprehensible—the union between body and spirit—and uncovers the scandal of this incomprehensible union in the paradoxical existence of a predestinate whose destiny is never accomplished. In the second version of the *Life*, which long remained unpublished, all of Pascal's existence could be read as the inconceivable struggle between a sainted spirit and an impure body:

He said the sinning body had to be punished, and punished relentlessly through constant penance, for it was incessantly rebellious to the mind and contradicted all sentiments of salvation. [Mesnard, 1, 625]

The *Lives* tell the story of a progression toward sainthood, through mortification of a body marching toward the grave, and the disappearance of the word "body" leaves us to read the physical dwindling recounted by this *Life*.

A BODY FOR SUFFERING

The body exists and is saved only as the locus of suffering. It is not enough to forsake all pleasures; one must welcome pain, not avoid it; thus the aliments apportioned to the stomach must not depend on taste or distaste; and the famous iron girdle, "incorporated" by Pascal, adds a new organ to the body, specifically for pain. Sickness is that which puts the body in its true place. It prevents the corporeal and fleshly illusion, that illusion which attributes to the body and the flesh an evident and fundamental vitality. A paragraph in the 1684 *Life* describes the morbid bodily torture as it relates both to the victim's placid acceptance and the horrified awe of those around him:

> Among other inconveniences, he had that, that he could not swallow any liquid thing, unless 'twere warm, and not then neither but drop by drop; and . . . the Physicians order'd he should be purged every other day for three Months together; so that he must take all this Physick warmed and drop by drop, which was no small Torture, and grieved them that were about him, yet he never seem'd to repine at it. [*Life*, 12]

Only at the very end of the work, in the last chapter, does the key to such fortitude appear:

> Thou gavest me Health to serve thee, and I have converted it to a profane use, now thou sendest me Sickness to correct me, . . . make me uncapable of enjoying the World . . . that I might enjoy thee only. [*Thoughts* XXXII, "Prayer to desire of God the right use of Sickness," 251]

In the *Life of Jacqueline Pascal*, also written, as tradition has it, by Gilberte, sickness plays an essential role in authentic conversion, not by replacing pleasure and strength by pain and weakness, but by substituting ugliness for beauty:

> She was struck by smallpox, and very nearly died. . . . She was then thirteen years old, and of such advanced mind that she was able to love her own beauty and feel its loss. But she was not troubled by this accident; on the contrary, she considered it a blessing and wrote verse to thank God. [Mesnard, 1, 660]

As for Pascal, his beauty, or his ugliness, are irrelevant; in his *Life*, however, a wariness of female beauty is mentioned twice; not on his account, protected as he is by his "purity," but on account of others, the "young men" and "valets" before whom the beauty of a woman should not even be evoked, and a young woman from the country alone in

Paris—"possessed of Good Features" according to a detail given only in the published version—and whom Pascal will place in the care of a priest (*Life*, 23). One can well imagine what prejudice this may have induced in the mind of a reader of the late seventeenth century, or the following century; first reading through the *Life* to reach the *Pensées*, he was bound to differentiate between the different kinds of beauty given in the fragments on fancy [*agrément*], where a house, a verse, or a woman, without any distinction among them, support general considerations on the judgment of aesthetic taste.[9]

The attitude towards pleasure introduces a similar gap between the *Pensées* and the *Life*. Gradually, Pascal would have succeeded in forsaking sensual pleasures entirely, in exchange for a superlative pleasure, of a different order:

> He settled the manner of his living in this retirement upon those chief Maxims, of denying himself all Pleasures and Superfluities. . . . He spent his whole time in Praying and Reading the Holy Scriptures, and therein took unspeakable Pleasure. [*Life*, 13–14]

The famous fragment on diversion [*divertissement*], however, establishes unequivocally the necessity of the pursuit of pleasure—a pleasure in keeping with the misery of man—and the longing for a sort of lost natural pleasure:

> A Man that has Means sufficient to live if he knew how to keep at home with pleasure, would not go abroad to Sea, nor to a Siege; . . . *And one seeks conversations and the diversion of games only because one does not know how to keep at home with pleasure.* . . . Hence it is Men so much love the noise and bustle of the World; that Imprisonment is esteem'd such a great Affliction. . . . *Hence it is that the pleasure of solitude is incomprehensible.* [*Thoughts*, 164, 165; Lafuma, 77]

But this anthropological assessment of the prominence of pleasure, (italicized in the quote above), which lays on a righteous foundation the substitution of the false pleasures of diversion (in a postlapsarian state) for the true pleasure of self (in a state of innocence), is missing from the chapter "Of the Misery of Man" in the Port-Royal editions:

> A Man that has Means sufficient to live if he knew how to keep at home, would not go abroad to Sea, nor to a Siege; and if one fought only enough to live, one should not much need such dangerous Occupations.

9. *Thoughts* XXXI, "Sundry Meditations," 247.

> Hence it is Men so much love the noise and bustle of the World; that Imprisonment is esteem'd such a great Affliction, and that there are so few Persons capable of enduring Solitude. [*Thoughts*, 164, 165]

Suffering replaces pleasure in the here and now. For the first editors, it appears essential to mark clearly the difference between the author of the *Pensées* and those who believe in the reality of pleasure after the fall:

> A Gentleman does verily think there is something Great and Noble in Hunting; hee'l say, 'tis a Royal Divertisement. It is the same of other things wherein most Men are exercis'd: One imagines there is Something that is Real and Solid in the Objects themselves: One fancies that if they could but attain such an Office, one would afterwards sit down satisfied. [*Thoughts* XXVI, "Of the Misery of Man," 168]

In this world, man can only pursue pleasure without ever reaching it, or experience it as an illusion; therefore, the editors in 1669–70, scrupulous to the extreme, are careful not to use the word in sentences where it might refer to a real pleasure without specifying that, since the fall, we are no longer worthy of it. The presence or absence of a word, "pleasure" in this instance—or "body" in the *Life*—, is not as insignificant as details are sometimes said to be; the whole chapter "Of the Misery of Man" tends to turn the theme of diversion very explicitly into an apology: diversion reveals the boredom it appears to conceal, thereby founding the pursuit of true happiness. In this perspective, the use of a term which can evoke sensuality, the sensitive condition of a body, among other, more spiritual terms—"misfortune," "happiness," "felicity," "beatitude," "misery"—cannot be condoned; even less so the use of the same term both to evoke the ideal condition of man without misery and to describe the daily experience of fallen man. "Pleasure" is a problematic term, an aporetical apex of the commingling of corporeal and material substances:

> What is it that feels Pleasure in us? Is it the Hand? Is it the Arm? Is it the Flesh? Is it the Blood? It will be found 'tis something that is immaterial. [*Thoughts* XXIII, "The Greatness of Man," 148]

The shift from corporeal to immaterial in this way, without logical steps, through a sort of exhaustion of interrogatives after they have touched upon what seems to be the essential element of corporality—blood, the "matter" of the body—transforms the phrase "it will be found" into the mere assertion of a moral imperative taking into account only the necessity to preserve the conjoining of body and soul where precisely one might think that the body alone is at stake.

PHYSICAL BODY AND SCRIPTURAL BODY

Neither pleasure, nor beauty, nor strength, nor health: only suffering, the natural condition and sign of a sainted body, justifies the interest taken in it, to the point of opening it up after death, as revealed by Pascal's autopsy report, which remained unpublished until 1740. Certain phrases of the minutes indicate that a *post mortem* diagnosis of the causes of suffering and death was the ostensible motive for the dissection:

> The stomach and the liver were found to be withered, but it could not be determined whether this state was the cause or the effect of his abdominal pains. . . .
>
> But what was remarkable, to which his death and the last accidents he suffered were particularly attributed, was that there were, inside the skull, opposite the ventricles of the brain, two marks, resembling the trace left by a finger on wax, which were engorged with clotted and corrupted blood which had begun to infect the *dura mater.* [Mesnard, 1, 646]

The greater part of this report is devoted to the skull, deemed "more particular"; it is free of sutures, "which apparently caused the great headaches he suffered all his life." It contains "a prodigious quantity of brain tissue," whose substance is "solid" and "condensed." There is no mention in this very brief report of possible links between these physiological particularities and the singular force of his apologetics.[10] Still, one cannot help but wonder what finger is capable of finding its way into a skull and leaving its impression in the bone as easily as in a piece of wax. All the more so since its action is recent, since the "corrupted" blood—the saint's body would then be a doubly corrupted body—has only "begun" its gangrenous action, as if this finger had come, finally, to put an end to the suffering and the life of this body.

Here we find a paradoxical presence of a body in a book: a body both absent and present, a suffering and mortified body, not even an organ-

10. An interesting parallel may be drawn with Richelieu's own skull and brain, which present characteristics very similar to Pascal's: lack of sutures, exceptional quality of the substance; the autopsy report clearly established a link between the form of a body and the power of a mind. See Christian Jouhaud, *La main de Richelieu, ou le pouvoir cardinal* (Paris: Gallimard, Coll. L'un et l'autre, 1991), 43–47.

ism, but a collection of organs, dispersed, disseminated in a book which gathers it in this condition and gives it to the public, thus transmitting it to posterity, as two "approbations" attest:

> One is obliged to the friends of this Christian philosopher for having offered to the public the precious relics of his spirit . . . remains of a marvelous loftiness . . . Precious remains indeed; and if one may be so bold, honorable relics of an illustrious deceased. [Lafuma, 79]

The bulk of the tumular operation, at the beginning of the *Pensées* series, can be discerned in the manner in which the "approbations" placed at the opening of the first book assert—though not completely— that the relics of a spirit, the remains of thought, are the relics of the deceased, of a corpse, of the body of the deceased. Here again, what is said about Pascal, about his writings, in the book that collects them, echoes chapter 30, "Meditations of Death":

> For we know the Holy Ghost dwells in the Bodies of Saints till the Resurrection, and that they shall be raised by the Power of the Spirit that resides in them to this effect. . . . [It is for this reason that we honor the relics of the dead]. It was upon this account that the Eucharist was heretofore put in the Mouths of the Dead. [*Thoughts*, 230]

It is the Spirit that vitalizes certain bodies in death and revitalizes them beyond death. One can say that the transubstantiation—the word may be too strong, but this is what the first editors are aiming at—of Pascal's body into relics of writing gathered in a book/sepulchre leaves open the mouth of the deceased, offered to the largest audience. The change in corporeal substance is again marked in the painstaking care not to give to the public fragments unintelligible to anyone who would not have "often heard him by Word of Mouth": for his thoughts to be published, the scriptural, typographical mouth, still open and alive, must take the place of the physical mouth, closed by death.

This transubstantiation is effected by the reader's itinerary through the mirror-like structure that links the thresholds of the book and the last chapters. The biographical presentation of an author in a *Preface* and a *Life*, both of which offer as pre-text a relatively large number of excerpts from the *Pensées*, or from reported remarks made by Pascal, first gives us access to the book; the reader exits from the book by traveling through two chapters of autobiographical thoughts—not narratives ("Letter on Death," "Of the right use of Sickness"). We are given, to begin with, words or writings in place of a life, and to conclude, fragments of life in place of thoughts; or rather, for our purpose, Pascal's body raised up through his writings and his speeches, then writings by Pascal attesting to the corporeal misery of man. This reflexive architecture transforms a man into an author, substitutes a book for a grave, replaces one substance by another, a physical body by a scriptural body.

FROM BODY AT WORK TO BODY OF WORK

My concern here is not to show how the *Pensées* have been transmitted to us as Pascal's real body, and not simply as an analogue of this same body; nor is it to show more specifically how the trend toward an alleged return to the so-called original text (i.e., the manuscript) begun in 1842–44 with the editorial and critical work of Victor Cousin and Armand-Prosper Faugères has, while destroying the *Port-Royal* editions, renewed and redoubled the incorporation of writings, the transformation of writings called *Pensées* into the real body of their author.

Let us turn instead to the way in which, for us today, Pascal lies in the book of his *Pensées*. The initial gesture of concealment, of dispersion and dissolution of Pascal's body into a book/shrine, into a written tomb, into a living body, where the Spirit still dwells, now finds its extension in a particular hermeneutic approach which reverses this gesture and tries, in so doing, to uncover what appears to have been hidden: a quest for Pascal's physical body, among the traces he may have left in the scriptural body that remains of him after his death. The printed text is deemed too inauthentic for this purpose, and textual genetics, scrutinizing the autographic manuscripts, seems to reach its very foundation when attempting to reveal Pascal's writing body through the traces of his penmanship left on a few sheets of paper. From 1956 on, the strange design formed by the lines covering one of the pages bearing the famous argument of the "wager," conjures up the condition and posture of a writing body:

> One is struck at first glance by the increasing margin and the progressive elongation of the stroke, as if Pascal, holding the paper with his left hand, had first crossed his other hand over, before drawing it nearer the right side, while inclining his body sideways—just as a man lying half down would do, a sick man reclining on his seat, writing on a paper placed to his right. If page 7 of the manuscript were the result of a sleepless night, the difficulties it raises might appear less insoluble.[11]

11. Georges Brunet, *Le Pari de Pascal* (Paris: Desclée de Brouwer, 1956), 76.

What possible solution could the hypothesis of a night of insomnia bring? It would be hazardous to see in it more than mere circumstance, since granting it a deeper causality would have to be predicated upon another, overly audacious hypothesis: in his normal condition, Pascal would not have written anything so confused. Be that as it may, even if the source of some difficulties is thereby revealed, the problem still remains. For the postures of the Pascalian persona conjured up by the critic do not help in the least with the deciphering of the page, nor its ordering, in contrast with the system of autographic symbols present on the same page and on those surrounding it, of somewhat greater authority in this matter.[12]

The vision thus acquires a stunning degree of precision, especially in the amplifying critique formulated by Henri Gouhier:

> One cannot help thinking: everything looks as if Pascal, while covering these two sheets with his handwriting, did not have any other paper at hand. . . . Indeed, one may very well imagine him, strolling and meditating in a garden or in the country with a writing case clipped to his belt. . . . Yet it does not fit his work habit. The scene calls for an interior setting. But if Pascal is sitting at his table, why this lack of paper? The handwriting on page 3 causes Georges Brunet to retain one image: Pascal in bed, writing in a reclining position. . . . [13] A night of insomnia, he adds: beautiful but doubtful; one would like to be sure; it is impossible to exclude some illness which would explain the daylight setting. The scene . . . but is the singular warranted? Everything looks, let us say now, as if Pascal had been writing the first sheet at his table; then . . . he would have continued in his bed, on a second sheet; finally, still in bed, he would have jotted down notes on these two scraps of paper. . . . As for further speculation . . . were additions and corrections made immediately following the first draft? Did they happen at different times during the same night or the same day? . . . Should this meditation be spread over several days? [249]

What, then, is the beauty of a night of insomnia? Indeed, it might explain, by the auto-graphy, the graphical uncertainty of this page; which in turn might very well be explained by illness; first and foremost, the hypothesis of sleeplessness would establish a link between the pages of the "wager" and those of the *mémorial*—which constitutes a privileged support for Henri Gouhier's *Commentaires*—

12. See the presentation of the sheets "Infini rien" in Georges Brunet's *Le Pari*, as well as Henri Gouhier, *Blaise Pascal. Commentaires* (Paris: Vrin, 1971), and Per Lønning, *Cet effrayant pari* (Paris: Vrin, 1980).

13. Gouhier cites here part of Brunet's text quoted above.

thereby granting existential authority to what then become truly graphical traces. This renewal of a dream, of a fantasy, extended and amplified, takes on the air of an attempt at critical rationalizing: imagination knows no bounds, and some imaginings, such as the strolling Pascal with his writing case, for instance, will be deemed grotesque by a Pascalian scholar, and dismissed as such; on the other hand, some images will be "retained," otherwise the fantasy could not hold sway. One must, however, be wary of their beauty; one would like "to be sure," to reach the certainty of a conviction. But it cannot be, and the attempt at rationalizing, while expatiating on the fanciful musing, reveals the concern for an ever-increasing refinement of the dream, an even higher definition of the image, as evidence of the demands of skepticism over the products of imagination. Criticism proceeds by alternatives: insomnia *or* disease, day *or* night, one scene *or* multiple scenes, until the fantasy is acknowledged for what it is, but controlled by a reflecting authority which puts it in its place and assigns it a positive role in critical thought: "It looks as if." This turn of phrase illuminates the fantasy, as an object placed on a stand for observation is illuminated.

What does reflection make of this fantasy? It does not cancel it; it gives it more amplitude and stability, enabling it to expand its dominion over not a single page, but two whole pages, and to return to the scriptural traces from which the musings had taken flight:

> Should this meditation be spread over several days? No material clue, no change in the ink or pen, for instance, can help us decide. In the absence of specific findings which experts on Pascalian handwriting alone could provide, we will distinguish three layers in the manuscript: The first coincides with an initial time-frame: Pascal, at his table . . . he is writing there the complete synopsis of an exposé. . . .The second coincides with a second time-frame: Pascal, in bed, revises . . . themes insufficiently developed. . . . The third consists of additions . . . for which chronological ordering in relation to the previously written texts is difficult to discern. [Gouhier, 249]

Since the "layers" are determined and identified by criteria which do not refer to the various positions of a physical body in a given place, but to the different stages of the writing process as it progresses, the hypothesis of the manuscript composition could have omitted the corporeal fantasy, especially for the third layer, which is given no specific place in this daydream. The fundamental motive for the musing on the position of the body is the irrepressible sensation that the traces call for it. Thus the first occurrence of the phrase "everything looks as if" does not correspond to a leaning toward a rational discourse of what is imagined; rather, it announces the spontaneous exposition of something that "one can't help thinking," of an image impossible to resist. It is important to note that the "certainty" established by this critical fantasy (the three layers) does not differ in the least from the simple fantasy, and that there is an effortless transition from "it looks as if" to what I would call "and so it is."

We may be offered here a glimpse into the heart of genetic criticism, a desire to see the author at work, to track him in his autographic traces, to ground the body of work by showing that the "fore-text" [*avant-texte*], to use a term coined by Jean Bellemin-Noël,[14] now stands for the author's missing body. The thrust of textual genetics would therefore be, instead of a search for the author through the text, a radical instituting of the *corpus* as a relation between an actual living body and the corpse of its author.

PASCALIAN CORPUS

What lies here, in this series of books, and in these autographic pages, collected under the title *Pensées*, are not writings designated, through the metaphor of the name, as a body lying in a book/grave; nor is it a corpse substituted for another which it would represent, through a real metaphor; it is the actual living body of Pascal dead, that is to say, the only body of Pascal present among the living since his death. Each editor tries to give this body its integrity and its true aspect, blaming his predecessors for having mutilated and disfigured it. We know that this scriptural incorporation is not natural, that it was effected through an early editorial effort, in the published dwindling, oblivion, of Pascal's physical body; and it finds its dialectical prolongation in a hopeless effort to summon Pascal's physical body through his scriptural body, essentially in its autographic form; it is this active relation, and not simply a vague analogical connection, which gradually constituted a *corpus* called the *Pensées*. Obviously, the phrases "literary *corpus*," "author's *corpus*," are often merely metaphorical, and nothing more. As regards the *Pensées*, however, the tradition offers an empirical object where the critical eye can invent a form which may be used as a transcendental model for the notion of "literary *corpus*," ill-defined in most cases.

14. Jean Bellemin-Noël, *Le texte et l'avant-texte* (Paris: Larousse, 1972).

It is significant that this model appears in the study of a tradition linked to Port-Royal. It is well known that the elaboration of a critical theory of the sign in the Port-Royal *Logique*[15] took shape in particular as a long and profound debate on the nature of the consecrating phrase "this is my body," in which Pascal, Arnauld, and Nicole asserted the real efficacy of transubstantiation, against the Reformed Church belief in a mere metaphorical formula. One should not, however, assume that the original editors have applied a Christological model; to imagine an objective structure transcending various subjective intentions, or even a subterranean, unconscious working of this model, is equally unnecessary. It remains that the editors and those around them create the locus for a critique of the body which, as we have seen, came into play, operated, and developed in the 1684 book, thereafter to produce its effects: man's physical body must be reduced to its organic components; but once achieved, when the body demonstrates the ability to welcome suffering, it is no longer a "filthy carrion," but the locus of potential redemption. As a body of suffering, Pascal's physical body deserves to survive after his death, to be inscribed in his scriptural body. The dwindling of Pascal's physical body—but not its suppression—its preservation, instead, as a locus of suffering and sickness initiated a movement of melancholic hermeneutic musings on Pascal's pathetic physical body. The Pascalian *corpus* named *Pensées-de-Pascal* is precisely the continued relation, instituted between 1669 and 1684 and chronically passed on since, between a dead physical body and a live scriptural one. Most likely, a disaffection of Pascal's pathetic body would be the sign, the cause and effect of the extinction of this *corpus* and the disappearance of this scriptural body.

—Translated by Françoise Jaouën

15. On this point, see especially Louis Marin, *La critique du discours* (Paris: Minuit, 1975).

BRIGITTE CAZELLES

Bodies on Stage and the Production of Meaning

The dual connotation of the Latin *sacer* in evoking phenomena that are both "cursed" and "blessed" calls attention to the significance of the sacred as a concept embedded in ambivalence. That the unknown—that is, phenomena that appear to have no rational explanation—has the capacity to arouse fright as well as wonderment indicates that the source of ambivalence lies not in the concept itself so much as in the reactions that it inspires. At the root of the contradictory feelings that are typically provoked by the embodiment of the unordinariness is the effect of generating disturbance among its witnesses, while at the same time inducing them to reaffirm their own communal identity as members of a group that shares the same values and accepts the same natural and social laws.

As a collective experience, therefore, the sacred takes the form of a spectacle targeted on beings and events whose nature belongs to no classifiable category. From the standpoint of the collectivity, such phenomena are deemed dangerous to the extent that, lacking a specific identity, they are therefore enigmatic and unreadable. In the context of a community whose order finds itself threatened by the appearance of individuals who seem to transgress the boundaries of ordinary humanity, what is at stake is the possibility of determining the origin—demonic or divine—of their abnormality and, in the latter case, of "domesticating" their power so as to insure that it will assume a protective function. In that sense, what characterizes the sacred as a collective experience is a mechanism of appropriation whose constitutive properties point to the following paradox: if, on the one hand, an indi-

YFS 86, *Corps Mystique, Corps Sacré: Textual Transfigurations of the Body from the Middle Ages to the Seventeenth Century,* ed. Françoise Jaouën and Benjamin Semple,

vidual is sacralized by virtue of the difference that distinguishes him from ordinary humanity, then it is essential that he retain his unexplainable character; on the other hand, public recognition of his sanctity also entails a process of domestication by means of which the unknown becomes a known quantity. At issue in the collective appropriation of the sacred is thus a problematic normalization of that which is by definition abnormal: how can an unexplainable phenomenon be translated into intelligible terms? Is there a privileged locus guaranteeing that this translation will take place? What kind of representation is involved, and what is the meaning thus produced?

These issues find a preliminary response in the essentially theatricalized character of the sacred understood as a collective reaction to the embodiment of the unknown. Specifically, this paper examines the representation of the sacred in those works whose delivery to their intended public involves performance—regardless of their generic form (narrative or dramatic) and content (religious or secular)—as entailing a spectacle whose focal point is the exposure of the human body at center stage. The "truth" of the script—in the theatrical sense of the word—lies here in a scene of revelation that has both a spectacular component (consistent with the Greek *theatron* as the locus of a visual spectacle) and a speculative one (in reference to the Greek *theoria* as contemplation and meditation). Giving the unknown a corporeal manifestation, the theatricalized representation of the sacred invites its witnesses to act as both viewers and interpreters of a spectacle whose script produces meaning to the extent that its climactic moment translates the unexplainable into flesh, thereby enabling the collectivity to assign meaning to the heretofore unreadable body exposed at center stage, by means of a second translation, that of the flesh into words.

Having identified elsewhere the sacrificial mechanism operative in the somatic imagery that is the trademark of the Old French portrayal of sanctity,[1] I propose here to explore further the effect of this mechanism in implying a theatricalized production of meaning. Three examples, selected on the basis of their variety in terms of medium and dating, will serve as illustrations of the tendency to visualize unexplainable phenomena for purposes of protecting the collectivity and reaffirming its cohesiveness in the face of the unknown. The first two documents under consideration, beginning with the thirteenth-

---

1. Brigitte Cazelles, *Le corps de sainteté. D'après Jehan Bouche d'Or, Jehan Paulus et quelques vies des XIIe et XIIIe siècles* (Geneva: Droz, 1982).

century verse *Vie de Saint Jehan Paulus*,[2] belong to the medieval hagiographic tradition and, as such, provide evidence of a mythical assessment of holiness, one in which the saint's body elicits on the part of its witnesses both a sacralizing and sacrificial interpretation (*mythos*). By contrast, the third example, by virtue of its resolutely scientific conception of the world, suggests the presence of an interpretative discourse grounded on the rational *logos* of humanistic thought, one by which the orchestrator of the spectacle—here, Andreas Vesalius— seeks to decode the enigma of the human body so as to include it in the body of human knowledge.

A specific aspect of the narrative *Vie de Saint Jehan Paulus* is the fact that this thirteenth-century vernacular text has no known Latin antecedent, pointing to its status as a product of imaginative literature. Like many of the Old French hagiographic poems composed during the period, the narration of *Jehan Paulus*, while devotional in content, also relies on strategies borrowed from the courtly tradition, the effect of which is a form of composition that can be described as hagiographic romance.[3]

The climactic scene of the "script"—the exposure of Jehan Paulus's body—takes place in the context of a plot focusing on the familial circumstances that account for the emergence of the hero as saint. Thus the first part of the narrative recounts how the soul of Pope Basile is transported to Hell, where he meets a woman who tells him that she will be delivered from her torments through the intercession of a great-grandson not yet born. On his return to earth, Basile seeks out the grandparents of Jehan Paulus and announces to them that their daughter will bear a son, who will be the agent of his ancestor's deliverance from Hell. When told of his assigned task by his grandmother, Jehan Paulus undertakes his mission of redeemer by abandoning the temporal world and leading a life of isolation in the wilderness. But the devil prompts Jehan to rape and kill the princess of Toulouse. To make amends for this murder, Jehan resumes his eremitic existence in the forest. Several years pass, until the king of Toulouse decides to organize

2. *La Vie de Saint Jehan Paulus*, ed. Louis Allen, in *The German Legends of the Hairy Anchorite*, ed. Charles Allyn William. Illinois Studies in Language and Literature 18 (Urbana, Illinois: University of Illinois Press, 1935), 83–133.

3. See Brigitte Cazelles, *The Lady as Saint: A Collection of French Hagiographic Romances of the Thirteenth Century* (Philadelphia: University of Pennsylvania Press, 1991), 11–21.

a hunting party in the part of the woodlands where Jehan's shelter happens to be located.

The hunting episode is the initial moment in the progressive recognition of Jehan as a saintly protagonist, a process whose successive stages comprise the discovery scene (*Jehan Paulus*, ll. 1590–1656), the exposure scene (ll. 1657–1731), and the revelation scene proper (ll. 1732–2056). In the opening part of the discovery scene, the royal hunting party, undertaking its search of a prey, has circled the forest ("avirone," l. 1605), in vain. Meanwhile, Jehan Paulus is under a tree, on a small elevation, praying. The poet elaborates a dramatic contrast between the saint, who is motionless and silent, and the hunting party, which is a noisy affair. It is, indeed, the barking of the dogs ("noise" and "bruit," l. 1615) that first attracts the hunters to the sacred site. From the perspective of both dogs and huntsmen, the silent, immobile creature on the elevation is an unsettling sight, inspiring their fear; whence the distance observed by the hunting party as it proceeds to surround the sacred site. In the resulting picturelike scene, dogs and hunters stand still, like Jehan; unlike Jehan, however, who does not look at them, dogs and hunters react as spectators and observe ("esgarde," l. 1626: "keep under close guard"), from below, the saint on his elevation. Here, the *spectacular* has a *speculative* function, inducing the hunters to gaze at this wild creature and to wonder about its significance. At this moment in the narrative, the sacred understood as accursed represents that which is untouchable, unnatural, and potentially dangerous.

The decision by one of the observers to approach the wild creature puts an end to this picturelike scene, which becomes animate, as the hunter dismounts, seizes the saint by his hair, and casts him to the ground. This action confirms the significance of the hunting motif in differentiating Jehan, a passive prey, from the king's men, who act as his pursuers. It also generates a transformation in the hunters' view of the sacred. No longer looking at the unidentifiable creature as a potentially threatening force, the hunters appropriate and tame it, thus reaffirming their superiority as human beings in the face of the wilderness. This is confirmed by the behavior of the hunters who, imitating their companion, proceed to examine the creature by turning it this way and that ("de chief en chief," l. 1645). The *spectacular* now takes on an *anatomical* significance, inducing the observers to marvel at the humanlike appearance of the creature (ll. 1647–52). However, Jehan's silence, together with his nakedness and hairiness (hence the title of the Miracle play—mentioned below—as Saint Jehan "le Pelu," or "hairy"), also lead them to conclude that this is not a man, but the embodiment of a unique species.

In contrast to these intratextual witnesses, both the poet and his public are aware of the merit of the "creature" as an exceptional product of God's creation, one whose uniqueness consists of an uncommon capacity to renounce the amenities of worldly life. In amplifying the spectacular at the expense of the spiritual, however, the text also appears to sacralize (that is, to emphasize Jehan's difference in terms of dangerous abnormality), rather than sanctify (that is, stress the exceptional character of his piety), its holy protagonist. In that sense, the textual revelation of Jehan's saintliness, which reenacts the dramatic event of his ostracism, thus transforms its listeners into voyeurs.

The following event, which initiates the second stage of the protagonist's exposure, provides evidence—at least at the intratextual level—of the profanatory character of the circumstances that lead the hunting party to acknowledge Jehan's distinction as an unusual, unnatural, and unique specimen. Anatomical examination, which now focuses on a specific aspect of the wild creature (its private parts, ll. 1677 and 1681), convinces the royal hunters and, soon after, the king himself (l. 1683) that this creature deserves to be brought to the city and displayed in public. The queen's inquiry to the royal messenger ("queus noveles?," l. 1692) testifies to the unusual, novel value of Jehan as prey, as is confirmed by the scene of exposure that takes place in the middle of the palace square. In a gesture invoking the ritual of the breaking of a quarry, the king's men proceed to grab Jehan by his arms and legs (the "four members" evoked at l. 1718) and throw him on the ground. The saint's examination by the hunters in the forest now gives way to his public humiliation, as all the citizens ("clers et lais," l. 1706), including the richly-clothed queen and her ladies (dressed in "vair et ermines," l. 1710) rush to the site and appreciate collectively the spectacle of this naked, defenseless, and ridiculous creature.

Jehan's position at center stage discloses the centrality of space—rather than time—as the privileged element used by the French poet to assess the place and function of self in society. In this spatialized representation of social order, Jehan as he finds himself encircled by the citizenry of Toulouse is the focal point that insures its unanimity. All the surrounding witnesses experience a similar feeling of reassurance in looking at a creature that is both like them and different from them. It is Jehan's difference—his silence and his nakedness—that confirms the cohesiveness of the collectivity, just as it is Jehan's unique position at center stage that delineates, by contrast, the terrain of proper behavior. The staging of Jehan's exposure thus functions as a *trial*, consistent with the etymological meaning of the word "try" in evoking a process of "distinction" and "separation" between good and evil, natural and unnatural, human and inhuman. In the social context of the narrative, the primary beneficiary of Jehan's exposure is the king himself to the extent that the result of his action as supreme hunter, by reaffirming spectacularly the identity of the collectivity as belonging to the human species, also confirms the value of royal rule in insuring the preservation of order.

The role of the king of Toulouse as beneficent center of the intratextual community reflects, it appears, that of the poet himself in contributing, by reenacting Jehan's trial, to the cohesiveness of the extratextual community, that is, the listeners of the performed text. From this resemblance between the witnesses within and without the text emerges a similarly sacrificial perception of social order, disclosing a notion of communal identity defined and experienced in the face of difference and singularity. Yet the hagiographer's intention is clearly not to indict but, on the contrary, to glorify his protagonist, as confirmed, at this moment in the narrative, by the implicit distinction that the text establishes between the admiring stance of the extratextual audience and the persecutive behavior of the intratextual public. Jehan's tormentors, however, are soon given the opportunity to recognize the divine significance of the hero's abnormal appearance, in the course of what constitutes the third and final stage of the exposing of the protagonist.

A dramatic incident initiates the rehabilitation of Jehan as an exception to the norm, pointing, this time, to the blessed rather than cursed value of his singularity. Among the citizens gathered around the creature stands a woman holding her newborn infant, who proceeds to tell Jehan Paulus that God has forgiven him for his crime. The miracle of the talking infant, together with Jehan's miraculous action in resurrecting Sabine, the murdered princess of Toulouse, prompt the public to display their admiration for a creature whom they henceforth venerate as the embodiment of holiness. The former fright inspired by the spectacle of Jehan's body henceforth turns into reverence, eliciting on the part of the intratextual witnesses a series of reactions that stand in radical opposition to those manifested during the initial discovery scene. An example is the assessment of those miraculous events in terms of "les bones noveles" (1. 2001): echoing the earlier appraisal of the wild creature as a novelty worthy of public exposure, the "good news" has, this time, a scriptural connotation, indicating the witnesses' awareness that they are dealing with a Christ-like figure. Another example is the manner in which the identification of Jehan Paulus as a holy man leads to a noisy celebration, as was the case of his discovery by the hunting party; but the soundscape has now a divine rather than predatory significance, as the bells of the city churches begin ringing on their own (l. 1996). Once again, all the citizens— including "clergie" and "chevalerie" (ll. 2025–6), "lais" and "clers" (l. 2031)—gather around Jehan, who thus, once again, occupies the center of the stage ("vient entre aus," l. 2005). This time, however, the protagonist is dressed in rich clothing, as befits the embodiment of the sacred in its blessed dimension.

A noteworthy aspect of this recognition scene is the fact that the spectacular is no longer a matter of *looking* at the saint's body, but of *touching* it, suggesting a treatment of the sacred focusing on the protagonist's corporeal rather than spiritual identity. The intratextual witnesses do not appraise Jehan as an individual entity, but as an object capable of working miracles. Thus, in the last analysis, the recognition scene functions in a manner perfectly similar to the discovery scene. In the forest as in the city, the protagonist is projected at center stage in an effort to dispel—literally, to break the spell of—the sacred. Indeed, the appropriation of Jehan Paulus as a saintly creature by the intratextual public anticipates the eventual fragmentation of his body into relics endowed with curative power. Whether the exposing of Jehan converges on his body as potentially maleficent or as beneficent, the public manifests a similar tendency to treat the sacred as an abnormal phenomenon. In both cases, the staging of the saint's entry into public life takes the form of a "trial," one that seeks to unveil and dissect, and in so doing to exorcize, the elements that account for Jehan Paulus's exceptional nature. The protagonist occupies center stage not because he is reintegrated within society but, to the contrary, because his uniqueness signifies that he has no place within society.

The spatialized representation of social order in this narrative thus elaborates a paradoxical treatment of center and margin. It is because Jehan Paulus becomes the focal point of a public spectacle that he is marginalized; and it is through the dramatic exposing of his difference that the intratextual or extratextual public reaffirms itself as a homogeneous collectivity.

What emerges from this analysis of the climactic moment of the narration of Jehan Paulus is an embodiment of the sacred for purposes of exorcising the fear of the collectivity. In this process of revelation, the saint is recognized as such to the extent that he remains an anomaly. The exposure of his body involves a sacrificial mechanism whose function is to protect the community from the danger of abnormality, as effected by the spectacle of Jehan's difference at center stage. Considering that the themes and motifs constitutive of the Jehan Paulus legend lend themselves to a theatricalized representation of the sacred, the fourteenth-century Miracle play[4] inspired by it should in principle amplify those elements which, in the thirteenth-century poem, articulate a domestication of the sacred involving expulsion and scapegoating.[5] Unlike its narrative counterpart, however, the play stresses the normal rather than abnormal or superhuman appearance of its protagonist, in part because the staging of Jehan Paulus's story increases the hero's proximity with the social realm in its familiar and localized dimension[6]; and in part because the theatrical text minimizes the sacred character of the protagonist as either a wild or a saintly creature.[7] The emphasis is on Jehan's defenselessness against the devil's deceit, leading to the protagonist's presentation as an embodiment of the human condition.[8] Consequently, the attention of

4. "Miracle de saint Jehan le Paulu, hermite," in *Miracles de Nostre Dame par personnages, d'après le manuscrit de la Bibliothèque Nationale* [BN, f. fr., 819–20], ed. Gaston Paris et Ulysse Robert (Paris: Société des Anciens Textes Français, 1876–93, 8 vols.), 1880, vol. 5, 89–151.

5. For a seminal analysis of the significance of scapegoating as reinforcement of social order, see René Girard, *Le Bouc émissaire* (Paris: Grasset, 1982).

6. For example, the play no longer alludes to such sites as Rome or Toulouse. The fact that one of the characters (the king) exalts the Virgin Mary as "our sweet lady of Boulogne" (143) also suggests that the Miracle was presented to, and probably acted by, members of that particular community. Some scholars, for example Jeanroy, have suggested that the collection of Miracles which contains our text was represented on stage (at the rate of one Miracle per year between 1362 and 1382) by the corporation of goldsmiths in Paris on the feast day—1 December—of their patron, Saint Eloy. See Alfred Jeanroy, "Le Théâtre religieux en langue française jusqu'à la fin du XIVe siècle," *Histoire Littéraire de la France* 39 (1962), 258.

7. Testimony to Jehan Paulus's ordinariness is provided in the final act of the play, which ends with the princess's miraculous resurrection as effected by God rather than by Jehan Paulus, thus eliminating the transformation of the hero into a saint endowed with thaumaturgic power as narrated in the poetic rendition of the legend.

8. As Francis Edwards remarks, the humanization of the plot in the Miracle plays reflects an atemporal conception of history, hence the anachronistic character of a spectacle whose central issues are not only the difficulties encountered by the average Christian on his quest for God, but also those incurred by the average man in his daily life. A recurring theme is man's solitary confrontation with death, as is the case of the respective protagonists of the *Castle of Perseverance* (early fifteenth century) and of *Everyman* (late fifteenth century): Francis Edwards, *Ritual and Drama: The Medieval Theatre* (Guildford and London: Lutterworth, 1976), 101–13.

the public is drawn to the centrality of the Virgin Mary as the sole mediating figure in the play, a sort of "Dea ex machina." The mechanical aspect of Mary's intercession in the theatrical text, together with its de-sanctifying presentation of Jehan Paulus, contribute to a de-dramatization of the legend.[9] If the legend takes on a more truly theatricalized representation in the thirteenth-century narrative than in the Miracle play, a primary reason lies, therefore, in a treatment of the Jehan Paulus story wherein the saint occupies center stage as a result of his being different from the norm.

Like the narrative *Vie de Jehan Paulus*, the second example under consideration provides a theatricalized account of the embodiment of the sacred understood as the locus of difference. A salient feature of the *Martyrdom of Saint Apollonia* by Jean Fouquet (ca. 1452–1456)[10] is, indeed, a staging of the holy body that, here too, takes the form of a circular configuration (see Fig. 1).[11] Another noteworthy aspect of Fouquet's image is that it reproduces visually a stage representation. Considering that the text of the play on which the miniature was based has not survived, we have here the final stage of a dual process of translation, first, from text to theatrical performance and, second, from performance to visual art.

Fouquet's illumination as the final stage of this process discloses the centrality of the circular configuration that I have explored in the Jehan Paulus poem.[12] Apollonia serves as the central point of a specta-

9. As Nagler notes, the miniatures of the manuscript in which the Miracle plays are preserved (BN, f. fr., 819–20) themselves offer an untheatrical rendition of the texts: Alois Maria Nagler, *The Medieval Religious Stage: Shapes and Phantoms* (New Haven: Yale University Press, 1976), 77.

10. The miniature was part of a Book of Hours commissioned by Etienne Chevalier, the Treasurer of France during the reign of King Charles VII. The Book of Hours "seems to have remained in the hands of the Chevalier family until 1630," after which time the miniatures were cut out of the book, pasted on oak panels, and dispersed; "about 1803, forty of the miniatures were sold by an art merchant in Basel to George Brentano of Franckfurt, from whose son, Louis, the Duc d'Aumale, bought the collection in 1891. Ever since that time, the forty miniatures have remained in the Château de Chantilly, bequeathed by the duke to the Institut de France": see Claude Schaefer's introduction to the *Hours of Etienne Chevalier by Jean Fouquet. Musée Condé, Chantilly*, trans. Marianne Sinclair (New York: George Braziller, 1971), 19.

11. The *Martyrdom of Saint Apollonia* is reproduced in Schaefer's edition of *The Hours of Etienne Chevalier*, Plate 45, 113.

12. According to Rey-Flaud, the circular staging of the martyrdom of Saint Apollonia as reproduced in Fouquet's illustration reflects a desire to obfuscate the passing of time: "le rond dramatique est le lieu magique à l'intérieur duquel le temps s'abolit, et où se recrée l'Eternité de Dieu." Henri Rey-Flaud, *Le cercle magique. Essai sur le théâtre en rond à la fin du moyen âge* (Paris: Gallimard, 1973), 278. Nagler (102–105) calls into

cle whose staging is in part constituted by the half-circle theatre that shelters the intrapictorial spectators, including the ladies located in two of the mansions at upper stage, and the crowd standing in the back of the lower stage. This half-circle is completed by a second—albeit invisible—one, the center of which is Etienne Chevalier, the recipient of Fouquet's work. It may be that Fouquet intended to induce Etienne, as extrapictorial center, to identify with Apollonia both as victim and intrapictorial center. Yet the difference in terms of attitude that distinguishes Apollonia from both the intra- and extrapictorial viewers tends to counteract the didactic import of Fouquet's illumination. Like Jehan Paulus in the thirteenth-century narrative, Apollonia does not look at the public but keeps her eyes closed. While the viewers of Fouquet's picture are asked to commemorate and admire Apollonia as an innocent martyr, nonetheless, the staging of the scene suggests that all the participants in this spectacle act as voyeurs and, hence, as persecutors.

Thus the core of the drama is not the injustice done in the past to the heroine, but the event of her torture as it is relived in the present. In this reenactment of the martyrdom of Apollonia, the past is actualized, theatricalized, in such a way as to focus on her mutilated body rather than on her spiritual value. The result of this circular configuration is a process of reification forcing on Apollonia the role of a tormented and passive object. Evidence of the significance of the scene of torture as drama is the spatial centrality of the tormented heroine, of her tormentors, and of the instrument of torture. Indeed, the organization of the pictorial space calls attention to the grossly disproportionate forceps, as well as to the four tormentors, who emblematize brute force. In a variety of ways, the function of Apollonia's body in Fouquet's image recalls that of Jehan Paulus in the thirteenth-century narrative. First, both protagonists are subjected to an anatomical examination that they endure silently and passively. Second, this examination entails a mistreatment invoking, in each case, a quartering of the body, as sug-

---

question the view—advanced by Richard Southern in *The Medieval Theatre in the Round: A Study of the Staging of the "Castle of Perseverance" and Related Matters* (London: Faber, 1957), 91–120, by Schaefer in *The Hours of Etienne Chevalier* (112), and by Rey-Flaud in *Le cercle magique* (134–36)—that Fouquet was a man of the theatre and that his miniature provides a realistic rendition of the performance on stage. According to Nagler, the theatrical (i.e., theatricalized) quality of Fouquet's image has a strictly pictorial function. In the perspective developed in this paper, the circular configuration characterizing Fouquet's image as well as the other three selected documents serves as a locus emblematic of a spectacle whose focal point is the victimization of the protagonist at center stage. See also Brigitte Cazelles, "Le cercle maudit," *Stanford French Review* 10 (1986): 259–80.

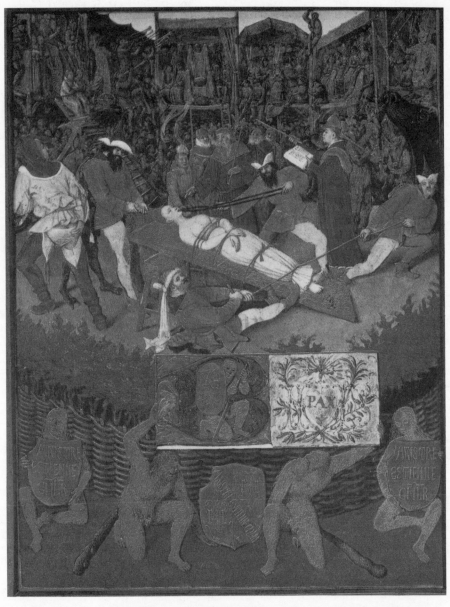

1. Jean Fouquet, "The Martyrdom of Saint Apollonia" in the *Livre d'Heures pour Etienne Chevalier*. Reprinted from a plate that appears in color in Jean Fouquet, *The Hours of Etienne Chevalier*, trans. Marianne Sinclair (New York: George Braziller, 1971).

66

gested, in Fouquet's image, by the position of the four tormentors and, in the thirteenth-century poem, by the gesture of the king's men when they grab Jehan by his arms and legs. Third, the result is a similar torturing of the body. Although in principle the story of Jehan Paulus the hermit takes place in a Christian rather than pagan social context, his Life is in effect a Passion. Anatomical scrutiny as it occurs in these two examples is not conducive to the exploration, hence understanding, of the unknown. Rather, it suggests a sacrificial treatment of difference, which is exposed, dismantled, and appropriated by the collectivity as a means of insuring its homogeneity and welfare.

The textual and iconographic documents mentioned above suggest the presence of two distinct categories of medieval theatricality. The first may be characterized as *dramatic*, in reference to the sacrificial effect of the circular configuration as it functions in both the thirteenth-century narrative and in Fouquet's image. The second points forward to a *mechanical* organization of space, in reference to the architectural rather than somatized representation of the world in the fourteenth-century Miracle play. Considering that Jehan serves here as an emblem of Everyman, it is *stricto sensu* that this body can be said to have an "edifying" value. His role is to serve as monument, or shield, securing and consolidating the distance between the secular and the sacred.

In contrast with these three examples, which illustrate a mythical perception of Creation, the final document analyzed in this paper bespeaks a scientific perception of the cosmos. The circular staging of this particular image thus appears to invoke a third category of theatricality, consistent with a *technical*, rather than dramatic or mechanical, approach to the exposed body.[13] Indeed, it is by now traditional to see in Andreas Vesalius of Brussels (1514–1564) the initiator of modern science. His *Fabric of the Human Body (De Humani Corporis Fabrica)*, which serves as a medium for the communication of observational and descriptive science, testifies forcefully to Vesalius's deserved reputation.[14] What distinguishes Vesalius's *Fabric*, which is justifiably renowned as a masterpiece within the context of both the history of

13. The primary purpose of scientific visualization is to standardize the human body. In Michel Melot's analysis, the image thus obtained is then "able to be memorized, classified, archived, transported, cut up: it enters in books, in files, in banks. It can also be reproduced": "L'image de la science," in *Image et science* (Collection Sémaphore; Paris: Centre Georges Pompidou/B.P.I. and Editions Herscher, 1985), 7.

14. The date of Vesalius's *Fabric* is also, significantly, that of Copernicus's *Motion of the Heavenly Bodies*. For a pictorial reproduction of Vesalius's *Fabric*, see J. B. deC. M. Saunders and Charles D. O'Malley, *The Illustrations From the Works of Andreas Vesalius of Brussels* (Cleveland and New York: The World Publishing Company, 1950).

medecine and the history of printing, is the manner in which text and image are integrated as a whole.

The scene illustrated in the frontispiece of the first edition of the *Fabric* in 1543 takes place outside a palace typical of the Italian Renaissance (see Fig. 2).[15] A temporary wooden structure accommodates the intrapictorial viewers. This out-of-doors setting is consistent with custom, as confirmed by the description of a public dissection that Vesalius conducted in Pisa, on 22 January 1544: a temporary scaffolding, erected for the occasion, proceeded to collapse, so great was the press to view Vesalius's demonstration.[16] Public dissections in the Renaissance were, indeed, much attended events, as illustrated in the Frontispiece by the turbulent and admiring public surrounding Vesalius, in recognition of his role in reintroducing dissection of cadavers in Western Europe.[17] Dissections of cadavers were forbidden during the Middle Ages, for this was seen as a profanation of the human body. However, it was not forbidden to dissect the living body, as during the Inquisition, the only prerequisite being that the body be clothed and not naked.[18] Although Vesalius's *Fabric* was in the main acclaimed as a scientific revolution, it also elicited hostile reactions. Representatives of the Church argued against a description of the male body that contained an even number of ribs, for this contradicted Genesis and the creation of Eve from one of Adam's rib—whence the odd number of ribs characterizing the male body. Scientists such as Sylvius of Amiens contested Vesalius's corrections of Galen's work, and Sylvius henceforth qualified Vesalius as a monster of arrogance and ignorance, changing his name, *Vesalius*, into *Vesanus* ("the mad man").

Like Fouquet's image, the staging of the 1543 frontispiece is constituted by two half-circles, including the visible, intrapictorial one, and the invisible, extrapictorial one. Yet a major difference distinguishes Vesalius's engraving from both Fouquet's miniature and our two textual examples. Here, the spectacle no longer focuses on the sacred but

15. The frontispiece of the 1543 edition is reproduced by Saunders and O'Malley (Illustrations, 43), whose work also provides a series of three preliminary stages of this particular engraving (see Plates 93–95, 249–51).

16. A permanent anatomical theatre—still standing today—was constructed at Padua in 1594. See the description of the 1543 frontispiece by Saunders and O'Malley (42).

17. The first scientific dissections were done by the Greeks, from 500 B.C. (Alcmeon) to 300 A.D. (Erasistratus, and Herophilus of Alexandria).

18. See Marc-Alain Descamps, *L'invention du corps* (Paris: Presses Universitaires de France, 1986), 18–19.

2. Frontispiece of the first edition (1543) of Vesalius's *Fabric of the Human Body.*
Reprinted from J.B. deC.M. Saunders and Charles D. O'Malley, *The Illustrations from
the Works of Andreas Vesalius of Brussels* (Cleveland and New York: The World
Publishing Company, 1950).

on the secular. Testifying to the technical rather than the dramatic function of the exposed body is the fact that, to all appearances, it is not the exposed body but Vesalius himself who serves as link between the intra- and extrapictorial public. Vesalius invites both the spectators within and the viewers without to understand the workings of human anatomy. The exploration of the unknown is not governed by a mythical perception of the cosmos, as was the case in our first three examples, but by a rational process focusing on the human body as the sum total of signification.[19] The resulting discourse is thus not a *mythos*—that is, a fictional, fabulous, and sacralizing interpretative act—but, on the contrary, a *logos*, in reference to a mode of expression producing meaning by dissecting, enumerating, and articulating the syntax of reality. Like taxonomy, anatomical scrutiny here consists of an inventory that disassembles the parts in order to reach an understanding of the whole. Once exposed, the secret of the body becomes *science*, in the etymological sense of that which is known; and the effect of science is both to dispel man's fear and to contribute to man's control over nature.

Yet, while the artistic and scientific value of this frontispiece cannot be questioned, there subsist, I suggest, traces of a victimizing understanding of order. First, here as in our medieval documents, the foundation of order is a dead body—and we may note, in passing, that the dead body is the only female figure represented in the scene. Second, the focal point that structures this circular staging is, in effect, dual: one is the corpse, emblematized by its closed eyes; the other is

19. In the Preface to his *Fabric,* Vesalius expresses his certainty that Charles V, to whom he dedicated his work, will be charmed by this exploration of the organism of the most perfect of all creatures, and will appreciate the detailed examination of what serves as both shelter and vehicle of "our immortal soul," justly described by the great thinkers of Antiquity in terms of microcosm: "Adeo ut haud fieri queat, quin ut mundi scientia unice teneris, ita etiam aliquando omnium creaturarum absolutissim[e] fabricatione expendenda delecteris, et immortalis animae diuersorio instrumentoque considerando uoluptatem capias: quod quia permultis nominibus mundo egregie correspondet, ueteribus haud ab re paruus mundus nuncupabatur" (So great is [your love of the study of the stars] that it can hardly be but that you are attracted in a unique degree by the science of the universe, so also you should at all times delight in considering the most perfectly constructed among all created things, and should take pleasure in considering what is the temporary dwelling-place and instrument of the immortal soul. For this in many particulars exhibits a marvellous correspondence with the universe, and for that reason was by them of old not inappropriately styled "a little universe" [microcosm]). See Benjamin Farrington, trans., "The Preface of Andreas Versalius to *De Fabrica Corporis Humani 1543,*" in *Proceedings of the Royal Society of Medecine* 25/5 (July 1932), 1365. See also *La fabrique du corps humain,* introduced by Claire Ambroselli, Anne Fabot-Largeault, and Christiane Sinding (Arles: Actes Sud, 1987), 48.

Vesalius himself, who is the only figure in the scene whose eyes are fully open. By contrast, the eyes of the spectators are only half-open, indicating that the public constitutes a middle stage between death of the body and life of the mind, between blind ignorance and scientific lucidity. Consequently, Vesalius stands out as a god-like figure, a Creator, by virtue of his unique capacity to turn the flesh into word. Thus, although anatomical scrutiny here articulates a desacralizing view of the world, the result is nonetheless a theatricalized rendition of the signified. The text constructed on the exposed body elaborates a hierarchical construct of order, one that assigns to the expert, and through his mediation, to man at large, a position of dominance and authority. It is not fortuitous that Vesalius, the master producer of the *Fabric of the Human Body*, calls the legend that accompanies each illustration a "cast of characters." Neither is it incidental that one of the modifications characterizing the frontispiece of the second edition (1555) of Vesalius's *Fabric* is the addition of a goat, observed at the right-hand lower corner of the picture (fig. 3),[20] for the presence of this particular animal serves as a discreet, yet unmistakable, reminder of the scapegoating mechanism that guarantees, traditionally, the preservation of order. The quest for control—whether it is the control of woman by man, of nature by mankind, or of myth (that is, the discourse produced by the "Humanities") by science—culminates here in a scene of exposure that is not entirely devoid of mythical import insofar as its script functions as a "scenario of fulfillment,"[21] that of the expert who confirms his right to supremacy and who realizes his dream of conquest by producing a spectacle in which he is both the leading player and the sole author of the script.

On the basis of the trial-like staging characterizing each of the three selected examples, it appears that the representation of the unknown converges on an unreadable body for purposes of extracting its meaning. The body exposed at center stage is at first empty, a white page, inasmuch as it is located between two poles of signification. An example in the thirteenth-century narrative is Jehan's body, which is neither entirely human nor animal; another is the body dissected in Vesalius's frontispiece, a body which is no longer alive but not yet reduced to dust. Only when the exposed body is inscribed by the logos of the

20. The frontispiece of the 1555 edition is reproduced by Saunders and O'Malley, *Illustrations*, 45.

21. To quote Peter Brooks's remark, in a lecture on "Invasions of Privacy: The Body and the Novel" presented at Stanford University, 4 November 1991.

ANDREAE VESALII
BRVXELLENSIS, INVI-
ctiſsimi CAROLI V. Imperatoris
medici, de Humani corporis
fabrica Libri ſeptem.

CVM CAESAREAE
Maieſt. Galliarum Regu,ac Senatus Veneti gratia &
priuilegio,vt in diplomate eorundem continetur.

3. Frontispiece of the second edition (1555) of Vesalius's *Fabric of the Human Body*.
Reprinted from Saunders and O'Malley.

72

collectivity does it become meaningful, signifiable, in reference to its middle status as threshold or border, shield, between the pole of the known and the pole of the unknown. Thus the founding myth fabricated on stage focuses on the exposed body as what seems to be a singular, hence, unreadable specimen. But the creation of the myth results, in reality, from a reverse process: it is not because it is singular that the body is at center stage but, to the contrary, because it is exposed at center stage that it becomes singular. The core of the drama, therefore, is essentially a violation of private space.

In this perspective, what defines a typically *theatricalized situation* is a confrontation between private space and public space. In the thirteenth-century rendition of the Jehan Paulus legend, for example, this confrontation undergoes two distinct stages. In the first, what sets Jehan apart is the spectacle of his naked body, a spectacle that concretizes, by giving it flesh and substance, the difference between normality (the public) and abnormality (the protagonist). In the second stage, what sets Jehan apart is his status as allegory to the second degree: not only does the public recognize that his hidden reality has a holy rather than abnormal character; public attention now focuses on Jehan's clothing as an allegory of his sacred nature.

By contrast, a *nontheatricalized situation* refers to a type of somatic representation that gives priority to private space. An emblematic episode is the Pygmalion myth as narrated by Jean de Meun in what constitutes the second part of the *Roman de la Rose* (ca. 1268–78).[22] In both the Pygmalion myth and in the Jehan Paulus myth, the exposed body becomes signifiable at the moment when it is initialized by desire. However, unlike the Jehan Paulus myth, wherein the fabrication of the body takes place in front, and requires the presence of a public, in the Pygmalion myth it occurs in *camera obscura*. Also noteworthy is the significance of the construction of the body of Galathea in effecting the construction of Pygmalion's—that is, Jean's—text. The staging of Galathea's body is thus integral to the author's attempt to affirm his status as a distinct and autonomous entity. In that sense, somatic representations that take place in a private (mental) space produce a script—in the scriptural rather than theatrical sense of the word— whose function is primarily self-descriptive. What emerges is a notion of selfhood grounded on singularity, focusing on the creative subject as a unique, original specimen. The interest of a nontheatricalized ap-

22. See the edition of Félix Lecoy, *Guillaume de Lorris et Jean de Meun. Le roman de la rose* (Paris: Champion, 1970), vol. 3, ll. 20787–21280.

proach to the body lies in the light it sheds on the concept of individualism: far from a historically-rooted phenomenon, individualism is, I suggest, the mark of a glorifying view of difference as a prerequisite to self-identity. What distinguishes Pygmalion as artist (Jean as author) is a reinscription of the Rose whose goal is to substantiate the exceptional and inimitable merit of its creator.[23] Nonindividualistic cultural productions, on the other hand, articulate a collective view of identity as experienced and reaffirmed in the course of a communal rejection of singularity.

Whether taking place in a public or in a private space, the exposure of the body has for its main characteristic a violation of privacy. The core of the trial, in effect, is the body in pain: what takes place on stage (in a torture chamber designated as "production room" in the Philippines or "cinema room" in South Vietnam) is, as Elaine Scarry notes, the translation of pain into power, that is, of the victim's body into the tormentor's voice.[24] As in the case of the Pygmalion myth, wherein the body of Galathea becomes Jean's text and, ultimately, the source of his self-glorification as author, the body of Jehan Paulus serves as a script of collective empowerment in the face of the unknown. Particularly interesting is the manner in which the protagonist of the verse narrative becomes a text for and by women, as occurs at the moment when the richly clothed queen and her ladies gather around the naked creature exposed in the middle of the palace square. In this metonymic spectacle, not only is Jehan the individual reduced to a body; his body is also reduced to an organ. The masterpiece of sanctity functions here as a centerpiece of erotic significance. In the last analysis, it may be that, regardless of the circumstances—public or private—of the representation, the textualization and fragmentation of the body at center stage are bound to constitute a kind of *Summa Sadistica*.

23. To adapt Dornbush's observation, what characterizes Pygmalion's statue as an "ymage sourde" is the absence of speech and hearing, features that are, by contrast, integral to Jean's success in praising his distinctive privilege as a creator inspired by a divine-like logos. Jean M. Dornbush, *Pygmalion's Figure: Reading Old French Romance* (Lexington, Kentucky: French Forum Publishers, 1990), 96.

24. Elaine Scarry, *The Body in Pain: The Making and Unmaking of the World* (New York and Oxford: Oxford University Press, 1985), 45–51.

THOMAS M. GREENE

The King's One Body in the *Balet Comique de la Royne*

During the year 1581, the unnecessary queen of France Louise de Vaudemont summoned to her apartments in the Louvre the Savoyard musician and choreographer Balthazar de Beaujoyeulx in order to make a request. She knew that her husband, King Henri III, was preparing a series of spectacular celebrations in order to fete the imminent wedding of his favorite Anne d'Arques, Duc de Joyeuse, with her sister Marguerite. She was unwilling to be excluded from these *magnificences* or to appear detached from them. Thus she asked Beaujoyeulx to plan an evening's entertainment which could form a part of the extended celebrations and which she herself could sponsor. According to his own account, Beaujoyeulx, after a delay for reflection, submitted a plan to the queen which won her approval and which would in fact lead to a performance during a fortnight of banqueting, pageantry, fireworks, and jousts following the sumptuous wedding. Of all those events, we have the most detailed description of the entertainment produced by Beaujoyeulx and his collaborators, a *Gesamtkunstwerk* combining theater, music, dance, poetry, and elaborate scenic effects lasting five and a half hours. The description is available because the choreographer himself published his book-length account of the spectacle, including the music and engraved representations of several stage devices. The title he assigned to the production was *Balet Comique de la Royne*. It has never apparently been reperformed since the original occasion on Sunday, 15 October 1581, but it marked a date in French court spectacle, and its textual description, amplified by

YFS 86, *Corps Mystique, Corps Sacré: Textual Transfigurations of the Body from the Middle Ages to the Seventeenth Century,* ed. Françoise Jaouën and Benjamin Semple, © 1994 by Yale University.

musical and visual supplements, remains an arresting legacy of early modern spectacular invention.

It must be admitted that in view of the royal finances and the state of the realm, this ballet, together with the other fetes that accompanied it, comprised a project of criminal folly. In 1581 France was enjoying an uneasy respite from the intermittent religious wars which had devastated the kingdom for twenty years and would continue for many more. The king's treasury was virtually empty and his people impoverished by the costs of seemingly endless warfare. To spend, as was rumored, over a million *écus* for the celebration of a wedding appeared to many as an act of royal irresponsibility, all the more gross because motivated apparently by the sole wish to honor the favorite d'Arques, named Duc de Joyeuse shortly before the ceremony. It is true that the marriage of Joyeuse to Marguerite de Lorraine, like the king's marriage to her sister, could be said to have a dynastic goal. Both marriages were doubtless intended to improve the Valois's troubled relations with the ambitious and threatening house of Guise, to which the sisters were connected. Henri de Guise, leader of the reactionary Catholic faction menacing the throne, so to speak, from the right, was present at the performance of the *Balet Comique*. But the political goal of the wedding failed to justify the madness of its expense. If anything at all justified this beyond the king's whim, the rationale would have to be found, as Frances Yates has suggested, in a magical basis of the various spectacles, including Beaujoyeulx's.[1]

Internal evidence does exist to support this hypothesis in the one case we can study in detail. It begins to emerge in the impresario's dedicatory epistle addressed significantly not to the queen, as might have been expected, but to King Henri. In this dedication, Beaujoyeulx refers to the disorders through which the kingdom has passed, comparing them to a disease (*maladie*) which the king and his mother Catherine de' Medici, longtime queen regent, have succeeded in healing. Now, he says, the kingdom has regained its robust appetite, its fresh color, and the strength of its limbs. This healing in fact is dramatized, writes Beaujoyeulx, in the action of the ballet, which stages the defeat of the enchantress Circe:

1. Frances Yates, *Astraea: The Imperial Theme in the Sixteenth Century* (London: Routledge and Kegan Paul, 1975), 159 ff. Yates writes: "The plot and the themes of the performance [of *Le Balet Comique*] relate it to the themes of the Magnificences as a whole, the invocation of cosmic forces in aid of the French monarchy"(165). See also Yates's *The French Academies of the Sixteenth Century* (London: Warburg Institute, 1946), ch. 11.

Le discours de tout cela, Sire, vous est icy au vif & plaisamment repre-
senté souz la fabuleuse narration de l'enchanteresse Circé, laquelle
avez vaincue par vostre vertu avec trop plus de louange qu Ulysse.

The telling of all this, Sire, is here vividly and agreeably represented in
the fabulous narration of the sorceress Circe, whom you have vanquished by your virtue with greater praise than Ulysses.[2]

It is suggestively unclear whether, in this sentence, the king's victory
consists solely in his supposed pacification of his realm or whether it
includes as well the victory over Circe staged by the ballet. What is
essential to learn from this remark (even if one might have divined it) is
that Beaujoyeulx understood his fable to have a specific political application, and wanted the application to be recognized. The scenario of
the ballet would have, according to this formulation, a *historical* function, representing allegorically what the king and his mother had already achieved in the world of public affairs.

This formulation accords well with the routine extravagance of the
dedication's flattery, but it would have deceived no one into believing
that the disease of the French body politic had in fact been healed. The
ballet's scenario as history was inaccurate, since all the conditions
continued to exist which had produced such grave symptoms of infirmity. What is more likely, and what indeed has been argued, is that the
creators of the ballet wanted it to bring about that healing process
which its dedication falsely asserted already to have occurred. It does
apparently represent a healing of the body politic in order to induce the
process to take place.

An impresario of the sixteenth century was not, according to an
influential philosophy, altogether powerless when confronted with the
illness of his nation. This philosophy assumed sympathetic resonances between the three levels of music first codified by Boethius as
musica mundana, cosmic harmony; *musica humana,* harmony of the

---

2. French quotations from the work under study are taken from Balthazar de Beaujoyeulx, *Le Balet Comique,* a facsimile with an introduction by Margaret M. McGowan
(Binghamton, N.Y.: MRTS, 1982). I have modernized slightly the French usages of this
edition while retaining the original spelling. English translations are based on *Le Balet
Comique de la Royne,* trans. Carol and Lander MacClintock, published by the American
Institute of Musicology, 1971, Musicological Studies and Documents, 25. This edition
contains a modern transcription of the music. The translation, however, is imperfect, and
I have taken the liberty of altering it in some instances. Page references to both editions
will be supplied hereafter in parentheses following the quotation. The passage quoted
above appears on page a.iii.r of the McGowan edition and page 28 of the MacClintock
edition.

human soul and community; and *musica instrumentalis*, the harmony of what we normally call music. A long tradition of thinkers beginning with Plato (who was himself influenced by Pythagoras) believed that the harmony of audible music could induce the absolute harmony of the spheres to correct discordances of the psyche, and this belief had received fresh authoritative support during the century preceding the *Balet Comique*. There is no reason to think that Beaujoyeulx himself had read philosophy or was well-educated; the sentence quoted in part above ends with a howler suggesting that he was not.[3] But he appears to have resembled many artists of most eras who could make use at second hand of fashionable theories available in the cultural climate while supposing them to be true. Thus Beaujoyeulx could refer to Platonic doctrine in his text without necessarily having read the *Timaeus* or Ficino or Pontus de Tyard. He does make this reference when he first speaks of the ravishing power of his ballet's music: the singing, he writes,

> pour ses voix repercussives, aucuns de l'assistance estimerent estre la mesme voix qui fut convertie en air repercussif, appelé depuis Echo: & d'aultres plus instruits en la discipline Platonique l'estimerent estre la vraye harmonie du ciel, de laquelle toutes les choses qui sont en estre, sont conservees & maintenues. [5v]

> because of the repercussive voices, was thought by some of those present to be the same voice converted into repercussive air, since called Echo. Others more learned in Platonic philosophy thought it was the true harmony of heaven, by which all living things are preserved and maintained. [38]

The more learned interpretation is clearly understood to be the correct one. From this and other passages, one can plausibly conclude that the impresario did wish to induce through his staged performance the descent of celestial harmony to a realm which at that moment desperately needed it.

The platonic doctrine Beaujoyeulx invokes has its roots in the *Timaeus* where Plato speaks of the effects of music within the context of cosmic creation.

> So much of music as is adapted to the sound of the voice and to the sense of hearing is granted to us for the sake of harmony. And harmony,

3. "... plus de louange qu Ulysse: auquel le grand Alexandre porta envie, pour avoir esté se dignement celebré par Homere " [. . . greater praise than Ulysses, of whom the great Alexander was envious for having been so worthily celebrated by Homer]. Beaujoyeulx confuses Ulysses with Achilles.

which has motions akin to the revolutions of our souls, is not regarded
by the intelligent votary of the Muses as given by them with a view to
irrational pleasure . . . but as meant to correct any discord which may
have arisen in the courses of the soul, and to be our ally in bringing her
into harmony and agreement with herself. [47c–d]

A long and complex strand of intellectual history connects this passage
and its context with the "discipline Platonique" of the sixteenth century. It has been traced by a number of scholars, most recently and
exhaustively by Gary Tomlinson.[4] But this complexity does not blur
the millennial agreement that harmony is at once celestial, audible,
and moral, and that music can operate beneficently on human beings
through a kind of magical *paideia*.

Ten years before the performance of the *Balet Comique*, an institu-
tionalized attempt to harness musical power systematically was made
in the foundation of the Académie de Musique et de Poésie by the poet
Antoine de Baïf and the composer Thibault de Courville. The Académie attempted to reproduce ancient music, despite the fact that
nothing was known of it, in order better to link all three Boethian levels
of harmony; specifically, it developed a type of choral music whose
rhythms followed those of poetic texts composed according to a quan-
titative prosody. These experiments rejected polyphonic composition
for choral songs in which all voices sang the same syllable in harmony
together, sacrificing the lively interweaving of musical lines for a more
solemn unanimity. The music of the *Balet Comique*, composed by a
certain Lambert de Beaulieu, does not introduce qualitative rhythms
but it does on the whole maintain a stately movement of all voices
from syllable to syllable. That this compositional style was perceived
as calculated to reflect or capture celestial harmony through the imitation of the ancients is affirmed by a complimentary poem introducing
the ballet's published text.

> Tu [Beaujoyeulx] nous fais veoir . . .
> . . . la façon tant estimee
> De nos poëtes anciens,

4. Gary Tomlinson, *Music in Renaissance Magic: Towards a Historiography of
Others* (Chicago: University of Chicago Press, 1993). Other discussions of the history of
musical theory can be found in Frances Yates, *French Academies*; John Hollander, *The
Untuning of the Sky* (Princeton: Princeton University Press, 1961); D. P. Walker, *Music,
Spirit and Language in the Renaissance* (London: Warburg Institute, 1985); and Claude
V. Palisca, *Humanism in Italian Renaissance Musical Thought* (New Haven: Yale Uni-
versity Press, 1985).

Les vers avecques la musique,
Le Balet confus mesuré,
Demonstrant du ciel azuré
L'accord par un effect mystique. [é.ii.v–é.iii.r]

You show us . . . the highly esteemed manner of our ancient poets,
verses with music, the complicated ballet brought into order, showing
by a mystical effect the consonance of the azure heaven. [32]

There appears to be no reason to doubt that Beaujoyeulx shared with
Volusian, the author of these verses, a belief in the "mystical effect" of
his production.

Volusian's reference to the "complicated ballet brought into order,"
as well as to music and poetry, can serve to remind us that choreography was perceived by many to embody harmony equally with music
and to possess music's capacity to order the soul. Another dedicatory
poem praises the enchantment of the "subtils destours" (subtle figures) performed by the corps de ballet, whose perpetually shifting geometric patterns the text describes in some detail. The geometric character of the dance figures participates in what could be termed the
quadrivial sublime of the early modern period, which assigned cosmic
patterns and effects to arithmetic, geometric, astronomic (or astrologi-
cal), and musical relations. Beaujoyeulx ("Geometre, inventif, . . .
parangon d'Archimede" as he is called in still another complimentary
poem [é.i.r]) attempted to tap this sublime through choreographic imitation in order to introduce its celestial order on earth. The perceived
movement of astral bodies as a cosmic dance was a cliché which still
held deep meaning in 1581 and which challenged the ingenuity of the
choreographer-metaphysician. What heightened the possibility of inducing harmony within the body politic was the *combination* of music, dance, and verse, a reinforcement of the powers of each through the
incantatory effects of their mingling in a single performance. Beaujoyeulx boasts that he has "within a single well-proportioned body . . .
pleased eye, ear, and mind" (33). Thus the production itself was a *body*
whose three major elements, skillfully mingled, corresponded to the
workings of the three faculties within each member of the audience,
integrating in his/her own body the impressions of the various senses.

This triple "proportioning" of performative media was heightened
in the *Balet Comique* by still another artistic device, namely allegory.
One of the most learned students of this work, Margaret McGowan,
quotes Tasso on the power of allegory to represent essences:

L'allegoria . . . rimira le Passioni, e le opinioni, i costumi, non solo in quanto essi appriono; ma principalmente ne lor essere intrinseco, e più oscuramente le significa con note (per cosi dire) misteriose, et che solo da i conoscitori della natura delle cose possono essere à pieno comprese.

Allegory . . . reflects passions, beliefs, customs, not only in their appearances, but chiefly in their intrinsic being, and denotes them more darkly through, so to speak, mysterious signs which can only fully be understood by those who know the nature of things.[5]

This ontological penetration of allegory confers upon it also a quasi-occult power, a "mysterious" power, since its signs (note) capture the intrinsic truths of things with a power unavailable to conventional forms of artistic representation. The allegorical sign reaches more profoundly to the core of the thing represented, implicitly breaking down the distinction between *signum* and *res*. In the civic ceremonial of the Renaissance, E. H. Gombrich suggests, the quality of abstract Justice could be understood as actually embodied in the girl given that name for the duration of a royal entry.[6] Allegory can thus be appropriated, like the other media we have been considering, for the purposes of magic, since magic depends precisely upon that linkage of signifier and referent which Tasso hints at and Gombrich analyzes. For the system of cosmic sympathies to operate which musical and choreographic enchantment presuppose, that kinship already present in the *Timaeus*, the audible sound or physical movement must be understood to be *interpenetrated* by the cosmic realities to which they correspond. A sign such as a gesture or a word must itself become a thing, must be hypostatized, in order to correspond adequately with supreme things. Without that incipient semiotic unity cutting across Boethius's three orders of harmony, nothing efficacious can be supposed to result from a given performance; there can be no "effect mystique."

These assumptions lay in the background as a large audience gathered on the Sunday evening within the Salle de Bourbon in the Louvre to witness the unprecedented production. The published account con-

5. Torquato Tasso, "Allegoria del poema" in *Opere*, ed. G. Rosini, 33 vols. (Pisa: Niccoló Capurro, 1830), 24, v–vi. Quoted by Margaret M. McGowan, *L'Art du Ballet de Cour en France 1581–1643* (Paris: CNRS, 1963), 25. My translation.

6. "Justice welcoming the King at the city gate during a 'Glorious Entry' was perhaps conceived as more than just a pretty girl wearing a strange costume. In and through her Justice herself had come down to earth to greet the ruler and to act as a spell and an augury." E. H. Gombrich, *Symbolic Images: Studies in the Art of the Renaissance* (New York: Phaidon, 1972), 176.

tains a useful engraving which supplements Beaujoyeulx's description of the stage space (see figure). From this it is clear that the performance took place within a rectangular area surrounded on three sides by spectators seated in graduated ranks above the action and thus able to follow the intricate geometric transformations figured by the dancers. At one end of the rectangle, and closer to the floor than the other spectators, sat the king, flanked by the two persons he most cared for, his mother Catherine and Joyeuse. At the far end of the rectangular stage space, facing Henri, was located the bower of the enchantress Circe, adorned with flowers and fruit trees, behind which a castle could be discerned. At certain moments, one could see within this bower some of the beasts into which the enchantress had transformed her human lovers. On either side, trellised arches permitted entrances and exits. To the king's right, half-way down the long side of the rectangle, was a small grove sacred to Pan. Opposite this grove to the left was a structure containing musicians and supposed to be covered with clouds; this was called the "voulte doree" (golden vault). Another mass of clouds (not visible in the engraving) was placed in the center overhead; from here Mercury and Jupiter would descend to earth.

The action of the ballet, interrupted frequently by instrumental music, song, and dance, centers on the ambiguous figure of Circe. The action opens with a long speech (here as elsewhere in verse) by a survivor of her malignant charms who takes refuge below the king and begs him to rescue those remaining in her control. It is Circe who later will immobilize with a touch of her golden wand twelve naiads (including the queen and the bride) as they dance in homage to the king, and when Mercury descends to save them with drops of moly, he too is immobilized and led off with the others to the sorceress's garden. This victory produces a crisis which will only be resolved by the progressive gathering of a coalition even stronger than she. Eight satyrs are joined by four dryads who successfully appeal to Pan for his support; these are joined by the still more powerful cardinal virtues, and then climactically by Minerva in a magnificent chariot and Jupiter descending from the clouds. These redoubtable powers advance toward Circe's garden in a formation which can be understood as an extension of the power of the king seated behind them and symbolically supporting them. Indeed, as she awaits her foes, Circe states that it is only the king of the French ("*ce Roy des François*") (54v) who can overcome her and to whose power she now yields. After a skirmish, Circe's wand loses its transformative power, her bower is successfully invaded, and she her-

Reprinted, by permission, from *Balthazar de Beaujoyeulx: Le Balet Comique, 1581*, ed. Margaret M. McGowan. Medieval & Renaissance Texts & Studies, vol. 6 (Binghamton, New York: 1982), 4r. Copyright, Center for Medieval and Early Renaissance Studies, SUNY Binghamton.

self is led by Minerva, followed by the other victors, to the place of the king, where she seats herself at his feet in token of defeat, and where the gods pay homage to Henri, his mother Catherine, and his wife Louise. The disarming and humbling of Circe before the king dramatizes at the level of the narrative that harmonization of the body politic supposedly induced at the artistic level by the incantatory power of the mingled arts. The action thus terminated, the performance closes with an elaborate Grand Ballet moving through forty geometric figures. This was followed in turn by the presentation by individual performers of eighteen medals bearing symbolic devices to distinguished members of the audience, beginning with the king. When these talismanic gifts had been presented, the *Balet Comique* came to a close.

A summary of the action of the ballet is incomplete if it fails to underscore the crucial centrality of the king. Henri is, with Circe, the most important personage of the allegory, even though he presumably remained motionless and silent. Circe is understood to be overcome by his surrogates, so that the physical confrontation of the two at opposite ends of the theatrical space corresponds to a moral and metaphysical opposition. Many of the songs sung by the various mythological figures who participate in the action—the sirens, the satyrs, Minerva, Jupiter—refer to him explicitly, and doubtless these and others gestured toward him. His place in the hall, above the theatrical space but closer to it than other members of the audience, allowed him to assume a dual role as spectator and actor. At the close, even this ambiguity is resolved when Minerva and Jupiter address him directly and he is seen to be a dominant presence within the fable.

When the ballet ended, the initiated spectator might well have believed, or wanted to believe, that something more than a fabulous narrative (*"fabuleuse narration"*) had been acted out and that the action of the performance as a whole was properly perceived as metaphysical. The victory of the male royal power over the inferior, but still considerable, female subversive power could be seen as a manipulation of a celestial magic more potent and more sublime than hers. McGowan comments:

> The power struggle between good and evil, between order and disorder, is not simply happening in a world of metaphor . . . , but in another part of the real universe. It is not merely a question of imposing an artistic view of things upon an uncomfortable or rejected reality, but rather the discovery of a different part of reality, which reflects the lived reality, and has the power to transmute it.[7]

7. McGowan, Introduction to *Le Balet Comique,* 33.

In theory, this transmuting coincides with the conclusion of the work. The potent mingling of hypostatized signs achieves a marvelous *paideia* of the kind Plato had first theorized. But in practice, the *Balet Comique* seems to me to render this achievement problematic, even if one remains within the conceptual limits which its published description sets. I would distinguish two sources of potential damage to the ballet's hermetic efficacy at work within the text.

The first of these can be attributed to the traces here betrayed of frivolous self-absorption on the part of that corrupt and effete court which the ballet was designed to entertain. One detects this self-absorption notably in the way Beaujoyeulx introduces the courtiers who served as performers. His account is always careful to supply the name of the individual who is playing a given role, thus diffusing some of the splendor of the evening on most of its participants. He is also careful to describe the elegant costume in which each actor performed. Thus we know, for example, that Circe was played by a certain Mlle de Sainte Mesme, Mercury by the Sieur du Pont, Minerva by a Mlle de Chaumont, and we are given detailed impressions of their gorgeous and costly garb. (We also learn that one of the Dryads was Hélène de Surgères, the Hélène of Ronsard's sonnets.) The description of the courtier playing Jupiter is representative:

> La musique finie le sieur de Savornin (qui est au Roy, pour estre doué de beaucoup de bonnes parties, & principalement tresexcellent au chant, & en la composition des airs de musique) representant Jupiter, s'apparut en la nuee vestu d'un habillementt de toile d'or, ses brodequins estoyent de cuir doré, & son manteau de satin jaulne, chamarré de franges d'or, double de camelot d'or: portant en une main son sceptre, en l'autre le foudre effroyable, & en sa teste une belle couronne, le tout fait d'or bruny. A travers de son corps il estoit paré d'une riche escharpe reluisante comme le soleil, pour les perles & pierreries dont il estoit couvert, & entre ses jambes une grande aigle d'or bruny. [51v]

> When the music ended Lord Savornin (who is in the service of the King, as he is endowed with many fine talents, being principally a very fine singer and composer of music), representing Jupiter, appeared in the cloud. He was clad in a suit of cloth of gold; his boots were of gilded leather and his cloak of yellow satin, trimmed with gold fringes, lined with golden camlet. He bore in one hand his sceptre, in the other the frightful thunderbolt, and on his head a fine crown, all made of burnished gold. Across his body he wore a rich scarf shining like the sun, because of the pearls and jewels that covered it. Between his legs was a great eagle of burnished gold. [81–85]

This fullness of description tells us something, I think, about the perception of the allegorical personages by the spectators. They surely recognized the Sieur de Savornin as himself when he descended in his dazzling costume from the ceiling; they did not forget that it was he who spoke Jupiter's lines and claimed Jupiter's powers. One saw the god through the person of the courtier. Beaujoyeulx's account corresponds doubtless to what might be called a courtly narcissism within the Salle de Bourbon; one was not so ravished by the (second-rate) verse or the music as to forget that a person one recognized was playing a role enabling him or her to shine, often literally. It was important, as a member of the court, to know who was performing and doubtless to judge the quality of the performance. The figure before one was thus always double, Savornin and Jupiter at once. But this duality, this space between the actor and the role, must be admitted to subvert that interpenetration or identification which we perceived above to be necessary for effective allegory, and most particularly for the magic of harmonic induction. The communal narcissism which prevents the actor from becoming the power he represents must then be recognized as an obstacle to the efficacy of enchantment and a blurring of the mystical effect. Celestial reality remains at one remove and is held there by an incorrigible worldliness. We never forget that Savornin playing Jupiter is Savornin.

One personage however escapes this fatal duality: the king himself, and in his presence the breakdown of magical hypostatization might be said to reach a limit and in some measure a restoration. The king has a single name, not two, and he remains himself both inside and outside the fable. When the performers refer to him and include him at the end in the action, he is to some degree a concrete presence; he is not a myth. He is a bridge between the fiction and the world. If the performance requires for its efficacy a linkage between representation and essence, then the linkage is present, and only present, in the person of Henri III. If the magic depends on identification, then it is there, embodied by the human, all too human figure of the last of the Valois. In him, representation and reality coincide; insofar as royal authority existed in France, it is incarnate in him. Mark Franko describes the king's role in analogous terms:

> For the golden age of France to come into being—and to remain after the performance has concluded—the king will have to perform, even if only symbolically by watching the ballet from his unique perspective. His presence as a spectator was as conspicuous as to make him a

performer. Thus, there is a hermetic dimension to the ballet embedded in the relationship between it and the monarch. Inasmuch as the king is an actor rather than merely a spectator, allegory becomes history as its own representation, its power to transform itself in the understanding glance of its prime mover.[8]

The king's presence, one might say, serves as a living copula between representation and reality.

It might be argued that, according to a familiar formula of recent scholarship, the king had two bodies which were essentially separate and which thus subverted the semiotic identification which a hermetic theater required. All students of early modern politics have become familiar with the distinction, somewhat simplified since its first formulation by Ernst Kantorowicz, between the perennial mystical body of the immortal king and the perishable body of the individual who occupies the throne for a limited period. But it is important to recall that many of the documents cited by Kantorowicz stress the essential *unity* of these two bodies, which can only be distinguished theoretically by a kind of legal abstraction. Thus the very first document cited in his book, and dating from the Elizabethan period, stresses the mystery of the inseparability of the two bodies. The opinion of the Elizabethan judges insists that the king

> has not a body natural distinct and divided by itself from the Office and Dignity royal, but a Body natural and a Body politic together indivisible; and these two Bodies are incorporated in one Person, and make one Body and not divers.[9]

There is no reason to assume that French theorists conceived of this matter any differently than their English counterparts. At the Louvre, it was this royal indivisibility which undergirded the hermetic assumptions of Beaujoyeulx's production. Insofar as Henri is and remains the monarch of France who incorporates his realm, it can be said of him what one of the dryads says of Jupiter—he is always self-identical, "tousjours semblable à soy" (38r).

But the self-identity of the king and his surrogate Jupiter is offset by the symbolism attaching to Circe, and in the conceptualization of this

8. Mark Franko, *Dance as Text: Ideologies of the Baroque Body* (Cambridge: Cambridge University Press, 1993), 36–38. Franko adds to the passage above: "I believe this is what Frances Yates was intimating when she called *Le Balet Comique* an incantation rather than a narrative." A note refers to Yates's *Astraea*, 159–162.

9. Quoted by Ernst H. Kantorowicz, *The King's Two Bodies* (Princeton: Princeton University Press, 1957), 9.

blocking figure I think we find the second threat to the hermetic efficacy of the work. The precise meaning or meanings of her symbolic
role are by no means transparent as one studies the precise language of
the *Balet Comique*, and it is quite possible that these meanings were
blurred rather than clarified by the familiarity of Beaujoyeulx and the
versifier he recruited, de la Chesnaye, with the farraginous Bible of late
Renaissance poets, Natalis Comes's *Mythologiae*. A brief passage devoted to Circe by this overstuffed mythographic manual is quoted,
along with other interpretations of her appearance in Homer, in a kind
of appendix to the published *Balet Comique*. But the symbolic density
surrounding her in the ballet is thicker than the comments of any
mythographer. Her propensity to change men into beasts links her
with self-indulgence and concupiscence. Her hostility to forces loyal
to the king links her with political sedition. But the flourishing flowers
and trees in her garden link her with natural abundance, a link rein-
forced by the brilliant sun placed just above the garden. She identifies
herself, echoing Comes, as the daughter of the sun. And in a long
versified apologia, recited just after her immobilization of Mercury,
she pieces together various facets of her role to form the most coherent
definition we are given. It rests upon an embryonic theory of human
society, whose achievements, she claims, stem from a restless quest for
pleasure, the itch of desire which leads away from the bland idleness of
the so-called golden age toward labor and achievement. According to
this theory, man is driven by false nostalgia for an imagined past, or by
yearning for the alluring promises of war or wealth. The cause of this
passion for change, the true arbiter of human will, is, says Circe, Circe
herself:

> Seule cause je suis de tout ce changement
> Qui fuit de rang en rang, de moment en moment:
> Mon pere, sans repos qui se meut & se tourne,
> La fin d'une saison d'un nouveau siecle bourne,
> Le Soleil fait tout seul ces âges varier.
> Ainsi veut le Destin toutes Choses lier. [25v–26r]

> I am the only cause of all this change, which occurs from rank to rank,
> from moment to moment. My father, ceaselessly moving and revolv-
> ing, limits the end of one season with another. The Sun alone makes the
> ages change. Destiny in this way links all things together. [62]

The long speech from which this passage is taken invests its speaker
with a kind of metaphysical dignity, despite the occasional traces of

sophistry in its reasoning. The sorceress's fickle (*muable*) changes of disposition, brought to her charge earlier, and her debasing changes of lovers into beasts can now be seen as the minor caprices of a goddess of mutability who is also governor of that cycle of generation and corruption Comes has already attributed to Circe. If the king's role is to be immobile, self-sufficient, self-identical, then his adversary fittingly embodies a principle of generative metamorphosis.

In this antithetical relation of constancy and change, immobility and diversity, lies the thematic core of the *Balet Comique*. But it must be admitted that this relation problematizes the magical project of the ballet, since the supposedly necessary exorcism of Circe seems to require the exorcism of natural dynamism. Even if one disregards the threat of courtly narcissism to this project, the banishment of Circe threatens to leave any achieved harmony a static, monotonous conformity divorced from the cycle of life. The problem in fact lies still deeper since the same antithesis also lies at the structural core of the performance itself, as this structure is defined by Beaujoyeulx. The definition is found in a brief prefatory notice "Au lecteur" in which the author justifies the two words which make up his title. The term "Balet" as he uses it involves the mingling of diverse elements:

> des meslanges geometriques de plusieurs personnes dansans ensemble sous une diverse harmonie de plusieurs instruments. . . . Je me suis advisé qu'il ne seroit point indecent de mesler l'un & l'autre ensemblément, & diversifier la musique de poesie, & entrelacer la poesie de musique, & le plus souvent les confondre toutes deux ensemble. [é.iii.v]

> some geometric mixtures of several persons dancing together to a diverse harmony of several instruments. . . . I decided it would not be a bad idea to mix one and the other together and to diversify the music with poetry and weave music into the poetry, and most often to merge the two together. [33]

Beaujoyeulx will return repeatedly and proudly to this element of diversity in the account which follows. In fact, it is already uppermost in his thoughts when he first describes his project to the queen:

> Je luy remonstray que mon dessein estoit composé de trois parties, sçavoir des poësies, qui devoyent estre recitees: de la diversité des musiques, qui devoyent estre chantees: & de la varieté des choses, qui devoyent estre representees par la peinture. [2v]

> I pointed out to her that my plan was composed of three parts, that is,

verse which must be recited, diverse musical compositions which
must be sung, and a variety of things which must be present in painting
[stage design and devices]. [35]

This proportioning of diversities was inherent to Beaujoyeulx's conception of ballet, as he himself explicates it. The word "comique," on
the other hand, seems to have had for him an almost Dantesque reference to reassuring closure:

La substance . . . j'ay inscrite Comique, plus pour la belle, tranquille, &
heureuse conclusion où elle se termine, que pour la qualité des personnages. [é.iii.v]

The matter . . . I have called "comic" more for the beautiful, tranquil
and happy conclusion than for the quality of the personages. [33]

The conclusion imposes a tranquil order on the diversity of the art,
thus justifying a title which, after this analysis, begins to sound oxy-
moronic. The opposition of monumental identity to dynamic or subversive change, that opposition which organizes the thematic action,
is correspondingly present in the structural tensions of the work as its
creator conceived it. And within this opposition, one is obliged to
point out that the performance itself depended much more on "diversity" than "order," much more on what is implied by "ballet" than on
what is implied by "comedy." For most of the five and a half hours of its
staging, the active pleasure principle is what matters. Minerva, addressing the king, compares Mercury to the senses in that they are
"plus legers que les vents, / Incertains comme luy, muables & vol-
ages " (47v) [lighter than winds, unstable like him, changeable and
flighty (79)]; but what does this ballet flatter, if not the senses? Circe
is in charge in at least two ways, and her predominance may lead us
once again to question the efficacy of the operation supposed to sup-
press her.

It is not clear that Beaujoyeulx was fully in control of the apparent
inconsistencies and ironies in his text. But it would be wrong to neglect
the attempts it clearly makes to resolve its own tensions. One of these
appears in the song of Jupiter as he makes his climactic descent to
earth, a song which reformulates the topic of universal change:

Tout ce qui vit de corps & sentiment
Sujet tousjours à divers changement,
En un estat durable ne demeure:
La liaison s'en corrompt & desfait

Et sans perir par apres se refait,
Et prent de moy une vie meilleure. [52r]

Nothing which has a living body and feelings, subject to many changes,
remains in a permanent state. Bonds grow corrupt and come unbound,
and then later, without dying, are remade and take on from me a better
existence. [86]

These lines envisage a spiral which incorporates change in a gradual
meliorative process. The Circean cycle of corruption and regeneration
permits a progressive ascent to a higher life. The closing stanza of the
song offers a concrete example of this ascent by commanding Minerva
to paralyze the king's enemies and gather his people, humbly obedient,
under his just law. Thus the king would himself become a figure of
redemptive transformation, capable of employing change to impose
orderly peace, capable of endowing those released from Circean de-
basements with forms of superior beauty. Jupiter/Henri would use the
movement of the universal ballet to achieve a "comic" conclusion.

Here is a kind of resolution of the work's thematic tensions. But the
most powerful and suggestive resolution was produced not in the un-
distinguished verse of the poet de la Chesnaye but in the choreography
of the ballet's creator Beaujoyeulx. After Circe has been led to the feet
of the king—not, we note, banished or imprisoned—the final and most
elaborate dance of the night is performed, the dance most fully described by its designer. This ultimate moment of the long performance
requires extended quotation:

> Ce fut lors que les violons changerent de son & se prindrent à sonner
> l'entree du grand Balet, composé de quinze passages, disposez de telle
> façon qu'à la fin du passage toutes tournoyent tousjours la face vers le
> Roy: devant la majesté duquel estans arrivees, danserent le grand Balet à
> quarante passages ou figures Geometriques: & icelles toutes justes &
> considerees en leur diametre, tantost en quarré, & ores en rond, & de
> plusieurs & diverse façons, & aussi tost en triangle, accompagné de
> quelque autre petit quarré, & autres petites figures. Lesquelles figures
> n' estoyent si tost marquees par les douze Naiades, vestues de blanc . . .
> que les quatre Dryades habillees de verd ne les veinssent rompre: de
> sorte que l'une finissant, l'autre soudain prenoit son
> commencement. . . . Chacun creut qu'Archimede n'eust peu mieux
> entendre les proportions Geometriques, que ces princesses & dames les
> pratiquoyent en ce Balet. [55v–56r]

At this point the violins changed their tone, and began to play the
entrée of the Grand Ballet. It was composed of fifteen figures, arranged

in such a way that at the end of each figure all the ladies turned to face the King. When they had appeared before the King's Majesty, they danced the Grand Ballet with forty passages or geometric figures. These were all exact and well-planned in their forms, sometimes square, sometimes round, in several diverse fashions; then in triangles accompanied by a small square, and other small figures. These figures were no sooner formed by the Naiads, dressed . . . in white, than the four Dryads, dressed in green, arrived to change the shape, so that as one ended, the other began. . . . The spectators thought that Archimedes could not have understood geometric proportions any better than the princesses and the ladies performed them in this Ballet. [90–91]

This memorable passage recalls nothing so much as Plato's description of the dance of the stars in the *Timaeus*.[10] The phrasing makes it clear that all of this dazzling metamorphic movement was oriented toward the person of the immobile king, the representamen of everything in the evening's symbolism. The first fifteen "passages" lead the dancers progressively closer to his place, after which the forty passages of the Grand Ballet proper are addressed to his majesty. But in the shimmering formations, disruptions, displacements, and reformations of these Archimedean patterns, one discerns a Circe who is alive and well, a Circe who has herself perhaps graduated to a "meilleure vie" in the spiral progress of mutability. Without the physical presence of the king, the body of royal power, the dance would have no orientation and no meaning. But the dance for its part might best be regarded as an investment of the king with its own shifting dynamism, a *penetration* of the king with the exuberant energy of celestial motion. The bodies of the dancers could be understood ideally to communicate to him the eurythmic precision they collectively demonstrate. The choreographic figures are signifiers at one with their meaningful play of pattern and disruption. The dance offers the paradox of a timeless geometry invaded by change only, briefly, to overcome it again. Here, surely, Beaujoyeulx reached the most satisfying resolution of the antitheses which govern his ballet.

Less satisfying however was the experience of the unnecessary Queen Louise, one of the naiads participating in the Grand Ballet. The

10. Plato, *Timaeus*, 40c, on the dance of the stars: "Vain would be the attempt to tell all the figures of them circling as in dance, and their juxtapositions, and the return of them in their revolutions upon themselves, and their approximations, and to say which of these deities in their conjunctions meet, and which of them are in opposition, and in what order they get behind and before one another."

medal she presented to the king after the performance bore the representation of a dolphin, a punning allusion to the dauphin she wanted to give him. But the dauphin would never be born and the house of Valois, for better or worse, would die out at the assassination of her husband. We can think of Louise moving in vain through all those brilliant and subtle formations, displaying herself in the great production she sponsored, performing in front of a trio who did not love her, and achieving in her case no magical harmony at all.

SARAH KAY

The Life of the Dead Body:
Death and the Sacred in the
chansons de geste

Death in the *chansons de geste* is characterized by a combination of features which is peculiar to the genre. It is violent; it strikes down a male hero in the prime of life; it forms a part of a pattern of conflict in which all the characters of these poems are embroiled. It takes place, then, amid a storm of energy, a generalized discharge of violence, which distinguishes it from the unilateral destruction of martyrdom, or from the typically one-sided encounters of chivalric romance, where the protagonist, set upon by often unexpected and anonymous adversaries, may despatch them yet sustain little or no injury himself. In these other narrative genres, violence, which is restricted almost exclusively to the protagonists' opponents, seems curiously sanitized. In hagiography, it is a haloed performance staged by the martyr for our edification. In romances, it appears mere trompe-l'oeil, allegorizing a brief phase of the hero's progress. In the *chansons de geste*, on the other hand, the history and experience of a whole society is violently inscribed on the bodies of its people. Whether suffered or inflicted on others, death is the lifestyle to which epic warriors are dedicated, the raison d'être of their upbringing, and the motivation for conflict eternally renewed. It is an obligation, a compulsion even. Also, of course, it is the means by which the dead accede to textual life as 'heroes' of these poems.

The body of a dying hero may assume the quality of a "mystical" or "sacred" body. The interference between epic and hagiography—which has been well documented from formal as well as substantive

YFS 86, *Corps Mystique, Corps Sacré: Textual Transfigurations of the Body from the Middle Ages to the Seventeenth Century,* ed. Françoise Jaouën and Benjamin Semple, © 1994 by Yale University.

similarities between the genres[1]—and the historical fact that many early *chanson de geste* heroes were venerated as saints,[2] have amply justified reading epic deaths in Christian terms. As Roland, in the Oxford text, is dying, he lists the fragments of the bodies of martyrs in the pommel of his sword (vv. 2445–8).[3] Sacred history was written on the bodies of these martyrs as now on his own. When Vivien, in the *Chançun de Willame* and in *Aliscans,* is on the point of death, he receives the viaticum from William (*Willame* v. 2049–51; *Aliscans* v. 947 ff.). This communion with *corpus Christi,* like the enumeration of relics in the *Roland,* is a reduplicative gesture, confirming the extent to which Vivien, as he lies in a paradise landscape and exhales an odor of sanctity, already partakes of Christ's sacrifice. Christological interpretations have been advanced for other *chansons de geste,* not necessarily the earliest ones, or ones whose setting is that of crusade.[4]

This well-established link between heroic death and the mystical bodies of Christ and the saints has, however, discouraged readers of these poems from seeing them in any other light. Although Le Gentil charts the progressive secularization of epic death scenes, he presents this shift as purely negative, as a move *away* from the Christian.[5] Micheline de Combarieu invokes a similar dichotomy between more and less Christian deaths. She distinguishes "positive" from "negative" heroes, the former assuming a Christological character in death,

1. For a recent review of this literature, see Dominique Boutet, *La Chanson de geste. Forme et signification d'une écriture épique du Moyen Age* (Paris: PUF, 1993), 44–6, 95–6.

2. For example, Roland, Ogier, Renaut de Montauban, Girart de Roussillon, Ami and Amile, William.

3. The editions of *chansons de geste* cited in this essay are as follows: *Aliscans,* ed. Claude Régnier (Paris: Champion, 1990); *Ami et Amile,* ed. Peter Dembowski (Paris: Champion, 1969); *Boeve de Haumtone,* ed. Albert Stimming (Halle: Niemeyer, Bibliotheca Normannica, 1899); *La Chanson de Roland,* ed. Ian Short (Paris: Livre de Poche, 1990); *La Chançun de Willame,* ed. Duncan McMillan (Paris: Picard, 1949–50); *Daurel et Beton,* ed. Arthur S. Kimmel (Chapel Hill: University of North Carolina Press, Studies in the Romance Languages and Literatures 108, 1971); *Garin le Loheren,* ed. Josephine Elvira Vallerie (Michigan: Edwards Bros., Inc., 1947); *Gormont et Isembart,* ed. Alphonse Bayot (Paris: Champion, 1931); *Raoul de Cambrai,* ed. Sarah Kay (Oxford: Oxford University Press, 1992); *Renaut de Montauban,* ed. Jacques Thomas (Geneva: Droz, 1989).

4. For example, William in the *Couronnement Louis.* See Stephen G. Nichols, "Sign as (Hi)story in the *Couronnement de Louis,*" *Romanic Review* 71 (1980): 1–9. The sacrifice of Amile's sons to cure Ami's leprosy is a good example of the Christological in a noncrusading context.

5. Pierre Le Gentil, "Réflexions sur le thème de la mort dans les chansons de geste," *Mélanges . . . Rita Lejeune* (Gembloux: Duculot, 1969), 801–9.

the latter deprived of it.[6] Claude Blum stresses the links between the *chansons de geste* and a generalized medieval Christian culture of death conceived in relation to sin and redemption. He then follows Combarieu's lead: the death of the "positive" character is seen as confirming his claim on the life eternal, whereas the "negative," traitor's death functions as a narrative reduplication of his earlier, spiritual death through sin.[7]

This essay seeks to define the sacrality of death in the *chansons de geste* in different terms. I shall argue that the death of the youthful hero has, indeed, a religious or "spiritual" character, but that this is not uniquely Christian; a "primitive" account of the sacred proves more illuminating than an orthodox Christian one. By appealing to pre- or non-Christian beliefs, we can discern features common to all the texts, and so avoid this often problematic and sometimes arbitrary division into "positive" and "negative" exemplars. The hero's death is generally the pretext for retelling his career as a secular warrior and may be described using non-Christian imagery, such as that of the earth, or animal life. The violence released in death may be "spiritual," but not necessarily in a theological sense. The "spirit" of the dead lives on, and communicates itself to other characters, affecting (or infecting) their behavior in a way not fully explained within a Christian framework. I shall briefly illustrate these points from a number of poems, before turning to the works of René Girard and Sigmund Freud whose theorization of the "primitive" sacred seems to me to offer fuller and more suggestive accounts of epic death than are furnished by traditional Christian commentaries. In conclusion, I shall offer a close reading of a single death scene from *Raoul de Cambrai*, a *chanson de geste* of the late twelfth century.

1. *The energy of the dying.* Like operatic *prime donne*, epic heroes experience greater bursts of energy the nearer they get to death. Roland does not manage to break his sword, but he has a pretty good try. Readers of the *Chançun de Willame* could be forgiven for assuming Vivien to be dead, until his uncle arrives. The "dead" man then launches into a 12-line speech (or, in *Aliscans*, several speeches total-

6. Micheline de Combarieu du Grès, *L'Idéal humain et l'expérience morale chez les héros de chansons de geste des origines à 1250* (Aix-en-Provence: Publications du CUERMA, 1979), 581–664.

7. Claude Blum, "L'Espace imaginaire de la mort dans les chansons de geste des origines à 1250," in *La Chanson de geste et le mythe carolingien. Mélanges René Louis* (Saint-Père-sous-Vézelay: Musée archéologique régional, 1982), 929–44.

ing 14 lines). Raoul's uncle, Guerri, also finds his nephew declared "dead" (*Raoul de Cambrai*, v. 2965) on the battlefield, but Raoul's body, although previously so immobile that the sword could not be wrested from his grasp (v. 3000), begins to writhe immediately before his death (vv. 3011–12). When Garin is struck down in *Garin le Loheren*, he is said to be "slain" (v. 16560). He is taken for dead by an over-eager relic hunter, who spots him as a likely martyr (v. 16569) and cuts off his right arm, whereupon Garin inquires, "Friend, fair brother, why have you slain me"? (v. 16576). In *Daurel et Beton*, the dying Bove, fatally wounded by his companion Gui on a boar hunt, elaborates a complex plan to save his friend from the consequences of his deed (v. 395 ff.). Another Beuve, whose ambushers in the opening episode of *Renaut de Montauban* are confident they have killed him (v. 1528), nevertheless has the energy to call on his son Maugis to avenge him (vv. 1536–8). These dying bodies, aflame with energy, seem to be all set for life in a different mode from that of their previous existence. *Vita mutatur, non tollitur* (Life is changed, not ended), says the office for the dead;[8] but only in very few cases (those of Roland and Vivien) does the poem narrowly identify that continuing life with the Christian resurrection.

2. *The story of life in death.* This vitality of the dying is often resumed in a retelling of their lives. Roland, typically for him, recounts his own glorious biography in the form of an address to his sword (v. 2318 ff.). Others, more self-effacing, leave this narrative responsibility to those who attend them in their last moments. Particularly full examples of the biographical *planctus* are those of William to Vivien in the *Chançun de Willame* (v. 1997 ff.) and in *Aliscans* (v. 810 ff.). Isembart, pronouncing a lament over the corpse of Gormont, takes the opportunity to review his enmity against Louis (vv. 470–96). In *Raoul de Cambrai*, Guerri briefly recalls Raoul's dealings with Bernier when he finds him dead on the battlefield; later, when Raoul's body has been brought back to Cambrai, no fewer than four people (his mother, sister, fiancée, and uncle) swoon over his corpse, while his courageous qualities are lengthily celebrated (v. 3370 ff.). Death, then, is the moment that focuses the vigor and energy of life, and casts it as a biography the narrative impetus of which is brutally interrupted. As I will show below (4), this narrative may be envisaged as continuing in another mode. My point here is that the poems' intentness on the achieve-

8. Cited in Combarieu, *Idéal*, 582.

ments of the dead locates their energies primarily in the cut-and-thrust of secular knighthood, and not in a Christian sphere.[9]

3. *The imagery of death.* Roland's sword, as he tries to break it, keeps rebounding heavenwards, a movement later followed by his glove in the hand of the angel. When Raoul is dying, however, raising his sword proves a futile gesture, and instead he strikes it deeply into the earth (vv. 2937–42). He has been fighting to win land for himself, and this blow, struck at the moment of his death, unites him with the desired object. In *Aliscans,* Vivien's end, following the viaticum, releases his soul to paradise (v. 1004; in the *Willame* its destination is unspecified, v. 2052). But for many others who die, the communion of *corpus Christi* is replaced by that with blades of grass or foliage. This is clearly a Christian rite, resorted to when no priest is at hand (*Raoul de Cambrai,* vv. 2249–50); yet its association is with the earth, and the natural order, albeit as God's work. It may well reflect ancient pagan beliefs, thinly veneered by Christianity.[10] The act of communion with the grass upon the ground is a reminder that the violence and abruptness of epic death return the body to the earth whence it came with alarming rapidity. Does the earth have any power to protect those who dwell upon it? Raoul says to Ernaut of Douai, "Neither the earth nor the green grass can preserve you," but in Ernaut's view they might (*Raoul de Cambrai,* vv. 2838, 2851).[11]

The possibility that communion with foliage may link the dying to the natural world, more than to a theological community, is most strikingly suggested in *Daurel et Beton,* where this communion is associated with other, non-Christian images of death. Bove is murdered on a boar hunt, and the details of his death scene make the boar an image of his life, and of the character of his assailant.[12] (Similarly,

9. Philippe Ariès locates the emergence of a link between biography and death in the twelfth century. See his *Western Attitudes towards Death: from the Middle Ages to the Present,* trans. Patricia M. Ranum (Baltimore and London: The Johns Hopkins University Press, 1974), ch. 2. This material is amplified in Part 2 of his *The Hour of our Death,* trans. Helen Weaver (New York: Knopf, 1981).

10. See the discussions by J. D. M. Ford, "'To bite the dust' and Symbolical Lay Communion," *PMLA* 20 (1905): 197–230, and by George L. Hamilton, "The Sources of the Symbolical Lay Communion," *Romanic Review* 4 (1914): 221–240. On the pagan origins of the rite, see especially Hamilton, 222–3.

11. For an early discussion of these lines, see the note in my edition of *Raoul de Cambrai,* cited in note 3.

12. See my "Compagnonnage, désordre social, et hétérotextualité," in *Actes du XIe Congrès International de la Société Rencesvals. Memorias de la Real Academia de Buenas Letras de Barcelona* 22 (1990): 353–67.

Begon's assassination beside the corpse of a boar has been seen [Combarieu, 591] as a powerful metaphor of the hero's abasement: see *Garin le Loheren*, v. 10313 ff.).[13] Bove asks Gui to grant him communion "with a leaf" (v. 428) and, when denied it, proposes instead that Gui should eat his heart. As Kimmel puts it, "if his courage and virility were to survive in the person of his assassin, he would reconcile himself to dying" (107). This motif of the heart in *Daurel* recalls the macabre moment in *Raoul de Cambrai* when Guerri extracts the dead Raoul's heart to admire its dimensions (v. 3059 ff.). The heart, center of vital energies, is seen as somehow focusing and perpetuating the heroism of the dead heroic body. The imagery of death, then, can link the hero not with a Christian heaven, but with the forces of nature, the animal kingdom, and the energies of the human organism.

4. *Narrative commitments.* Such imagery of death suggests that the life force of the dying man is somehow transmitted to the universe around him, rather than being transferred out of it to "heaven." In many cases, the death scene also contains a suggestion that this "spirit" will somehow survive to influence the course of narrative events. It is true that laments for the dead often contain a prayer expressing the hope that the hero's biography is to be continued in a Christian afterlife.[14] In many cases, however, what seems uppermost is a desire for vengeance in the here and now. Begon, Garin's brother in *Garin le Loheren*, reflects on the consequences of his death for his family and vassals ("How much you are losing today," v. 10616); they will later pursue reprisals against his assailants. Combarieu observes that death, in this poem, marks a moment of crisis in the irresolvable political conflict among the living (Combarieu, 587, 589, 593); the extension of this conflict in the form of revenge, then, merely continues a meaning which has been highlighted by death. There is a sense in which Begon's allies do not "lose" him at all; the crisis of his death lives with them, and the violence which he suffers still affects them. Similarly Isembart promises to fight on for Gormont's cause (vv. 487–8); Guerri swears to kill all Raoul's enemies, and tear out Bernier's liver and lights (vv.

13. Begon also takes communion with three blades of grass, which he apparently takes up in his feet! (v. 10621).

14. On the prayer as a formulaic element in laments for the dead in the *chansons de geste*, see Paul Zumthor, "Etude typologique des *planctus* contenus dans la *Chanson de Roland*," in *La Technique littéraire des chansons de geste. Actes du Colloque de Liège* (Paris: Les Belles Lettres, 1959): 219–34, and "Le *planctus* épique," *Romania* 84 (1963): 61–9.

2992–3, 3007–9, 3017–9). Even in the more "Christian" poems, *Roland* and *Willame*, thoughts of vengeance are crucial to the continuation of the plot after the hero's untimely removal from it.

An interesting example of a dead man's energy continuing the narrative of a poem with renewed, and unexpected, impetus is provided by *Renaut de Montauban*. As we saw, the dying Beuve calls on his son Maugis to avenge him. Maugis is a remarkable figure in the *chansons de geste*, since he is a magician and a thief.[15] His deviousness and his supernatural character are a striking illustration of the "spiritual" influence exerted by the dead on the world which they appear to have left. *Boeve de Haumtone*, likewise, opens with the death of the hero's father. This scene draws on animal imagery like the examples reviewed above; the hero himself only narrowly escapes a similar fate.[16] His subsequent extraordinary adventures (involving combats with animals, storms, and marvels) could be seen as powered by the poem's initial outburst of violence, as though some "spiritual" force resulting from this violence were somehow directing its narrative course into "supernatural" channels.

Thus whereas the prayers pronounced at death scenes may suggest the removal of the dead warrior to a transcendent sphere, in fact his "spirit," the energy of his fractured biography, often seems to infiltrate the social universe of the poem, and direct its subsequent action.

What this brief survey shows is that the energy associated with violent death, in the *chansons de geste*, is "religious" in a sense that does not conform with conventional Christian belief. Heroes may be dead, but they won't lie down. Some kind of "spiritual" energy reaches a peak in their bodies at the moment of death and remains among the living. This "sacrality" of death overrides the distinction between "positive" and "negative" heroes or between Christian (e.g. crusading) and non-Christian settings, since it is distinctive of the genre as a whole.

The idea that the dead continue somehow as "persons" among the

15. See the two studies by Philippe Verelst, "L'enchanteur d'épopée. Prolégomènes à une étude sur *Maugis*," *Romanica Gandensia* 16 (1976): 119–62, and ibid., 18 (1981): 73–152; also Wolfgang van Emden, "What Constitutes a 'bon larron'?," in *Guillaume d'Orange and the Chanson de geste: Studies presented to Duncan McMillan . . .* , ed. Wolfgang van Emden and Philip E. Bennett (Reading: Société Rencesvals [British Branch], 1984), 197–218.

16. His wife sends him on a boar hunt, in the course of which he is killed by her lover (v. 128 ff.). She then arranges for Boeve to be killed, but his tutor kills a pig instead and uses its blood to stain Boeve's clothes (vv. 329–39).

living is, of course, one to which medieval Christian thinkers sub-scribed.[17] Indeed, anxiety about the invasive energy released by violent death finds an echo in clerical thinking, as Philippe Ariès records:

> Because of this aversion to violent death among the clergy, and despite the emergence of a more moral and more reasonable attitude, [Guillelmus] Durandus [bishop of Mende in the thirteenth century] continued to invoke the primitive beliefs regarding the pollution of sacred places by the liquids of the human body, blood, or sperm: "Those who have been killed are not brought into the church for fear that their blood will soil the floor of the temple of God." In such cases, the Mass and the *Libera* were said in the absence of the body.[18]

If the emanations of the violently slain are capable of harming the sacred sites of Christian worship, they must themselves contain some "spiritual" force. The key term in this quotation, for my purposes, is "primitive." What "primitive beliefs" are operating in the *chansons de geste* (and elsewhere in medieval culture) to invest the dead with such mysterious powers? It is at this point that I turn to the works of Girard and Freud, who offer illuminating insights into the operations of a "primitive," pre- or non-Christian sacrality.

In *Violence and the Sacred*,[19] René Girard examines with reference to Greek tragedy the "primitive" identification between violence and religion. "Violence," he writes, "is the heart and secret soul of the sacred" (31). This is because violence is an unavoidable, uncontrollable impulse in human nature, and everything uncontrollable appears "sacred" to the primitive mentality. Violence, for Girard, forms part of a terrifying triad the other terms of which are imitation and desire. Everyone desires not just to be *like*, but to *be*, the other person; to annex to himself that being which, in the other, is perceived as grounded and secure. But the more he yields to the compulsion to imitate, the more the difference between himself and the other col-lapses; the desire to efface difference brings as its inevitable accom-paniment a violent destructiveness towards that very being which the subject is trying to assume. It also provokes, in the other, a surge of reciprocal violence: he desires to be imitated, to have his sense of self confirmed, but such imitation threatens that self with the loss of its

17. See Gerhard Oexle, "Die Gegenwart der Toten," in *Death in the Middle Ages,* ed. Herman Braet and Werner Verbeke (Leuven: Leuven University Press, 1983), 19–77.

18. Philippe Ariès, *The Hour of Our Death,* 13.

19. René Girard, *Violence and the Sacred,* trans. Patrick Gregory (Baltimore and London: The Johns Hopkins University Press, 1977).

being, and this is unbearable. The escalating whirl of desire, imitation, and violence produces what Girard calls a "sacrificial crisis" in which the collapse of difference fuels violence, and violence hastens the demise of difference. The sacrificial crisis is like a plague, a contamination that reduces everyone to undifferentiation and death. Thus legal systems have to evolve which will hold violence in some kind of check; but the means whereby they do this involves miming the very violence they seek to repress. And religions must be elaborated which recognize the sacred quality of violence and channel it towards the destruction of a mutually agreed upon object, whom members of a society agree to brand as "different" because they need to restore difference as the only possible antidote to the contagion of violence.

The *chansons de geste* seem to me to contain many of the "primitive" traits which Girard perceives in tragedy. The legal machinery of the *judicium Dei* stages violence within a confined, judicial theatre; yet many duels are inconclusive, and even when they are not, their outcome does not command universal acceptance, so that violence spills out once more into society. The genre devises sacrificial patterns of thought, forcing "Saracens" or "traitors" into the role of the-enemy-who-is-different, and thus restoring order to the community. But this ascription of difference is often hard to maintain (epic Saracens, for instance, are disconcertingly like epic Christians); and even the presence of Saracens and traitors does not prevent others from coming to blows, like Roland and Oliver in the *Roland*. A "sacrificial crisis" reigns, to some degree, in all the poems, drawing antagonists into interminable and reciprocal violence, and making epic characters all resemble one another in their fundamental aggression.

The death scenes with which this essay is concerned show this violence reaching its peak in the brutal curtailment of life. As I have shown, the abruptness of death does not eliminate the violence. On the contrary, the dying hero's energy, and the sense of the dynamism of life being arrested in mid-flow, lead to violence being diverted into the natural world, and affecting the actions of those who survive. Revenge, the mainstay of plot construction throughout the genre, exhibits in a frenzied form the Girardian triad of violence, desire, and imitation, since the desire to repeat, to reenact a previous instance of violence, is itself only a fresh act of violence that calls forth fresh desire for imitation. "Only violence can put an end to violence, and that is why violence is self-propagating. Everyone wants to strike the last blow, and reprisal can follow reprisal without any true conclusion ever being reached" (26). Girard's formulation admirably captures the generalized violence of the *chansons de geste,* so different, as I said at the outset, from the carefully delimited and unilateral character of violence in other genres.

By deconstructing religious (and specifically Christian) belief, Girard advances a more general theory of the "sacred" which is illuminating for these poems. However, there are shortcomings in his thinking which are highlighted by his very combativeness against those with whom he most disagrees: proponents of psychoanalysis. He devotes a chapter of *Violence and the Sacred* to an attack on Freud's *Totem and Taboo,* a work concerned, like his own, with the emergence of law and religion in the wake of inherited violence. Essentially he objects to Freud's insistence that this original violence was expressed against the Father; that it has a sexual, as well as an aggressive component; and that it requires interpretation via a notion of the unconscious as the place where repressed desires are lodged. This exposes weaknesses in Girard's own thought: his lack of any theory about what is meant by the term "instinct"; his unwillingness to countenance any libidinal dimension to violence (or, indeed, to engage more than fleetingly with difference as sexual difference); and his refusal to conceive of violence as other than overt and reciprocal. Thus, although Girard strenuously maintains that his own views replace and correct those of Freud, there are resources in psychoanalytic theory which exceed Girard's account of the sacred, just as a Girardian approach goes further than the account offered by traditional Christianity.

So as not to broaden the range of this argument unduly, I shall restrict my discussion of psychoanalytic texts to *Totem and Taboo,*[20] despite its notorious eccentricity. Freud is concerned throughout this work with the ambivalence inherent in social and religious practices, and in this regard his thinking has parallels with Girard's. For Girard, man is both compelled to imitate, and not to imitate; both admiration and antagonism are born of this contradiction. For Freud, a taboo (such as that concerning kingship) "unmistakably reveals its double meaning and its origin from ambivalent tendencies" (68). This ambivalence, here described as being between exalting and punishing, will later be theorized in relation to the murdered primal father, who inspires both love and guilt (185). (Unconscious) guilt for violence towards the father, then, fuels social acts just as it does neuroses; and in both cases, con-

20. Sigmund Freud, *Totem and Taboo,* trans. A. A. Brill (New York: Vintage Books, 1918).

flict with the father is sexually motivated, at least in part.[21] In pursuing the analogy with neuroses, Freud explicitly distinguishes between the conscious and unconscious aspects of primitive practices:

> [The taboo] would thus be the correct counterpart to the compulsive action of the neurosis in which the suppressed impulse and the impulse which suppresses it meet in mutual and simultaneous satisfaction. The compulsive action is nominally a protection against the forbidden action; but actually we would say that it is a repetition of what is forbidden. The word "nominally" is here applied to the conscious whereas the word "actually" applies to the unconscious instance of psychic life. Thus although the taboo ceremonial of kings is nominally an expression of the highest veneration and a means of guarding them, actually it is the punishment for their elevation, the revenge which their subjects take upon them. [68–9]

We seem to be a long way here from death in the *chansons de geste*, and yet this quotation provides useful material with which to speculate about the "sacred" quality of epic death. Freud's concern is with psychic processes that possess energy and deviousness to an equally extreme degree. Primitive construction of the "sacred," for him, is a response not just to the uncontrollable (as in Girard) but also to the unknowable, unacknowledgeable operations of the psyche. It is interesting to view the "sacred" quality of death in the *chansons de geste* as likewise reflecting unconscious investments. Thus, for example, revenge narratives might be seen as superimposing (conscious) protection on (unconscious) repetition. When a character seeks vengeance, is he perhaps not only motivated to "protect" (himself, his honour and lineage), but also driven by an unacknowledged desire to repeat an act of violence himself? The "spirit" of the dead man which calls for such revenge would be a striking representation of such a compulsion. And why do characters get killed in the first place? Death is linked to sexual considerations in more *chansons de geste* than one might think. Men are murdered out of desire for their wives in *Daurel* and *Boeve de Haumtone;* Garin in *Garin le Loheren* may also be killed partly for

21. Though as Girard points out (*Violence and the Sacred*, 209), the murder of the primal father is a literal crime carried out by adult men, whereas the inhibitions of the Oedipus complex involve a child's unconscious anxieties and fantasies. In *Totem and Taboo* (93–7), Freud distinguishes the greater sexual content of neuroses and its lesser importance in social institutions. It is, of course, misleading to limit the libidinal aspect of Freud's concept of aggression to unconscious desire for the mother. It is primarily the libidinal investment in the ego, as a result of narcissism, which gives aggressive instinct a libidinal dimension.

sexual reasons. It is striking that these are the texts that invoke animal imagery in connection with death.[22] Is the motif of the hunt a way of invoking a character's unconscious drives? Do the wild animals figure the killers' unacknowledged animality?

The biological or symbolic family may also provoke unconscious desires that find expression in the "sacrality" of death. Girard's account of reciprocal violence, considered in Freudian terms, limits conflict to that between "brothers" (as in *Raoul de Cambrai* or *Daurel*, where violence is initially sparked off between companions of the same age), and belongs in the specular, or narcissistic, domain of the ego.[23] The scenario these poems elaborate could be described in para-Freudian terminology, as a "peer romance." But other texts necessitate recourse to the "family romance," where the drama unfurls not within a generation but between them. Beuve in *Renaut* is killed in reprisal for the death of Charlemagne's son; and the main action of the poem then pits a childless Charles against a fatherless Maugis. Each finds in bereavement the gratification of a certain fantasy, Charles not to have to contemplate a successor, Maugis not to be subordinated to paternal control. Is the latter's elusive, magical quality another way of figuring unacknowledged desires? Similarly, could the strange adventures of Boeve in *Boeve de Haumtone* express the fantasy of liberation from the father's authority?

The section of *Totem and Taboo* in which Freud speaks of the cult of the dead throws further light on the *chansons de geste*. The dead patriarch, overthrown by his sons, proves more influential than the living one had been, since they find themselves instituting social and religious practices that embody his interdictions. The "primitive" attitudes encoded in this myth are paradoxical in that they simultaneously deny and affirm the power of death: the dead are attributed with influence over the living both *because* they are dead, and *despite* being dead. Thus, Freud argues, "primitive man would bow to the superior power of death with the same gesture with which he seems to deny it" (121). In the *chansons de geste*, likewise, the energy and mysterious agency of the dead may result from the violence of death, but they are also a refusal to admit that death can ever really sever a person

---

22. Admittedly in *Garin*, this imagery actually appears not in Garin's but in Begon's death.

23. For a study of narcissism and psychosis in *Raoul de Cambrai*, see Alexandre Leupin, "*Raoul de Cambrai*: the Illegitimacy of Writing," in *The New Medievalism*, ed. Marina S. Brownlee, Kevin Brownlee, and Stephen G. Nichols (Baltimore and London: The Johns Hopkins University Press, 1991), 131–154.

from his place among the living. The "sacrality" of death is an assertion that death, whilst inevitable, is also profoundly inadmissible.

I shall conclude this essay by analyzing the scene at the end of *Raoul de
Cambrai* where Bernier, returning with Raoul's uncle Guerri from a
pilgrimage to St James of Compostella, passes by the very spot at
Origny where, 5000 lines and many years previously, he had killed
Raoul. Bernier sighs, and at Guerri's insistence, explains why:

> Il me remenbre de Raooil le marchis
> qui desor lui avoit te[l] orguel pris
> qu'a .iiii. contes vaut lor terre tolirr.
> Vees ci le leu tot droit ou je l'ocis. [8198–201]

> I am reminded of Marquis Raoul who was consumed with such pride
> that he resolved to take the land of four counts for himself. This is the
> very place where I killed him.

Soon after hearing this, Guerri is seized by an "evil spirit" (*max esperis*,
v. 8228): detaching his stirrup iron, he dashes out Bernier's brains.
Bernier falls from his horse into a stream, from which he is pulled by
his companions. With the energy characteristic of the dying, he pro-
nounces a speech in which he first condemns Guerri for his treachery,
remembers that his wife (Guerri's daughter) had warned him against
her father, then recalls Christ's forgiveness of Longinus, and pardons
his assailant. Confessing his sins (which the text does not specify), he
takes communion with three blades of grass and expires. But his narrative goes on: the narrator prays that his soul may be received into
paradise (v. 8263), and shortly afterwards, his son swears to avenge him.
In the concluding lines of the poem, Guerri flees from his attackers and
is never heard of again.

This episode exhibits the features which I detailed earlier as typify-
ing epic death scenes: the energy of the dying; the sense (only briefly
evoked here) of a narrative cut brutally short; imagery of the earth
alongside more conventionally Christian images of death; and the
commitment to resume the hero's narrative through the avenging of
his death. Its Christian elements, although pronounced, form only a
part of a more broadly "sacred" character that includes the role of
premonition, the power of the ground as the place where Raoul died
and from which Bernier takes the last rites, and Guerri's invasion by an
"evil spirit."

Bernier's death is a mirroring response to that of Raoul. Although
he is not actually killed on the same spot, his death is linked to the site

of Raoul's. Both die from an injury to the head which causes their brains to spill out on the ground; both have been forewarned by a woman that they will die, and both are avenged. The greater sanctity, in the Christian sense, of Bernier's end is an inversion of the sacrilegious character of Raoul's, and thus still within a specular frame. Such mirroring encourages us to see Guerri as the agent of a Girardian violence, grounded in imitation. Indeed, Bernier and Raoul have been caught up in a typically Girardian triad of desire, imitation, and violence, since Raoul died trying to win the lands of Bernier's family (and thus in a sense seeking to assume his friend's position and being in the world); whereas Bernier has married Raoul's cousin and gained control of Raoul's estates, thereby responding to Raoul's aggression by imitating and displacing *him*. The "sacred" aspects (Christian and non-Christian) of Bernier's death, and the "spiritual" motivation of Guerri's attack, thus fall to some degree within the theoretical parameters of *Violence and the Sacred*.

However, this account is not adequate to the scene, since it passes over what the text also conceals, but nevertheless betrays: the influence of Bernier's mother. When Bernier remembers that Raoul was so proud as to "take the land of four counts for himself" (v. 8200), the audience can hardly forget that the first act of Raoul's campaign was to burn down the convent, also at Origny, where Bernier's mother Marsent was abbess. This crime was, indeed, the main motive for Bernier's killing Raoul. When Bernier, dying, forgives Guerri in the name of "Diex nostre pere" (v. 8249), he reminds the audience that he had earlier claimed God as his father when remonstrating with Raoul for causing Marsent's death. Condemned as a whore by Raoul because she bore Bernier out of wedlock, Marsent is represented by Bernier as a holy woman who chose God as her partner in preference to the husband offered her when she was abandoned by her seducer Ybert, Bernier's biological father. In an adventurous anticipation of the Freudian "family romance," Bernier asserts "that no one is a bastard unless they have denied God" (v. 1531), thus situating himself as the son not of Ybert and his concubine, but of God and a nun. Provoking Raoul to attack him, Bernier, in this quarrel, places himself in the position he assigns to his mother: that of the victim of Raoul's aggression. And in killing Raoul, Bernier continues to act on his mother's behalf, exacting revenge for her death. So, when Bernier recalls Raoul's crazy belligerence, dies near where his mother died, and appeals to the Father his mother chose for him, her influence is unmistakable.

The episode of Bernier's death, then, is an overt response to the death of Raoul, but a covert one to that of his mother. His last sight of her was of her lying on the ground with her psalter burning on her breast, as he lamented his impotence to save her (vv. 1325–33); he would later describe her breasts themselves as burning, as though her body were transformed into an altar:

> Celes mameles dont ele me norri
> vi je ardoir, par le cors Saint Geri! [1349–50]

> The very breasts with which she suckled me, I saw them burning, I swear by the body of St. Géri!

In his last moments, Bernier reproduces both the violence and the spirituality of this scene, consuming as he dies not the milk he received from her body at birth, but the grass of the earth redesignated as the body of the Father (v. 8258). The sacrality of Bernier's death, then, stems not only from the uncontrollable effects of violence, but also from their unspeakable inscription on the mother's body. In reenacting her death, Bernier follows her to a (relatively) pious end. He had reproached himself with failing as her heir (v. 1332), but this death *is* his inheritance. Furthermore, in simultaneously reenacting the death of Raoul, he places himself in the role of the man who killed her and, by dying, accepts punishment at the last for having failed to protect her earlier.

Ascribing these meanings to the text exceeds the framework advanced by Girard, and necessitates recourse to Freud. In relation to Raoul's death, Bernier's death may be Girardian; but in relation to his mother's it is Freudian. It betrays the irresistible influence of the family (real and symbolic), the libidinal dimension of epic violence, and the power of the repressed. The *chansons de geste*, like the unsophisticated or primitive mind, see violence as sacred not just because it is uncontrollable, but also because it is frighteningly unfathomable. They respond to it with a combination of admiration and reprobation, resignation and protest, Christian faith and despair. They know that the dead, who do not die, but continue to live amongst us, are the fears and desires we can neither face up to nor shake off.

FRANK LESTRINGANT

Travels in Eucharistia: Formosa and Ireland from George Psalmanaazaar to Jonathan Swift

For Claude Rawson

In the sixteenth century, the dispute or, rather, the "crisis" of the Eucharist was, in France, Holland and England at least, the decisive factor in the schism within Christianity. A symbol of community and a sign of ecclesiastical identity, the principal sacrament of Christianity abruptly became, for a large part of the faithful, a stumbling block and a potential cause of sin. The criticism of transubstantiation, by proposing a symbolic or commemorative conception of the Lord's Supper, directly weakened, fissured, and, for a certain period of time at least, eradicated the intimate solidarity of those twin bodies, the monarchical State and the Church. Here, I wish to examine, at the beginning of the Age of Enlightenment, the belated echo of this controversy with its innumerable consequences. It is a phenomenon which I call "travels in Eucharistia," a hybrid literary genre which is derived from utopian fictions and the allegorical novel, from pamphlets and travel narratives. This fictional narrative, which is both political and religious, is set in an isolated spot on the map, preferably an island, where it fashions, through the pronounced traits of a theocratic and anthropophagous society, a digest of the horror which Protestant Europe felt for an archaic act of violence continually renewed in the dogma of a demonized enemy. By this act of distancing and this nervous yet vigorous pursuit, the travels in Eucharistia contradictorily associate the rite of conjuration with the will to profanation. The mystical body is devalorized as a fleshly body, devouring and excreting, yet is simultaneously expanded to the legendary dimensions of a Moloch or a Leviathan.

YFS 86, *Corps Mystique, Corps Sacré: Textual Transfigurations of the Body from the Middle Ages to the Seventeenth Century,* ed. Françoise Jaouën and Benjamin Semple, © 1994 by Yale University.

109

GEORGE PSALMANAAZAAR'S ISLAND
OF FORMOSA

The *Description of Formosa* is one of the most famous forgeries produced by exotic literature.[1] This minutely detailed and supposedly
objective portrayal of a theocratic and cannibalistic society relocated
the bloody feasts of the Aztec religion to the Far East. Its goal was to
criticize the strong-arm missionary tactics of the Jesuits in that part of
the world, but the imaginary idolatry of the Formosans indirectly stigmatized the notion of sacrifice in the Catholic mass. Although well-
received in London, where everyone appreciated his apology for Anglicanism, George Psalmanaazaar was denounced as an imposter by
French Jesuits. Despite the protests of these Jesuits, the pseudo-
Japanese writer's account was generally received as authentic for
nearly thirty years.

It is pointless to become indignant over this literary hoax, as
Tzvetan Todorov has done in a recent book.[2] All things considered, it is

---

1. George Psalmanaazaar, *Description de l'Ile Formosa en Asie: Du Gouvernement,
des Loix, des Mœurs et de la Religion des habitans: Dressée sur les Mémoires du Sieur
George Psalmanaazaar natif de cette Ile* [. . .] *Par le Sieur N.F.D.B.R.* (Amsterdam: E.
Roger, 1705). On Psalmanaazaar, who was of French origin, and on the sources of his
work, see Percy G. Adams, *Travelers and Travel Liars, 1660–1800* (Berkeley and Los
Angeles: University of California Press, 1962), 93–97; or by the same author, *Travel
Literature and the Evolution of the Novel* (Lexington: The University Press of Kentucky,
1983), 71, 108. Psalmanaazaar, alias, Psalmanazar, became, in his old age, a friend of
Samuel Johnson. [Author's Note]

There are three editions of Psalmanaazaar's *Description*: a first English edition
of 1704, a second revised and updated English edition of 1705, and a French edition
published in Amsterdam in 1705. The author has used the French edition exclusively.
The English editions were published under the title, *An Historical and Geographical
Description of Formosa, an Island Subject to the Emperor of Japan . . . By George
Psalmanaazaar, a Native of the said Island, now in London* (London: Dan. Brown;
G. Strahan and W. Davis; and Fran. Coggan, 1704; and London: Mat. Wolton, Abel Roper
and B. Lintott; Fr. Coggan; G. Strahan and W. Davis, 1705), the 1705 version including a
subtitle: "The Second Edition corrected, with many large and useful Additions, particularly a new Preface clearly answering every thing that has been objected against the
Author and the Book." Since there are substantial variations among the three editions
and particularly between the English and French texts, I have generally provided my own
translations of the French. However, whenever possible, I have cited the English editions. Hereafter these texts will be cited as follows: Psalmanaazaar 1704 (first English
edition), Psalmanaazaar 1705a (second English edition), and Psalmanaazaar 1705b
(French edition). [Translator's Note]

2. Tzvetan Todorov, *Les Morales de l'histoire* (Paris: Grasset, 1991), 134–41; or *The
Morals of History*, trans. Alyson Waters (Minneapolis: University of Minnesota Press,
forthcoming). It goes without saying that I do not subscribe to the strictly moral conclusion of this chapter: "As a historical text, Psalmanazar's *Description* does not deserve

better to admire the feat of "this inspired mythomaniacal adventurer-imposter," whose fiction proved so convincing that he "was officially charged with teaching Formosan at Oxford in order to train future missionaries who were to be sent to that country."[3]

What strikes us first is the way in which the author knew how to produce a sense of familiarity leading his readers to accept the most implausible of accounts. For the parallel universe which he managed to create bears more than a passing resemblance to our own. The uncanniness, or, to borrow Freud's term, the *Unheimlichkeit* of the Formosan theocracy fascinates by its very familiarity. The horror of human sacrifices on the island of Formosa defies good sense. It mocks the rules of reason and contravenes all the evidence of observations reported by travelers up until then. Yet the horror is not unknown, for it lies at the heart of the Catholic sacrament of the Eucharist as it was spontaneously interpreted, and reviled, by Protestants. The Formosan utopia thus confers a spectacular brilliance on this rite, all the more scandalous for being perpetrated undisturbed in the neighboring countries of southern Europe, where the church of Rome reigned supreme. What is more, the travelers who preceded Psalmanaazaar in the Far East, although well-informed and enemies of sensationalism, were, for the most part, Jesuits, which was enough to discredit their testimony before the English elite, to whom, more than anyone, the *Description of Formosa* is addressed.

The pseudo-Formosan's strength was knowing how to play on the latent fears of his potential reader. Distanced from the reader and adorned with the glamour of exoticism, the holy terror of the bloody sacrifice created a perfectly believable fiction, up to and including its wild exaggerations. One example of these exaggerations: each year, it is said, no less than eighteen thousand male children under the age of nine perish at the hands of the sacrificers. The preface goes to great lengths to prevent possible objections to this point:

> Of all the customs observed in the pagans, those which pertain to religion are ordinarily examined with more curiosity than the others: the more distant they are from those which we practice, the stranger they seem to us. [Psalmanaazaar 1705b, xxv]

---

respect because it is false. As a fiction, it is not worthy of admiration because it does not present itself as such, and because its author was not particularly eloquent. But what if he *had* been?"

3. Jean-Michel Racault, *L'Utopie narrative en France et en Angleterre au XVIIIe siècle* (Oxford: The Voltaire Foundation, 1991), 304.

This rhetorical precaution betrays a profound irony. Of course the description of Formosa engages the reader on the subject of religion and indeed almost exclusively on the subject of the Christian religion, all under the guise of a geographical allegory. We have seen what the original readers must have thought of the supposed strangeness of the island's religious customs, and in particular of the principal one among these, the sacrifice of young children. The strangeness is not so radical that it prevents one from perceiving straightaway, though more or less indistinctly, a mysterious kinship to the ceremonies that can be observed in Europe. If the scandal is so great after all, it is that the conspicuous distance conceals a dangerous proximity. The reader's fear and discomfort are on the order of that certain feeling of unease caused by the recognition of the familiar concealed beneath the most monstrous of appearances, those which are the farthest removed from his or her frame of reference.

Before this glaring truth of a bloody sacrifice less distant and less exotic than it seems, the reader takes fright. He cries out in indignation at that enormous figure of eighteen thousand victims. Because it is so difficult to bring superficial verisimilitude to so tragic a story, Psalmanaazaar resorts to the voice of authority: the Ancients, first the Greeks and Romans, then the Israelites, are proposed as illustrious predecessors. There were precedents for Formosa's bloody theocracy among the most famous peoples of both profane and sacred history. The case of the ancient Hebrews offers a fine example, at least if one can pardon the chosen people for a temporary lapse:

> The scriptures teach us that they had established a place expressly for him [Moloch] in a valley near *Jerusalem*, where they had their children thrown in the fire and sacrificed them in honor of the sun and the moon, to which they made an idol; the idol was destroyed by the good king *Josiah*, who entirely abolished this impious and detestable cult. [Psalmanaazaar 1705b, xxvii]

A central character in Protestant readings of the Bible, Josiah is the symbol of the reform sovereigns who, like Edward VI or Elizabeth, destroyed idolatry and renewed the alliance with God, which had been momentarily compromised.[4] If one is to believe this allegorical deciphering of sacred history, fashionable in Huguenot France and in Cromwell and William of Orange's England, then the cult of Moloch becomes an exact prefiguration of papistic idolatry.

4. According to 2 Kings 22–23, Josiah purified the temple of Jerusalem and the territory of Judea of idolatry. Cf. Agrippa d'Aubigné, *Les Tragiques* vol. 3, l. 731.

The second argument in favor of the accuracy of Psalmanaazaar's testimony is of a different sort. The verisimilitude sought is no longer historical, but is at once sociological and geopolitical. Formosa, as we know, is an island. Its human resources are thus strictly limited. The question is how to know if the rate of fertility of a necessarily restricted population permits such sacrificial debauchery. Couldn't the end result be the extinction of the Formosan nation?

This line of questioning reveals in Psalmanaazaar and his interpreter a very modern preoccupation which reappears throughout the Age of Enlightenment, from Swift to Diderot and from Cornélius de Pauw to the Reverend Thomas Robert Malthus, passing through Voltaire and Sade.[5] The concern is, in a certain sense, an ecological one and consists of examining over a certain period of time the relationship between a given population and the territory it occupies. Malthusian pessimism evolves readily from this consideration, which it expands to encompass the entire globe. As for Diderot, he brings the argument back to the insular paradigm: the oceanic island, enclosed within its coral reef and protected from all exterior contact, represents, in his view, the ideal observatory for examining the evolution of society over several generations. One thus discovers the diverse solutions developed by a group to curb overpopulation, such as birth control, eugenics, human sacrifice, and anthropophagy. From this point of view, Formosa would represent an anthropological laboratory somewhat comparable to the tiny Ile des Lanciers discovered by Bougainville in the middle of the Pacific. It seems that a runaway birthrate, benefiting from the absence of sexual taboos, must imperil the precarious equilibrium of a location with limited resources. This natural growth, theoretically unlimited, can only be corrected by barbarous cultural practices, which seem barbarous, but which an inadequate site, when combined with an overly favorable climate, imposes and justifies.[6]

It so happens that, within Psalmanaazaar's social fiction, the difficulty is the reverse: the threat which hangs over the inhabitants of Formosa is not famine due to overpopulation, but extinction of the race by a sort of sacrificial consumption. What will happen later to the African kingdom of Butua, that bloody anti-utopia staged by Sade in his novel *Aline et Valcour*, could happen here. In Sade's tyrannical state situated at the heart of Africa and formerly stretching from one

5. On this point, see my book, *Le Cannibale, grandeur et décadence* (Paris: Perrin, 1994), ch. 12: "Cruelle nature: De Pauw, Sade."

6. Denis Diderot, *Supplément au Voyage de Bougainville* in *Le Neveu de Rameau et autres dialogues philosophiques* (Paris: Gallimard, 1972), 287.

ocean to the other, hatred for procreation, contempt for women, and a systematic destruction of them through cannibalistic orgies which were renewed day after day, led to a rapid decrease in the population. As a result, the kingdom of the despot Ben Mâacoro, who was both a sodomite and a cannibal, shrunk rapidly, and was supplanted by its less terribly barbarous neighbors, who were more concerned for their own future.[7] In many ways, the Formosan situation is diametrically opposed to this bestial brutality, yet there exists on the island a superstition which is almost as devastating. The author of the preface assures us, however, that this nation is not about to perish: polygamy provides the Formosans with an inexhaustible supply of progeny. Moreover, they do not strictly adhere to the figure of eighteen thousand: the "positivist law" which prescribes it "is not carried out literally."

The final argument is doubtless the weakest, although not the least ingenious: the obvious implausibility of so massive a number of human sacrifices is in fact hardly less shocking than Candidius's "flight of fancy" regarding repeated abortions by Formosan women, forbidden to bear children before the age of thirty-seven.[8] By a clever ruse,

7. Sade, *Aline et Valcour*, in *Œuvres*, ed. Michel Delon (Paris: Gallimard, Pléiade, 1990), letter 35, "Déterville à Valcour," vol. 1, 559–97.
8. Cited in Psalmanaazaar 1705b, xxviii. See George Candidius, *A Short Account of the Island of Formosa in the Indies, situated near the Coast of China; and of the Manners, Customs and Religions of its inhabitants. By George Candidius, Minister of the Word of God in that Island*, in *A Collection of Voyages and Travels, some now first printed* (London, 1704, BN: G.1218), 531: "But one thing is very remarkable in them, that their Wives are forbidden to bring forth any live Children till they are 36 or 37 Years of Age: wherefore they are obliged to kill their Children in the Womb, which they do thus: One of their Priestesses is called in, who lays the Woman with Child upon a Bed, and squeezes her so long, till the Child is forced thus from her, which puts them into more violent pains, than if they brought forth a Child according to the regular Course of Nature: they declare, they do this not for want of tenderness to them, but because they are forced to it by their Priestesses, who persuade them that they cannot commit a greater crime, than to bring Children into the World before the Age of 36, by which means many thousand are lost in a Year. I remember a certain Woman there, who told me her self, that she had thus been forced to miscarry sixteen several times, and she was then big with the seventeenth, which she promised she would bring forth alive. When they are arrived at the age of 36 or 37, they thus first begin to bring Children into the World as our Women do, and from that Age till 50." Cf. Arnoldus Van Bergen, *Ambassades de la Compagnie Hollandaise des Indes d'Orient, vers l'Empereur du Japon* (Leyde, 1685–86, BN: 8.0206), vol. 2, 279: "They have a horrible custom for women who find themselves pregnant before the age of 37 years, which is that the priestesses, who are called forth for this great mystery, lay them down in the beds of which we have already spoken; and they throw themselves on their stomachs, causing them to suffer frightful pains, until the point that they have brought the women to abort. George Candidius, Dutch minister on the island, reports that in the year 1628, he saw a woman there who was made to deliver

Psalmanaazaar, with the aid of his spokesperson, displaces the accusation of absurdity that is addressed to him back onto his principal source. In fact, the *Description of Formosa* in some spots plagiarizes Candidius word for word in order to furnish this "nowhere" with a few easily verifiable traits.

Having taken these precautions, the geographic fable can unfold in its ever-inventive folly. For the requirements of allegory are everywhere exceeded. As Jean-Michel Racault has noted (op. cit.), there is something Borgesian about this pseudo-Formosan. With impressive rigor, the *Description* methodically delivers up all the necessary elements of the country's statistics. A map, which stretches from Korea in the north to the Philippines in the south, resituates the island in the China Sea archipelago. An alphabet, which contains several Greek and Hebrew characters, offers the reader the opportunity to initiate himself into the rudiments of the Formosan language. A bit further on, this same armchair traveler discovers coins, engraved with curious hieroglyphs, which will permit him one day, should he so wish, to negotiate for unlikely commodities with the inhabitants of this imaginary country, whose clothes are described and distinguished according to gender and social condition. In fact, the *Description* is as much utopian fiction as travel guide. The name Formosa can in fact be found in all the atlases of the time. To substantiate his fiction, Psalmanaazaar had only to reproduce a preexisting map. At any given moment, the reader is under the impression that the dreamlike transports of reading could easily turn into travels through a practicable and very real space. To express such calm conviction, the author himself must have shared the illusion, at least from time to time.

The frame of the introduction, with its extremely neutral tone, prepares us for the most important thing, that *pièce de résistance* constituted by the religious anthropophagy of the Formosans. The ritual is meticulously described, without useless pathos—beyond the "innocent hearts" being roasted—and with all the requisite technical precision. There are neither screams, nor tears, nor useless convulsions during a sacrifice prolonged over a period of hours, in which the throats of chained victims are slit and their hearts torn out one by one. The most devout silence is interrupted only by the prayers of the offi-

---

in this detestable manner sixteen times, and that she was then pregnant with the seventeenth, which she hoped to carry to term, for she was at last at the required age to be able to bring it into the world." I wish to thank Christian Bartaud for verifying these various references for me.

ciating priests. Then sacred hymns, accompanied by flutes, drums "and other instruments " (Psalmanaazaar 1705b, 66–67) resound until the point at which the flesh is cut into small pieces, boiled in its own blood, divided into portions, and served to the faithful. The priests dexterously thread small pieces of human flesh onto skewers which will be distributed one by one to the assembled group, composed of adult men, women, and children over the age of nine. They advance one after the other toward the altar where they respectfully receive a piece of consecrated meat from the hands of the priest and eat it, after having knelt to the ground on one knee.

It is here that the process of the "sociological revolution," which will soon receive its pedigree from Montesquieu, intervenes.[9] The witness to the Formosan rites is naturally unmoved by ceremonies supposedly familiar to him. Yet he must also dedicate himself to enlightening the European reader by drawing the comparisons he deems appropriate, those which, by a backlash effect, make our countries' most acceptable practices seem unusual. Whence the use of ambiguous formulations such as "cette espece de Communion" [this kind of Communion] to designate the ritual anthropophagy of the Formosans. The astuteness lies in indirectly suggesting an allegorical reading by way of parenthetical remarks inserted into the text or of explanatory notes relegated to the bottom of the page.

The culinary precisions constitute an excellent medium for leading the reader's mind beyond obvious meaning and bringing him imperceptibly from Formosa back to papist Europe. One learns in passing that the pieces of human flesh thus distributed are "about the size of an egg, and when cooked, are no more than a mouthful." The similarity with the host used in the Catholic Eucharist cries out to be noticed all the more so when we learn thereafter, thanks to another note at the bottom of the page, that the priests set aside the best morsels for themselves, leaving only a "little mouthful" for the other members of the congregation. Since the Reformation, criticism was often directed at the Catholic rite, which kept the throng of believers from the eucharistic species, intending the consumption of the bread and wine only for the clergy. In addition, one can add to this observation one of

9. On the concept of "sociological revolution," see Roger Caillois's preface to Montesquieu, *Œuvres complètes* (Paris: Gallimard, Pléiade, 1947), vol. 1, v. Cf. Georges May, "Sens unique et double sens. Réflexions sur les voyages imaginaires," *Diogène* 152 (October–December 1990): 3–21.

the most traditional anticlerical criticisms: the Church dupes its flock and grows fat at its expense.

In a more subtle fashion, certain details of the Formosan rite can only be explained with reference to the holy sacrament of the altar. For example, the fact that the flesh is dipped in small pieces into the blood of the victim and boiled in it recalls the gesture of intinction which reconstitutes the unity of the body and blood of Christ, as the priest, at the moment of Communion, dips the host into the goblet of wine. Another indication: the mouthfuls of meat are taken one by one from the hand of the priest, as in the Catholic rite the host is taken from the ciborium. Protestants, on the other hand, insisted that the goblet and the bread circulate from hand to hand among those receiving Communion, without the priest acting as intermediary. The kneeling of the faithful for the occasion, an attitude which implies respect or even adoration, is another element of the ritual which the most radical members of the Reformed Church denounced as clear proof of idolatry.

Finally, the explicit meaning of the Formosan and Roman communions are identical: in both cases, it is requested that God "be pleas'd to accept these Sacrifices for the Remission of the Sins of the People" (Psalmanaazaar 1704, 182). Now the sacrifice of the Mass is very much the great scandal which the Reformed Church, wishing to return to the always relevant efficacity of Christ's death and passion and to break once and for all with the curse of the blood, denounced from the beginning. Protestant Holy Communion, in its Zwinglio-Calvinist variant, is in no sense a sacrifice, but is at most a symbol of alliance, and at the least a commemoration.

The rest of the exposé of the ceremonies observed in Formosa confirms that this kind of allegorical reading, which the notes addressed to the Christian reader recommend from page to page, is intended. It is thus that in the chapter entitled "Of the Priestly Garments," the mitre of the High Priest, whose privilege it is to rip out the hearts of children, recalls that of a bishop; and the band of violet cloth which he wears resembles the scapular worn by "the majority of the European monks." A clarification of this point emphasizes the superstitious spirit which sometimes governs the Catholic clergy: "Many among them contend that they received it from the hands of the Holy Virgin." Later on, the High Priest's shoes lead to a comparison with the Capuchins' sandals, and a footnote straightaway characterizes them as hypocrites: "These are the kind of monks who call themselves reformers of the Order of

Saint Francis and who flaunt a very poor and very austere life, they go barefoot" (Psalmanaazaar 1705b, 84–86).

We can no longer know to what kind of reader the *Description* was addressed: a Formosan star-worshipper? A practicing Catholic? Or, as is probable, an Anglican convinced in advance of the corruption and paganism fundamental to the Roman rite? Still it is only after the depiction of Formosa's religious and political institutions, which constitutes the *Description* proper, that we come to the second part of the novel, which recounts, sometimes in a picaresque mode but most often through interminable chapters of controversy, the adventure and conversion of the hero to the true religion. From the choreographic description of a faraway island and its customs, which links the *Description* to the genre of utopian fiction, we come presently to the bildungsroman. Religious discourse assures the deeper coherence of a work which, on a superficial level, is thus disjointed.[10]

The first part stigmatized Catholicism through the circumlocution of exotic allegory. The second part, to further this condemnation, uses the additional arguments of individual experience and reason. Noted because of his intelligence by a Jesuit father who takes him in and educates him, Psalmanaazaar soon becomes the victim of his protector. Brought to Europe, he notices too late that he has fallen into a veritable spiritual trap. At first he is taught only general truths about Christianity, which he receives with enthusiasm. And, in Avignon, the priest Alexander of Rhodes and his religious brothers seek to force him to embrace the dogma of transubstantiation, which the Formosan, although accustomed to spilt blood and the ingestion of human flesh, is averse to do. He is then threatened with the Inquisition. To avoid the issue, he flees and reaches Cologne where he meets some Lutherans and learns of their Consubstantiation, as shocking in his view as "la Transubstantiation Romaine." Calvinism tempts him more. (We should not forget that the "true" Psalmanaazaar was probably a defiant Huguenot who fled France after the revocation of the Edict of Nantes.)

The Formosan therefore consults a "Minister" of the Reformed Religion, who agrees with him about the "absurdities" to which Roman and Lutheran doctrine are subject, and he is then quite close to becoming a Christian. Yet the pastor reveals himself to be overly attached to the principle of absolute predestination. Rejected yet again, wandering from one religion to another, the Formosan ends up in Hol-

---

10. On this point, see Todorov's remark, 135.

land where he happily embraces Anglicanism, the only doctrine which, in his view, is in harmony with natural religion and which conforms, moreover, "to the Apostolic Institutions and to the practices accepted by the first Christians" (Psalmanaazaar 1705b, 296). A prayer of thanksgiving closes the thirty-ninth and final chapter: "May heaven grant that I never stray: and let there be unto God all honor and all glory, now and forever. *Amen.*"

In the end, the Formosan fable appears to be of a lucid simplicity. The enigma, in the form of a geographical rebus, is soon resolved by an edifying story, crowned by the most moral of conclusions. In those years following the revocation of the Edict of Nantes, testimony of this kind constitutes a weighty argument in the struggle against the Roman Catholic Church and the intolerance of the Catholic victor.

Yet at the same time the *Description* is more cunning than it at first seems. At the last moment, the author tricks the reader. The cannibalistic allegory could in fact take on another meaning. Certainly, Catholicism is anthropophagy, but it is not alone in transgressing the alimentary taboo—figuratively, that is. Absolute predestination, preached by Calvin and his disciples, is hardly less "monstrous" than the "absurd" dogma of transubstantiation. After a public argument organized in Holland, the Formosan, still hesitant to be baptized, has his chance to retaliate against those who are indignant over the inhumanity of child sacrifices and who reproach him for his "very cruel and very barbarous God":

> If you call our God cruel because he deprives some of his creatures of a temporal life in order to make them eternally happy, by what name shall I call him who expressly draws his creatures out of nothingness in order to make them supremely unhappy and who condemns them to eternal pains, before they have even existed, and without a care either for the good or for the evil that they might do? [Psalmanaazaar 1705b, 279]

The lesson of this unusual apostrophe is that the symbol could well be more horrifying than reality itself. The necessarily distant perspective of eternal pains inflicted on innocents is even more repugnant to the foreigner than the spectacle of young children dismembered and grilled for the greater glory of the Formosan god. Even if we must take into account here the irony and the pursuit of paradox, the fact remains that the tyranny of the mystical body is more intolerable than the cruelty inflicted on living bodies. Now, in their opposition to the Pope, Calvinists endeavored to reform and to purify their religion, distancing it from any trace of the sacrificial constraint of its origins. But they had not yet finished with the terror which weighed on their souls. On the contrary, they merely extended indefinitely—beyond History and to its very end—that which they had to lose.

Although his text may be seen as an improvised amalgam, Psalmanaazaar had grasped what can be called the return of the repressed. In the end we can question whether, in pursuing this effort at "reformation" and in adopting the rational middleground in religious matters, the Anglicans of the *Description* and their young neophyte found the path that will lead to a reconciliation, in the peace and serenity of a religion without sacrifice and threats, between the freedom of individual conscience and a universal Church, which is frightfully possessive and devouring.

SWIFT'S SATURNIAN IRELAND: *A MODEST PROPOSAL*

Like Formosa, Ireland is an island. It is an island where overpopulation has caused horrible famines, an island where, more than anywhere else, a single religion is observed, distinct from the one, so much more rational and true to natural law, which dominates the rest of the British Isles. In fact, this religion prescribes a belief in the corporeal presence of the Son of God in the round of dough which the faithful ritually chew and digest. It would not be surprising if, like the Formosans, the inhabitants of Ireland became authentic cannibals in the end.

From this observation, shared by a number of his contemporaries, Jonathan Swift comes to a recommendation. It is the *Modest Proposal*, a "modest" proposal which attempts to resolve the problem of subsistence in Catholic Ireland by sending year-old children to the slaughter.[11] As Claude Rawson has shown, the irony of the proposal is not what we would imagine today. Swift heartily detested beggars.[12] He was scandalized by parents so thoughtless to produce abundant offspring without worrying about the responsibility of having to feed them. Like most members of the Protestant elite, he thought that the

11. Jonathan Swift, *A Modest Proposal for Preventing the Children of poor People in Ireland from being a Burden to their Parents or Country; and for making them beneficial to the Publick. Written in the Year 1729*, in *Prose Works*, ed. Herbert Davis (Oxford: Blackwell, 1955), vol. 12.

12. On this point, see Claude Rawson, *Order from Confusion Sprung* (London: Humanities Press, 1992), 121–144: "A Reading of *A Modest Proposal*."

children of the poor classes should, from a very young age, play a role in society, rather than remaining a burden on the community. Why not henceforth make of them an edible commodity? The result is coldly logical. The recommended measure offers the additional advantage, valuable in Swift's view, of return to an autarkic economy. The flesh of the Catholic child is a local product, authentically Irish. Its consumption would allow the Irish considerable and honest self-sufficiency, rather than forcing them to continue to import mediocre goods at outrageous prices, mostly from England, with corrupting effects and ruinous repercussions.

In a fundamental way, the "humble" proposal is no stranger to the traditional prejudices targeted at the "savage" Irish, anthropophagous in intentions and in deeds, formerly and presently, or rather potentially, cannibals, probable descendants, as it was once thought, of the ancient Scythes or "Scoti," who drank with equal eagerness the blood of their horses and that of their enemies. "Our Savages,"[13] writes Swift, procreate without respect for the laws of marriage. They therefore deserve to be associated with the most exotic and the most barbarous peoples. It is not by chance that in the same pamphlet we find mention of the inhabitants of "TOPINAMBOO," those famous Topinamboux or Tupinamba of Brazil, anthropophagous Indians who enjoyed longstanding fame, especially in France, from Montaigne to Boileau.[14] These savages, known for their ferocity, seem in many ways more civilized than the Irish, whose case is almost desperate. Among "the other Expedients" that the author of the *Modest Proposal* dismisses as ineffective is the learning of civic duty, that love of country which even the Laplanders and the Tupinamba share.

In this respect, the Irish are closer to the Jews of the time of Titus, who, in besieged Jerusalem, killed each other under the enemy's gaze. This example, which Swift cites immediately after that of the "inhabitants of Topinamboo," still has a certain link with cannibalism. The siege of 70, immortalized by Flavius Josephus's narrative, had struck a chord not only because of the persistence and the horror of the fratricidal struggles, but also and perhaps especially, because of an anecdote, exaggerated in the Christian West and distorted by a long tradition of

13. Swift, 111. On the comparison of the Irish to the ancient Scythes in classical English literature, see Claude Rawson, "Indians and Irish: Montaigne, Swift, and the Cannibal Question," *Modern Language Quarterly* 53/3 (September 1992): 299–363.

14. Swift, 116. On the vogue of the Tupinamba in France, see my book, *Le Cannibale, grandeur et décadence*, chs. 3–8.

anti-Semitism: harassed and despoiled by soldiers, a woman was reduced to eating the child she was nursing.[15]

It is doubtful that these juxtapositions within the *Modest Proposal*
were innocent. The Irish in Swift's time were decidedly in good company: thus situated between the cannibals of Brazil and the devouring
mother of the besieged Jerusalem, they are themselves destined to be
child-eaters. By an unusual twist of fate, the crime for which the Jews
were reproached becomes the remedy prescribed to contemporaries,
the only one, at least, which they can still tolerate.

In its crude and meticulous expression, with its taste for figures and
statistical analysis—which far exceeds the demands for verisimilitude
of the utopian genre respected by the *Description of Formosa*—the
black humor of the *Modest Proposal* reaches vertiginous heights. Yet
the repulsive brutality of the text allows us to glimpse from time to
time an underlying allegorical depth. Thus, while he affirms that he
could call Ireland "a Country, which would be glad to eat up our whole
Nation without [salt]" (117)—of course he means England—, the author suggests that the curative and almost purely virtual pedophagy of
the Irish is quite benign compared with the economic exploitation
which they undergo at the hands of their neighbors who treat them as
subhuman, claiming their lands, monopolizing their trade, and reducing them to beggary.

Another glimpse of the allegorical substructure of the *Modest Proposal* is afforded by an explicit reference to George Psalmanaazaar—or
rather to the "famous *Salmanaazor*," "a Native of the Island of *Formosa*" (113). Formosa's ritual anthropophagy served as a model for
Swift's economic fiction. Or at least it underlies the anthropophagous
variant proposed by a friend of the author, who offered the following
refinement: instead of eating one-year-old babies, wouldn't it be prefer-
able to wait a bit and sacrifice adolescents from twelve to fourteen
years old, who in any case were destined to perish of malnutrition? In
this way, the nobility could obtain the venison they lacked since they
had long ago depleted the forest. In the end, although the author of the
Modest Proposal politely disputes this hypothesis in the name of the
sacrosanct economy and also for gastronomical reasons—young
people at that age are mere skin and bones and continuous exercise
makes their flesh tough and disagreeable—, he does not show himself
to be insensitive to the supposed observations of the pseudo-Formosan.

15. Flavius Josephus, *De bello Judaico*, vol. 6, ch. 3, §4.

As proof, he transcribes the remarks which the citizen of Formosa supposedly made to this worthy patriot ("a true Lover of his Country"): in this really quite sensible country, when it happens that young people are put to death, the executioner sells their remains to "People of Quality" as a choice delicacy. For example, a chubby fifteen-year-old girl, crucified for having attempted to poison the emperor, was sold for four hundred crowns to the prime minister and other Mandarins of the court. The author of the pamphlet concludes, for his part, that the same kind of measures taken against Dublin's young coquettes would not make Ireland the worst of kingdoms.

It is interesting to see that the religious motif of sacrifice, so visible in Psalmanaazaar's text, is here not invoked explicitly: it is a crime of lese-majesty which justifies the slaughter and consumption of the young and agreeable person. But the theological allusion is obvious and is even tinged with blasphemous intentions. The execution takes the unusual form of a crucifixion. On the cross, a plump pink damsel, destined to be eaten in a community meal by the dignitaries of the kingdom, has replaced the Son of God.

Finally, beneath the cold calculations of the exposé and the meticulous statistics of children's bodies destined to the slaughter, another body, this one mystical, can be glimpsed. The religious question, in Swift's time as today, is no small matter in this Ireland unequally divided between Catholics and Protestants. Is not one of the avowed goals of the *Modest Proposal* to "Greatly lessen the *Number of Papists*" (114), by making their overly abundant offspring the game of the Protestant aristocracy?

From the start, the grating humor of the pamphlet consists of translating the political metaphor, well-known to both fat and thin, eaters and eaten, into real terms. If Swift's *Modest Proposal* were to be followed literally, the rich would eat, once and for all, the poor. Moreover, Swift insists, this legal pedophagy would result in "the public Good of my country" and the nation's salvation, not to mention commercial prosperity and family harmony. In order for the redemption of the mystic body of the State to occur, individuals, preferably young and innocent, must pay the fair price. Their immolation constitutes, in fact, "a fair, cheap, and easy Method of making these Children sound and useful Members of the Commonwealth" (109). We can see how the allegory of the "body politic" is suddenly incarnated in the most tangible and disquieting manner possible. In this original and perverse version of the fable of the members and the belly, which vaguely recalls

Menenius Agrippa's apologia as recounted by Livy,[16] the health of the organism requires not only that the members work for the belly, but also that the most fragile and weakest of them be devoured by him. "Ton chef mange tes bras" [Your head is eating your arms], exclaimed d'Aubigné in his address to France during the religious wars.[17] Similarly, in the nightmarish Ireland which the *Modest Proposal* allows us to glimpse, social unanimity is broken down by mastication and digestion. The community which devours its own children takes on the appearance of a new Moloch. It evokes the ogre of fairytales who, in his canine rage, would have become autophagous.

Moreover, to advocate the slaughter of indigent children in the name of economic profitability is to legalize and systematize Herod's crime, in other words to practice on a large scale the Massacre of the Innocents. It would seem that Swift and his spokesperson ridicule Christ's message of love. Even more, they abolish the very foundation of the Gospel pronouncement and make redemption through the cross null and void. It is in vain that God gave his only Son for the salvation of humanity. At least such a blessing, which henceforth renders all bloody sacrifice invalid, is not suited to the Irish, who must organize the daily slaughter of their children—those sons and daughters too numerous to inherit the kingdom of the Father—in order to survive. In this sense, the green Erin, a recluse in the middle of the sea like Jerusalem within its walls, could very well contain another cursed people.

Finally, the height of irony is that the Protestants are meant to eat the Catholics. "Savagery" is thus not the exclusive domain of the dangerous classes, nor is anthropophagy particular to the "God-eaters." It is practiced in all serenity by gentlemen of good families, no longer within the context of a rite with the purpose of spiritual regeneration, but with a simple alimentary goal, at home on Sunday or at the inn, for the pleasure of jaded palates. The most frightening, or rather the most agonizing aspect of the *Modest Proposal*, of which I have just suggested a "Eucharistic reading," is, finally, the desymbolization which affects the many levels of social life. The metaphor is lost and we are returned to the triviality of the real: the rich really do devour the poor. Transcendence is destroyed, and religion is reduced to commercial and nutritional necessities. The "Souls" accounted for in the *Modest Proposal* are no more than the only livestock with which Ireland is

16. Livy, *History of Rome*, 2, 32.
17. Agrippa d'Aubigné, *Les Tragiques*, vol. 1, l. 618.

abundantly stocked: the prolific chattel of the innocent.[18] The Communion of Saints degenerates, in the end, into a cannibalistic meal, confirming the regression of the group to a point which falls far short of the law of Love. It goes so far that the theological debate, like class conflict, is reduced to the encounter of Catholic flesh and Protestant teeth.

As for the figure of the island, instead of representing on the world map the unity of a mystical body—ethnicity, nation, State, Church—, it expresses no more than the drastic constraint exercised by an unfeeling nature on a famished population which devours itself. This vision, which has been qualified as "proto-Malthusian,"[19] is, in addition, placed within the shadowy light of Saturn, the god who devoured his own children and whose melancholic influence marks this masterpiece of black humor from the very first words: "It is a melancholly Object to those, who walk through this great Town, or travel in the Country. . . ." Accentuated as much as it is tempered by the vertiginous height of this general irony about the world, such is the tragic vision of the social body and, beyond that, of a demystified humanity, reduced to its appetites and its brutal needs.

—Translated by Noah Guynn

---

18. Swift, 110. Cf. Claude Rawson, *Order from Confusion Sprung*, op. cit., 134.
19. See Rawson, ibid.: "Swift's celebrated, proto-Malthusian use of dehumanized economic jargon . . ." (134).

HÉLÈNE MERLIN

Fables of the "Mystical Body" in Seventeenth-Century France

> The term "mystic" is . . . a mediating one. It insures the unity
> between two times. It overcomes the division and makes them into a
> history. "Mystic" is the absent third term that joins two
> disconnected terms.
>
> —Michel de Certeau, *The Mystic Fable*

Under what circumstances can we speak of the "mystical body" in seventeenth-century France and in what sense? The question merits examination if we do not want to allow ourselves to be seduced by the charm of overly precipitous metaphorical links. According to Henri de Lubac, the *corpus mysticum* referred, in early Church history, to the *corpus Christi*, that is to say the sacramental body, the host consecrated by the Eucharist:

> Through the Eucharist, each person integrates himself in reality into the only true body. The Eucharist unites all the members among themselves, just as it unites them to their common head.[1]

It is a matter of a founding commemoration which reunites the Church with the historically *absent* body of Christ. It is a mystical process in the sense in which Michel de Certeau explains it in the following passage:

> The term "mystic" is . . . a mediating one. It insures the unity between two times. It overcomes the division and makes them into a history. "Mystic" is the absent third term that joins two disconnected terms.[2]

1. Henri de Lubac, *Corpus mysticum. L'Eucharistie et l'Eglise au Moyen Age* (Paris: Aubier, 1949), 33.
2. Michel de Certeau, *The Mystic Fable*, trans. Michael B. Smith (Chicago: University of Chicago Press, 1992), vol. 1, 83.

YFS 86, *Corps Mystique, Corps Sacré: Textual Transfigurations of the Body from the Middle Ages to the Seventeenth Century,* ed. Françoise Jaouën and Benjamin Semple, © 1994 by Yale University.

However, the Church body progressively detached itself from the mystery of the Eucharist and took the name of *corpus mysticum*: the formula *translatus est Christus ad Ecclesiam* indicated that the Church no longer needed the Eucharist in order to exist: from then on the Church constituted the *respublica christiana* of which Christ was the head. Similarly, the sacramental body took the name of *corpus verum*, previously reserved for the historical body of Christ, while at the same time, according to Michel de Certeau, its "mystery" was "reappropriated under the philosophic formality of the sign":

> the visibility of that object replaces the communal celebration, which is a community operation. It acts as a visible indicator of the proliferation of secret effects (of grace, of salvation) that make up the real life of the Church. There are, therefore, two positivities—one readable, the other visible—that refer the Church body to a carrying out and a totalization that are still "mystical." [84]

If the mystical body remains mystical, it is in the sense of this mysterious totalization. But the attribute *mystical* defines itself more particularly in relation to an absence, a loss, as in the first formula of the *corpus mysticum*. The second formula, on the contrary, will drift further, and will move from theological discourse to juridical discourse, as Ernst Kantorowicz has shown in *The King's Two Bodies*. The expression *mystical body* will refer to "the legal person or the institution."[3] Joining with other juridical concepts, those of the "fictitious person," the "corporation," or the *universitas*, it finally crosses paths specifically with the notion of the *political body* (Kantorowicz, 210): the syntagm becomes fixed and the epithet *mystical* no longer refers to any mystical quality.

However, Kantorowicz writes, "the designation *corpus mysticum* brought to the secular polity, as it were, a whiff of incense from another world" (210). According to Kantorowicz, this mystical trace in the juridical notion was particularly noticeable with French jurists:

> The comparison of the state with a *corpus mysticum* . . . fell in with the mysticism of French kingship, which reached its first growth in and after the times of Charles V, and at the same time it counterbalanced the royal mysticism by a mysticism of the estates. [218]

After having given as examples the concepts of Gerson, Jean de

---

3. Ernst Kantorowicz, *The King's Two Bodies: A Study in Medieval Political Theology* (Princeton: Princeton University Press, 1957), 210.

Terre Rouge, and Claude de Seyssel, Kantorowicz finally quotes Guy Coquille:

> At the end of the sixteenth century, Guy Coquille, a jurist going his own ways, stated in so many words that the king as the head and the three estates as the members "together form the body politic and mystic" of the realm. [220]

Yet, when it is put back in context, Guy Coquille's frequently cited expression reveals both its polemical and its definitional value. Coquille in effect evokes the question of royal counsel and the figure of the bad counsellor:

> And it could come to pass that such ordinary counsellors . . . in trying to aggrandize themselves . . . counsel the king in favor of things which are harmful to his people, and consequently to his State. Because the King is the head, and the people of the three orders are the members and all together they form the political and mystical body whose link is indivisible and inseparable and cannot suffer in one part without the rest of the body suffering as well . . . one of the best remedies for this is the convocation of the Estates; and for the king to seek counsel when it pleases him from those who are sent to him, those who are above all suspicion: because this charge in itself is costly and brings them nothing, and they should not expect any profit. Only zeal for the public good brings them there and they expect only the retribution of God, who recognizes and rewards all those who come to the aid of the suffering.[4]

The definition of the State as a "mystical body" composed of the King (its head) and "the three orders of the people" (its members) lends support to an implicit definition of the public good: if matters which are "harmful" to the people are equally harmful to the State, then the State's welfare is identical to the public good. The public good is therefore what is good for *all* members of the State *because the state is a "political and mystical body."*

Given during the meeting of the Estates-General at Blois where Guy Coquille was a delegate of the Third Estate (the very same meeting at Blois during which Henri III had Henri de Guise and his brother, the two heads of the League, assassinated), Guy Coquille's speech—while it can hardly be suspected of sympathy for the leaguers—takes on a very precise polemical tone. It opposes Tacitus's adage, which was beginning to acquire considerable importance in political discourse.

4. Guy Coquille, "Discours des Etats de France . . ." in *Œuvres* (Paris: Jean Guignard, 1665, orig. pub. 1588), vol. 1, 323.

Somewhat later, we find this adage, translated almost literally from Tacitus, in the writings of Cardin Le Bret:

> There are many things which, although they might seem unjust and tyrannical with respect to the individuals [*particuliers*], have another face when they are considered with respect to the public.[5]

Here, the members [*particuliers*] are not united in a political body and do not form a "people" which represents an extension of the State, but rather the "public" (the State) is at the same time superior and external; the "public" plane is separated from the plane of the individuals [*particuliers*], and two spheres are described whose heterogeneity destroys the beautiful ontological unity of the mystical body.[6] The affairs of the State cease from then on to be everyone's concern, and begin to concern only those with a specific political competence: this is what is at stake in the figure of the counsellor evoked at the beginning of Guy Coquille's discourse. However, in a certain sense, this conception of a detached State could appear as the fullest expression of the *mystical body*, in the strict juridical sense of the term: the State appears as a "fictitious person," abstract, autonomous, and perpetual, disengaged from all spiritual connotation, even if a "mystery" remains, that of its real nature.[7]

However, Guy Coquille's entire speech struggles against this notion of a divided *socius*. In his eyes, it only serves to justify a perverted political practice, fed by the actions of a *schismatic*[8] counsellor who seeks to govern the prince in order to further his own particular interests. On the contrary, he defines the dynamic of the public good according to a participatory logic: the public good, in order to be the common good of everyone, must proceed from individual zeal. Only the Estates-General, the political and public expression of this zeal, can constitute

5. Cardin Le Bret, *De la souveraineté du Roi, de son domaine et de sa couronne* (Paris: J. Quesnel, 1632).

6. Regarding the question of the breach between the public and private spheres, see Reinhart Koselleck, *Critique and Crisis: Enlightenment and the Pathogenesis of Modern Society* (Cambridge: MIT Press, 1988).

7. Jean de La Bruyère, *Les Caractères ou les mœurs de ce siècle*, in *Œuvres complètes* (Paris: Gallimard, Pléiade, 1951), "Du Souverain," 270.

8. I am borrowing this adjective from the jurist Guillaume de La Perrière: "Any republic will come to ruin if its citizens are not united by friendship: for if they are partial and schismatic, they come to grief. . . . He who prefers his private gain to the public (so says Aristotle in the third book of *The Politics*) loses the label 'citizen' and adopts the label 'wicked.'" *Le miroir politique, contenant diverses manières de gouverner et policer les républiques* (Paris: V. Norment et J. Bruneau, 1567, orig. pub. 1555), 20.

royal counsel. The sacrificial foundation of the mystical body is explicit, since "this charge in itself is onerous, they do not gain by it nor do seek any profit from it": the sacrifice of the members for the State makes manifest its value as a "mystical body." Such a sacrifice has nothing to do with the "individual evils" [*maux particuliers*] which the statist doctrine associates with the public good: in this last case, the wrongs done to individuals arise from a necessity that only the sovereign power can evaluate, and to which the individuals can only passively submit, as to something which is beyond their power. In Guy Coquille's speech, on the contrary, it is a question of a consensual and voluntary sacrifice which signals that both the subjects and the king, although they do not share sovereign power, share at least the same concern (and the same zeal) for the public good, that is to say for the good of the body to which they belong, the former as members and the latter as head.

The ontological reality of the State is therefore grafted onto the circulation of energy between the king and his subjects, the pooling of bodies. It is a dynamic process of incorporation which thus testifies, mystically, to the theological model of divine totality. But it is a precarious process: religious wars and statist theories threaten the corporeity of the State, a body which itself has for its reference point a bankrupt body, that of the Church, so that the figure of *absence* which marked the first formula of the *corpus mysticum* finds itself reactivated. If, above and beyond juridical convention, this "mystical body" of the State possesses, in the writings of Guy Coquille, a truly mystical dimension, it is because of this coalescence [*ce faire corps*] which occurs during the Estates-General with the establishment of a perpetually endangered communication. In this manner, Guy Coquille's phrase reveals not only hope but faith. It expresses the orator's ardent aspiration for the endangered term: the *mystical body* does not find itself simply *defined* but *summoned* as well. The discourse seeks to efface itself before a presence which it does not simply represent but to which it testifies: only one member need evoke and demonstrably endure suffering on behalf of the whole body for the body to appear in its virtual totality. An advisory speech which, justifying itself all the while, aims miraculously at conjuring up the very core on which it is built, Guy Coquille's discourse exhorts the king to beware the Tacitean maxims (or Machiavellian ones, which are one and the same by the late sixteenth century) of bad counsellors who turn the head away from the members and, governing from behind the closed doors of their private chambers—a location which is detached from the mystical body and perverts its organic integrity—transform the State into a separate entity, a sort of abstract and monstrous idol, with no reality other than that of a juridical fiction, upheld by institutions and by the subjection of everyone to this fiction.

However, the Estates-General did not meet between 1610 and 1789. The ontological unity of the political body, the mystical unity of the members and the head, ceased to appear effective. With Richelieu and Mazarin, the figure of the counsellor appeared to many contemporaries as emblematic of the changes which the religious wars had brought about within the State: a figure who, displacing the "head" of the political body from the center of the polity, symbolized by itself all the "schisms" which were rending it. According to Michel de Certeau, it is at this point that the mystical demand propagates itself in the sense of "the mystical":

> The task of producing a Republic or a State by a political "reason" that would take the place of a collapsed, illegible, divine order, is, as it were, paralleled by the task of founding places in which to hear the spoken Word that had become inaudible within corrupt institutions.   [154, translation modified]

Nonetheless, short of this absolute "mystical task," the ontological unity of the political body did not cease to appear desirable or even possible, even though it was in a state of collapse. In the eyes of many contemporary witnesses, it is clear that the perspective of its actualization, or of its *return*, had become distant: the model of the "mystical body," a model which became even more "mystical" since the body seems to have been attained through absence, is nonetheless evoked. The so-called "pious movement" (*courant dévot*), for example, which took shape in the fight against the "cabal of libertines,"[9] sought to restore the mystical corporeity of the political body through a spiritual reform of its members. This idea comes through clearly in a text by Father Caussin, *La Cour sainte*, of which the third volume, which appeared in 1631, is entitled *Les Maximes de la Cour sainte contre la cour profane*.[10]

9. The expression is from the Jesuit Father François Garasse, *La doctrine curieuse des beaux esprits de ce temps ou prétendus tels, contenant plusieurs maximes pernicieuses à la Religion, à l'Etat et aux bonnes mœurs* (Paris: Sébastien Chappelet, 1624).

10. Nicolas Caussin, *La Cour sainte* (Paris: Sébastien Chappelet, 1640, orig. pub. 1631), vol. 3: "Les maximes de la Cour sainte contre la cour profane." English translations throughout are from *The Holy Court, Maxims of the Holy Court against the Profane Court* (London: Printed for John Williams, 1663).

In this text, Caussin follows an agonistic method: each chapter is organized around a specific moral value or another abstract entity and these values are defined in two antithetical manners as they are considered both from the point of view of the "Holy Court" as well as from the perspective of the "Profane Court." Contrasting maxims are presented at the head of each chapter in a short tabular form: to the left and in italics, the maxim of the Profane Court; to the right and in roman, the maxim of the Holy Court, exposing in an immediately graphic fashion the moral rectitude of this maxim and correcting the maxim to the left. Then, the refutation begins in a unique and exhortative enunciation which sometimes places itself face to face with a hostile interlocutor, both fictitious and collective (as well as libertine), but whose voice, never presented in direct discourse, always finds itself framed and controlled by the enunciation of the Jesuit preacher.

The textual device imitates, therefore, a combat that aims at eliminating the adversary, whose presence threatens the *body*, in order to surmount the split: the division is first conveyed typographically, but in a typographical display that has already declared victory; a victory that is established once schismatic opinion, refuted, finds itself dissolved in the organic unity of the discourse.

The word fashions itself as the dramatic agent of a mystical reunion which it prompts, but which must be pursued in this privileged site which the Court constitutes. Maxim 10, "Of Proper Interest," attacks most particularly the ethic of self-interest which, in the eyes of the "pious" [*dévots*], constitutes the most fearsome motivating force of this ontological decomposition of the ecclesio-political body. This maxim, like all others, is articulated in two inverse propositions.

For the Profane Court, on the left side of the page, in italics:

> *Every Understanding man should do all for himself as if he were his own God and esteem no Gospel more sacred than his Proper Interest.*
> [Caussin, 389]

and for the Holy Court, to the right:

> That proper interest is a tyranny formed against the Divinity, and that a man who is the God of himself is a devil to the rest of the world. [389]

Next comes a discourse in which Nicolas Caussin castigates "proper interest" (i.e., self-interest) in its triple sense, at the same time moral, economic, and political. Addressed in this apostrophe: "And you, little worldling, you political spirit" (390), the courtier who is attacked here is the "political" libertine. In fact, beginning with Montaigne, an entire wave of opinion abandoned without nostalgia the reference to the "mystical" body and, on the contrary, denounced it as a lie:

> Most of the rules and precepts of the world take the course of forcing us out of ourselves and driving us into public view for the use of society as a whole; they have thought to produce a fine effect by diverting and distracting us from ourselves, presupposing that we were attached to ourselves only too closely and by a too natural tie; and to this end they have said all that could be said.[11]

Only the self possesses an ontological reality, not the "public society." Montaigne's famous phrase is well known: "The mayor and Montaigne have always been two, with a very distinct separation" (1379). The individual person does not *participate* in the public person, who in fact is not a *person* at all, but a *character*. There is no mystical correspondence between the two, and Montaigne plays with the organicist metaphor with extraordinary satirical efficacy:

> I see those who transform and metamorphose themselves into new shapes and new beings as numerous as the public duties that they assume, and who play the dignitary even to their hearts and bowels, and carry their office with them even into their retiring room. [1379][12]

The mystical formula of the political body is therefore a double mystification in his eyes, regarding oneself and others. The bodies that this formula concerns are only taken in a "farcical" manner. Zeal dissimulates, behind the *public good*, a passion which is no more than the perverted form of a legitimate "self-interest." But, if self-interest is the only real and legitimate driving force of human action,[13] then, instead

11. Michel de Montaigne, "On the Management of One's Will" in *The Essays of Montaigne*, trans. George B. Ives (New York: The Heritage Press, 1946), vol. 2, 1371.

12. See also: "If at times I have been forced into the handling of other people's affairs, I have promised to take them in hand, not to be completely engrossed by them; to burden myself with them, not to make them a part of myself. . . . I have enough to do to order and arrange the crowd of domestic concerns that I have at heart, without admitting there, and being overwhelmed by, outside concerns; and I am sufficiently occupied by my own essential affairs, proper and natural to me, without inviting others foreign to me" (1368).

13. On this question, see Albert O. Hirschman, *The Passions and the Interests: Political Arguments for Capitalism before Its Triumph* (Princeton: Princeton University Press, 1977), and *Vers une economie politique élargie* (Paris: Editions de Minuit, 1986); and Anna Maria Battista, "Morale 'privée' et utilitarisme politique en France au XVIIe siècle," in *Le pouvoir de la raison d'Etat*, ed. Christian Lazzeri and Dominique Reynié (Paris: PUF, 1992), 191–230.

of repressing it and risking its development into a fanatical form of zeal, it is more appropriate to transform it into the rational, objective, and transparent motivating force of the State: it is no longer, as in Tacitus's adage, that the State is above particular interests; it is, on the contrary, that the State must express these interests and guarantee them completely. According to the juridical model of *societies*, the State can define itself as the organism charged with overseeing this association of interests which "human society" constitutes. For example, here is what La Mothe le Vayer writes, reversing the *"mystical body"* formula:

> It is not the goal of the Legislator, nor the goal of civil societies to make it so that everyone is profitable to the public and the community by his work, but instead that there is no one to whom the community is not useful and who does not feel content to be one of the members that composes it. [Cited in Battista, 227]

In opposition to the statist doctrine which is implicit in the profane court, Nicolas Caussin develops at length the earlier concept of the onto-theology of the political body:

> So as soon as one is born with fair and worthy qualities, he is born for the public, and he who would retain to himself what Providence gave him for everyone, commits a Sacrilege in the great temple of the God of nature: if he perpetually reflects on himself in all things, and draws all to himself, as if all were made for him, he opposeth his judge, and makes himself a corrival to Sovereign Majesty. [390, translation modified]

For Father Caussin, the "public"—which must in this situation manifestly encompass the Church—must attest to the order of Creation, and such participation arises from the mutual collaboration of all the members in just such an order. Everyone must consequently participate without reserve in the public good, and one must contribute one's energy without any "holding back," without reserving for oneself a personal space or personal interest. Like other men of the cloth, Father Caussin would like to confer the role of motivating force upon the court in what could be called a dream of reincorporation of the *public*. An exemplary part of the political body, a mediator between mere individuals [*particuliers*] and the State, the court should restore the ontology of the political by suturing, around the sovereign, with all the force of attraction of its harmonious organicity, the gap introduced by the rational scission between individuals and the public. In this sense, the court constitutes, in Nicolas Caussin's mind, a mystical term, a *third term to be produced in order to reunite the two separate terms.*

Thus, in spite of the differences of grounding in their discourses, one in a juridical discipline and the other in a theological discipline, Guy Coquille and Nicolas Caussin share the same participatory conception of a *public* whose mystical unity is placed under God's watchful eye. But the scenes have changed: the political and advisory forum of the Estates-General was supposed to represent *all* of the kingdom. The forum of the court is, on the contrary, immediately something partial: the court stands in the absence of a lost totality, even if it must, in the mind of Nicolas Caussin, possess an expansive virtue, warding off by its organicist nature the irreparable loss of the body which affects the State.

By way of Nicolas Caussin's text, both an irreversible displacement of the concept of the mystical body and a desire to maintain its memory and its necessity, even its reality—in spite of everything—come to light: that is to say, in spite of the State and the reason of State [*la raison d'Etat*]. It is not certain, however, that the actual positions are generally so clear-cut: on the one hand, a persistent and unequivocal nostalgia for the mystical incorporation of the members in a present body; on the other, a rational critical position which would like to give a pragmatically realistic foundation to the State. The model of the mystical body continues to haunt political thought and to nourish dreams of a paradoxical reincorporation. Here, I will only develop one of the most remarkable examples. It concerns the first three *Political Discourses* by Guez de Balzac, addressed to Madame de Rambouillet: "The Roman," "The Conversation of the Romans," and "Maecenas."[14] They are presented as an annotated description of several aspects of Roman history as well as an allegorical transposition of recent French history.

"The Roman" offers a portrait of a typical Roman, more precisely of a Roman Consul-General, the veritable incarnation of the idea of the Republic:

> He knows neither nature, nor alliance, nor affection, where the interest
> of his Country is concerned; He hath no other particular interest but
> that, and neither loves nor hates, but for public concernments. [10]

Rapidly, Balzac focuses his description, which then becomes a dra-

14. Jean-Louis Guez de Balzac, "Le Romain," "La Conversation des Romains," and "Mécénas" in *Oeuvres*, published by Valentin Conrart (Paris: T. Jolly, 1665), vol 2. English translations are from "The Roman," "The Conversation of the Romans," and "Maecenas," in *Three Excellent Discourses* (London: J. Holden, 1652).

matic story, on the fact that the Roman is an army general instead of a magistrate in order to emphasize the dynamic virtue of his exemplarity and the contagious dimension of his action. Indeed, he infuses his subordinates with a mysterious energy which resembles a sort of ecstasy:

> Observe how with his Eyes he leads the whole army? How a Nod of his head keeps all the world in their duty? How his presence only establishes Order, and drives away Confusion? . . . that good Grace . . . is an admirable charm and enchantment for him to sweeten the bitterness of disgustfull Orders. . . . It hath a strange force to win the heart of the Soldiery. . . . By this charm they bind themselves not only to him, but they unloose themselves from all other things; They mind neither Pay, Plunder, or Recompense; They care neither for the feasts of Rome, nor for the delights of Italy; They demand and desire nothing but their General. [46]

The Consul, described as a miraculous presence which is also a self-absence, appears as the mystical center of a voluntary incorporating of the members of the army around his command:

> What a one, good God! must so passionate a Militia be; Tis not obedience in pursuit of command; Tis zeal which even prevents it; Tis not affection which obligeth them to the cause of their Chief; Tis a transport which ravisheth them from themselves. . . . So that, Madam, they are no more soldiers of his army which march with him; They are as the members of his body, which move when he stirs; They are as we may say, stranger parts of himself, which are more united to him than his natural. [20–22]

Here, Balzac makes an implicit comparison between this "zeal," this ardent desire to abandon all "self-interest," and the new basis of the State, founded on passive "obedience" to the orders of the public powers: by means of this "transport" the members are incorporated with their head and a body emerges, detached from Rome, but representing it in its entirety, not as institution but as spiritual entity. And the "charm" which the General exerts is carefully linked to a transcendent cause:

> Is not this, Madam, an effect of that Authority which comes from Heaven; of that Authority inherent in the person of him who hath it distinct and separate from that other authority bred by the power given him by the Republic, verified by the Senate, and to be read in Patents of Parchment, and confirmed with Eagles, and Dragons in picture, by Rods, Axes, and Archers? [26]

Two orders of visibility are delineated: one, institutional or representational—force coupled with imagination; the other, authority which refers back to an invisible source from which it draws its mysterious power. Balzac's discourse therefore celebrates in a sublime mode this assumption of everyone into the presentation, to itself and to the enemy, of a collective body which is itself sublime: the subject of enunciation, although not a contemporary of "The Roman," imagines himself present before such a chief[15] and such an event, and can find no better way to represent this than by imitating the transport of the soldiers toward their head: the enunciation, in itself mystical, seeks to (re)produce the event, to tie it to the present, to render it *truly present*,[16] in a time in which its absence is cruelly felt, since, as the beginning of the next discourse underlines, present times are sterile. It may still be possible to find today some "privileged soul" or some "extraordinary person" analogous to the Roman Consul-General; it remains, however, that the "others" necessary to complete the body are lacking, because:

> This one makes no number . . . there is not a multitude of Heroes.
> There is no people of extraordinary persons. There is no more a Rome,
> nor Romans. We must seek them under ruins, and in their Monuments.
> [44–45]

At what "army," at what *public* could this Balzacian celebration be aiming, by way of this address to Madame de Rambouillet?

In a certain sense, "The Conversation of the Romans" responds to this question, but in displacing the terms. "The Conversation" opens on a completely different note. If there is praise within "The Conversation," it is relative:

> It belongs not to us to be Camillas and Catos, we want the vigor of such
> Men as those instead to provoke our courages, they make our ambition
> despair. . . . By giving us examples, they have obliged us to an unprofitable
> trouble. They have given us what we cannot take. These examples
> being of that height that there is no way to attain unto them. [43]

15. The discourse opens, in fact, with an initial "contract in writing" which announces the mode of representation (sublime, more than mimetic) chosen by Balzac: "Can we find out no way to show you a Roman Consul? Is there no safer and more innocent means, than that of Magic to bring him whole from the place where he is? Because, undoubtedly, you would like to see him in both body and spirit" (3). On the question of seventeenth-century representation, see Hélène Merlin, "L'Epistémé classique ou l'épineuse question de la représentation," forthcoming in *Littératures classiques*.

16. See the quotation in the preceding note, in which Balzac announces his intention "to bring him whole from the place where he is."

Balzac has changed *styles*: from the sublime style, he has descended to a middle, yet sustained, style. Projected into a distant past, the mythic figure of the Roman explicitly becomes a legend whose illusory nature has been uncovered. The figure of Cato, for example, returns further on:

> You would desire, Madam, that I should show you the Romans when they hid themselves, and that I should open to you the doors of their Cabinets. . . . Twas there, Madam, for example, where Cicero was neither sophist, nor rhetorician . . . neither of this, nor of that party: There he was true Cicero, and after mocked himself privately of what he had adored publicly. Twas there he defined men and painted them not, where he spoke of Cato as a Pedant of the Portico, or at most but as of a Citizen of Plato's Republic. [71–72]

Where "The Roman" proposed to reinstate a past presence which is entirely public and marvelously efficient, "The Conversation of the Romans" proposes another sort of representation—the raising of a veil—but a fictive representation since no traces remain of this other side of Rome, a hidden side which reveals a duplicity or a non-self-presence, a difference which is within the man as well as the city.[17] And, from this new approach, in an entirely novel way, the model of the political body is presented as a derisory utopia in which only Cato can believe. The public has become a theatrical stage, built entirely upon conventions, even though its institution as such is necessary and its flip side paradoxically constitutes its only sphere of authenticity: it is the space of the "cabinet," a private space, that is to say a space which is secret and not civic. The scene of the City is therefore divided, its two faces together form a duplicitous whole, and no body is able to take shape within this space.

So while the soldiers of the first Rome—which, after the second discourse, is understood to refer mostly to earliest Rome—no longer dreamt "of either Roman feasts or the delights of Italy" once they were in the army, the Roman of "The Conversation," who is a Roman living at the end of the Republic, is, on the other hand, oriented toward "honest pleasures" and "the pleasures of the spirit" (46). There is the pleasure of Letters which is not a solitary pleasure but a communal one: conversation and the virtue of urbanity which it requires form the horizon of a society of individuals, an "assembly of men" which is in no way a mystical body but which is nonetheless truly founded in its

17. "They knew how to change virtue according to the diversity of time and place; they received at night in their closets, the favors they had in the morning rejected on the Tribunal," 65.

own right, since familiar and erudite exchanges create links between individuals, based on correspondence and harmony.[18]

Between the first and second discourse, it is possible to read the same opposition that Caussin traced between the Christian maxim of the *public good* and the libertine maxim of self-interest. But, as they are both projected onto Roman history and thus disengaged from theological reference, they enter into a historical relationship which places them within a hierarchy in a complex manner. On the one hand, on a temporal axis which is linear and directed, there is a progression from the first to the second: the civil society which is positively born from a private space is celebrated as superior to the primitiveness of ancient times, while public space is greatly devalued when seen from this point of view and in this specific moment, a necessary and splendid *trompe l'oeil*. On the other hand, however, on a less temporal and more eschatological axis, the progress evident in the development of civility is also witness to a regression of civic values. A contradiction is created between the two discourses: if "The Conversation of the Romans" describes that which is lacking in "The Roman"—civility—and casts suspicion on its perfection, "The Roman" is no less a measure of what is lacking in *the Romans*: unity in the extraordinary, the sublime virtue which, miraculously, provokes the assumption of the collectivity into a mystical totality. This lack also affects the present times, as we have seen:

> I do not say, Madam, that in the most miserable times, God cannot send some chosen soul to make us remember his first Magnificence. I will not deny but that he may take a particular care of that soul, and but that he hath means to preserve it from the vices of the Court, and the contagion of Custom. In the most general stupidity of the world, there is someone found to wake the rest, who breaks the bounds of the age, who is capable to conceive the idea of ancient virtue, and to shew us that the miracles of History are still possible things. It is true, Madam, there is such a one: But this one makes no number; he marks even fertility, neither doth he hinder this solitude. Is there a privileged soul, an extraordinary person, an Hero or two in all the world? There is not a multitude of Heroes. There is no people of extraordinary persons. There is no more a Rome, nor Romans. We must seek them under ruins, and in their Monuments. [43–45]

Placed within the context of this disappearance, even if it is not explicitly tied to Roman history, the context of a historical breach,

18. See, in particular, 49–50.

"The Conversation of the Romans" does not evoke a "race of extraordinary people," and its description of Roman private rooms seeks its model in the French historical present, completing the contamination of temporal frames of reference.

The third discourse, "Maecenas," is, however, centered on this "extraordinary soul" whose existence "The Conversation of the Romans" affirmed without ever giving a specific example. Maecenas will provide this example, and it is so exceptional that it is able to mitigate the lack of a "people," and Augustus's counsellor then appears as a type of synthesis of the two preceding figures: that of the Consul-General and that of the man of letters.

"Maecenas" opens with a brief summary of the passage from Republican Rome to Imperial Rome: the duplicity present in the preceding discourse explodes here into discord, exposing the *public* to the vicissitudes of Fortune until the Romans renounce their civic liberty in order to recover civil peace, preferring to assure the enjoyment of private space, since they cannot enjoy public space, henceforth impracticable in its republican form, monopolized by one person. At this point, a first "extraordinary soul" appears: Augustus.

But the scene moves from Augustus to his two counsellors, Agrippa and Maecenas, soon to concentrate only on Maecenas. An accomplished man of letters, Maecenas is particularly "extraordinary" because of his eloquence and his generosity:

> The same fountain whence individuals drew favors and courtesies, furnished the public with councils and resolutions. . . . He had the religion to receive nothing which could not be given justly: He did not want anything for which he could be reproached, not only by public complaints about his reputation, but also by the secret sighs of interested individuals. [135–36, translation modified]

Rejecting Tacitus's adage while entirely sacrificing his private self, "Maecenas" presents a polymorphous "zeal": he spends, or better yet, he spends himself on *both sides of the division* and expands his private self to the dimension of the *public*. Situated at the same time in private and public spaces, Maecenas reunites them: in the secrecy of the imperial chambers, he counsels Augustus to do nothing against the public good while in the secrecy of the individuals' chambers he exhorts them to serve Augustus:

> With this efficacious eloquence, which is nothing other than the right use of prudence, which is communicated to men through the word, he

gained for Augustus an infinity of servants, and after having persuaded him to moderation, he persuaded the others to obedience. [142–43]

Maecenas directs the individuals toward Augustus and Augustus toward the public good, that is to say, toward the individuals considered as a people, as a community. It is therefore he, by his eloquence, who turns each person toward the public good. The figure of Maecenas makes the two antagonistic dimensions of the political body, the principle of obedience and that of commanding, reflect upon themselves and meet each other, all the while softening them both:

> A man could not get from him without a sweet emotion able to waken the deadness of those who were not sensible to the felicity of the reign of Augustus, who never dreamt of the beauty of good things. The air of his face, the tone of his voice, and what the Rhetoricians comprehended under the eloquence of the body, gained the outward sense in an instant. [144–45]

A discreet but omnipresent mediator,[19] it is by him that communications, correspondences, and liaisons are maintained. In another discourse, Balzac writes this astonishing phrase regarding Maecenas:

> It was Maecenas who gilded an age of Iron, who made the Monarchy tolerable for those passionate souls calling for freedom; who spread his own happiness on all sides; who shared the friendship of Augustus; who only asked in order to give.[20]

Maecenas is a center of reconciliation: he redistributes the material and spiritual gifts that both Augustus and nature have given him. He appears as a dynamic principle of exchange and passage, he circulates words and money, and this circulation which irrigates the political body wards off the threat of its division. "The general good of the world," according to the text, Maecenas is himself a gift which he freely distributes to all, on all sides, without preserving anything for his own self. A sublime figure, Maecenas appears by himself, alone, as a hidden and mystical third party who reunites, in a single (hi)story, the Rome of the first and second discourses, who unites these two disunited faces of the public and the individual.

"It is true, Madame, that this someone exists," "The Conversation

19. See, for example, his miraculous apparition at the moment that Augustus is about to punish innocent victims during a session of the Imperial tribunal.

20. Jean-Louis Guez de Balzac, *Réponse à trois questions touchant Fabrice, Auguste et Mécénas*, in Œuvres, vol. 2, 421.

of the Romans" affirmed. Is there a historical counterpart to this mystical mediator, through whose power a body surfaces even when there are no members? It is impossible not to think of Richelieu. If Guy Coquille's speech, if Nicolas Caussin's position suggest how Richelieu could have been perceived as usurping a position, a *body*, the figure of Maecenas permits us conversely to measure the hope which could have been focused upon his person. Once the mystical totality, as Guy Coquille still called it, has been engulfed, there remains nothing but to dream of a counsellor who, in substituting for the whole, represents and accomplishes *all*, above and beyond all the fissures which affect the *socius*.

—Translated by Allison Tait

TIMOTHY MURRAY

Philosophical Antibodies: Grotesque Fantasy in a French Stoic Fiction

In Memory of Louis Marin

The baroque destroys every transcendent aura and desublimates fantasy. It compels fantasy to embody itself, to exhibit itself, to wear itself out in a sort of ostentatory apotheosis deprived at once of eschatology, delivered before itself to its visual and spectacular dimension. Such a *vision of fantasy in the body* and between bodies subjects the characters of the baroque theatre, like those of painting, to affect and its physical drive. . . . Constituted by this scopic drive, bodies can appear only in their most infuriating forms: deformed, convulsive in death or *jouissance*, fetishized in details, flesh in ecstasy and in *jouissance*.
— Christine Buci-Glucksmann, *La folie du voir*

What is entailed in raising anew the question of the mystical, even sacred body in seventeenth-century France? Methodologically, it might mean complicating the kinds of empirical data passed on by recent historical studies of "the body" and its sociological manifestations in order to focus on those more fluid outlines of the "vision of fantasy in the body."[1] I here refer to Buci-Glucksmann to foreground the consequences of those virtual details of corporeality which are almost always rendered frail by their specular framing in the scene of ecstasy—be it religious, sexual, or philosophical. The body stands out in this scene because it "images" something ecstatic, like the arrival of

1. Thomas Laqueur's *Making Sex: Body and Gender from the Greeks to Freud* (Cambridge, Massachusetts: Harvard University Press, 1990) provides an excellent "new historical" reading of the early-modern discourse on the body and its "metaphorical" resonance in scientific and philosophical treatises. My study focuses differently on the seventeenth-century scripting of fantasy's exhibition of the drives and traumas on the site of the body. In this context, I analyze how seventeenth-century literature and philosophy frequently rely on the passions and sentiments as the interiorized specular screen through which the subject knows itself as body.

YFS 86, *Corps Mystique, Corps Sacré: Textual Transfigurations of the Body from the Middle Ages to the Seventeenth Century,* ed. Françoise Jaouën and Benjamin Semple, © 1994 by Yale University.

faith, of knowledge, or of orgasm. Yet the image of ecstasy must always stand forth as the disturbing figure of the differences it resists, be they religious, sexual, national, or racial. It is as an image-field of the spectacular dimension of interiority that the body, I would like to suggest, comes to "infuriate" those most dependent on its visions.

However, Buci-Glucksmann's adjective, "infuriating," might be too universal a term to signify the early-modern subject's response to the fetish and its convulsive ecstasies. For "maddening," "destabilizing," "paralyzing," or even "tormenting" could suggest just as easily the broad cultural response to the enigma of the body in seventeenth-century culture. Her term does provide, however, a sense of how forcefully affect attached itself to the vision of fantasy in the body, as well as how the appearance or discourse of affect relied on the stabilizing detail of the fetish, at least when the horrific part stood in for the already deformed whole in the period's rhetoric of self-representation. This corporeal division, a division between body and soul as well as between bodies and sexes, is what I aim to pursue in reflecting on how a masculine anxiety over the destabilizing scene of ascetic self-representation haunted the cultural imagination and literary practice of seventeenth-century France.

THE BODY IN FANTASY

Seventeenth-century discussions of the site/sight of self-representation range from philosophical extensions of Montaigne's blatant linkage of castration with the loss of epistemological prowess to narrative equations of social and religious evil with the fleshy bodies of women and colonized peoples of color. Standing out among the many cultural sites in which this all comes to a head are the vehement Jansenist attacks on painting, theatre, and the novel as potential passion-spawning sites of erotic debauchery.[2] To the critics of figural representation, the artistic image and the literary text tend to embody in color, line, and sentiment the paranoid vision of a fatal attraction threatening the phallologocentric project of mental, spiritual, and linguistic constancy. Pierre Nicole sums up this threat in "De la comédie": "Dramas and novels excite not only the passions, but they also teach the language of the passions, that is to say, the art of expressing them and of making them appear in an agreeable and ingenious fashion, which is no small evil."[3]

2. See Louis Marin's unparalleled analysis of the philosophical significance of this attack in *La critique du discours* (Paris: Minuit, 1975).

3. Pierre Nicole, *Les visionnaires* (Liège: Adolphe Beyers, 1667), 484.

The danger of the arts, then, is that they give visual and linguistic body to the threatening display of otherwise internalized passions.

But it was not only the Jansenists who were exasperated by imagings of the body. A challenging aspect of seventeenth-century French philosophical attitudes is their almost universal ambivalence toward the figure of the body. Whether considered in relation to the rigorous experiments of the new science, the melancholic fascination with the specter of death, or the erotic fantasies of literature, spectacle, and the arts, the body seems to surface as a combined figure of fascination and repulsion. With the rise of the new science, philosophy seized on the body as a chartable site of scientific advance. Its attentions turned to the body as a scopic object of analysis lending credence to larger metaphysical claims of rationality and epistemological certitude. Of consequence is how these broader concerns with the advance and purity of mind were understood to transcend the body or, at least, to provide the early-modern subject with something tantamount to a conceptual out-of-body experience. For it provided the mindful subject with an apparatus for thinking alongside of, or in-difference to, the body. This proved true as well in terms of the baroque fascination with death in art and philosophy. When confronted with disruptive thoughts and fears of the ultimate loss of body, the seventeenth-century philosophical tradition returned consistently to an earlier call to arms. Regardless of the school, seventeenth-century philosophy carried on the charge earlier led by Montaigne: "To Philosophize is to Learn How to Die." The method of learning how to live in the carcass of death, that is, how to confront one's fear of a dying body, constituted a significant aspect of the early-modern philosophical project.[4]

Of equal, perhaps even greater, importance to reflections on literal manifestations of death and dying were the mental attentions given to the many figural aspects of the body and their threat to philosophical and religious confidence. One of my favorite examples stems from what appears to have been a popular exercise of the provincial salons

4. See Louis Marin, "Montaigne's Tomb, or Autobiographical Discourse," trans. Geoffrey Bennington, The Oxford Literary Review 4/3 (1981): 43–58; Timothy Murray, "Translating Montaigne's Crypts: Melancholic Relations and the Sites of Altarbiography," in Reconfiguring the Renaissance: Essays in Critical Materialism, ed. Jonathan Crewe, Bucknell Review 35 (1992): 121–49; Christine Buci-Glucksmann, La Folie du voir: De l'esthétique baroque (Paris: Galilée, 1986); Julianna Schiesari, The Gendering of Melancholia: Feminism, Psychoanalysis, and the Symbolics of Loss in Renaissance Literature (Ithaca: Cornell University Press, 1992), 233–67; Mitchell Greenberg, Subjectivity and Subjugation in Seventeenth-Century Drama and Prose: The Family Romance of French Classicism (Cambridge: Cambridge University Press, 1992), 65–86.

that trained young men to use the powers of figuration to separate themselves from their bodies, as it were. This exercise involved the written description of an imaginary "tableau enigmatique" followed by an allegorical explanation written in verse. In the painting of the young Christ imagined by an adolescent François Hédelin (later to become the Abbé d'Aubignac), a shepherd holding the little savior is flanked by two figures marked by the shame of their corporeality: "On the right side is shown a nude man holding a vase in his hands, and on the left another person whose only clothing is a dunce cap."[5] The subsequent explanations of these allegorical figurations of the body foreground a paradox of visualization that tormented baroque thought. The image on the right is revealed in verse to represent the "World" sporting the headdress of "madness." As d'Aubignac explains, even the wisest human is "mad" in comparison to God. Of particular significance is how the author manages to explicate the condition of madness whose confrontation usually renders him "uncertain and dumb." He does so with the aid of understanding, "As in a mirror, I will see the past / the present, the future, all great things / Which one believes to be secretly enclosed in destiny, / Man's thoughts, whims, actions, / Virtues, vices, pleasures, aims, & passions." In keeping with philosophical conventions of the period, the understanding is said to be mediated by the ordering procedures of visual reflection and its ability to collate disparate mental phenomena through ocular projection. As if a mirror, the subject fixes in sight the figure of the eternal presence of all human qualities. However, the stability of such a visual apparatus of self-reflection has already been rendered suspect by the author's prior explication of the other "personnage nud": "Shameful and nude Flesh with a vase between its hands, / A true portrait of the pleasures that charm mankind, / Sees dissolved its wiles, its pride, its audacity, / As if a sheet of frozen water held in front of the face." Here the mirrorical device, an anamorphic "sheet of frozen water," is dismissed as the virtualized specter of shameful flesh whose momentary reflection displays only the subject's arrest in the face of the aggressivedissolution of audacity, pride, and, most significantly, feminine wiles or charms ("ses apas"). Rather than order sight, this mirrorical configuration merely enlivens vision's proximity to the distorting attractions of false virtue and feminine allure, not to mention vision's

5. François Hédelin, Abbé d'Aubignac, *Explication du tableau enigmatique proposé en la ville de Nemours, le dimanche xxiv du mois de Mars, 1624* (Paris: Jean Laquehay, 1625).

distance from the suturing comfort of eternal presence. Much like the subject described by Lacan, this one comes to know the self-loathing of narcissism primarily in relation to the scopic drive which first casts the developing subject outside itself through the figuration of the body.[6] Faced with the natural distortion of his imaging, this subject stands transfixed by the grotesque arrest of the pleasurable representation of Narcissus. When revealed as a figure, in the flesh, the subject will always stand against itself as the image of gendered Otherness.

D'Aubignac therefore presents to his reader a two-sided mirror. One permits the subject to imagine itself in relation to a confident plenitude repelling the follies of representation. But the Other suggests that the mirror as well as its subject are distorted and inconstant, that reflection itself has a different aspect, an Other side that confronts the subject with the arrest of the perfections of reflection. It is thus in view of this destabilizing double vision that the mirror represents the grotesque excess of specularization from its very inception.[7]

Even though the seventeenth-century system of virtuality, whether philosophical or religious, understands all subjects to be naturally at risk, I wish to stress that d'Aubignac's imagery follows the lead of religious and philosophical doctrine by figuring the masculine subject as the one with the most to lose, that is, as the one understood to be most unnaturally transformed by the dual threat of wily flesh and corporeal figuration, of body and phantasm. Some readers may object to my basing this claim on the significance of only one feminized attribute, "ses apas," since early-modern philosophy and theology frequently collapse gender distinctions when treating the passions, the body, and the negative effects wrought by both. I now point to this collapse, however, not to engage in a defense of gender claims, but to pursue the paradox of the passions in seventeenth-century French thought, a consideration which will eventually return to the different ways that gender marks the representation of the ascetic body.

Consider two contrasting positions. One is Antoine Coypel's enthusiastic Aristotelian endorsement, in *Excellence de la peinture*, of painting's arousal of the passions:

6. Jacques Lacan, *Écrits: A Selection*, trans. Alan Sheridan (New York: Norton, 1977), 1–7, and *The Four Fundamental Concepts of Psychoanalysis*, trans. Alan Sheridan (New York: Norton, 1978).

7. See Louis Marin, *Des pouvoirs de l'image: Gloses* (Paris: Seuil, 1993), 25–39; and Jean-Luc Nancy, "Larvatus Pro Deo," trans. Daniel A. Brewer, *Glyph 2* (Baltimore: The Johns Hopkins University Press, 1977), 14–36.

The great painter must not only please but also move and enrapture, as do great poets and great orators. Like those musicians so praised by antiquity, he must sometimes inspire sadness to the point of drawing tears, sometimes provoke laughter, sometimes inflame anger and force the spectators to display their admiration and surprise. In fact, this is what is sublime in painting and the painter's greatest merit.[8]

Much less enthusiastic about the positive nature of these sublime effects is the Abbé d'Aubignac, whose treatise "Abbregé de la philosophie des stoïques" links the inconstancy of passions to "the interference of the corporeal senses which is contrary to great virtues, and whose outbursts must never be indulged."[9] Asserting the popular stoic position, d'Aubignac echoes his more youthful discomfort with bodily passions. With the Stoics, he affirms that "they [the passions] are diseases which one must completely remedy, that one must not leave such a dangerous poison in our heart, and that virtue is not so unfortunate as to need its enemies in order to enable itself to do good" (APS, 97–98). In keeping with Nicole's precedent of associating these dangers with the corpus of popular culture, d'Aubignac joins Nicole in critiquing the novel for being one of the most virulent carriers of pedagogical poison: "But if all of these novels were as perfect as one might desire them to be, reading would be no more the better for it; I reserve for another occasion the consideration of morals which are not always completely governed in the novel, and I do not claim to condemn here the evil sentiments that the reading of novels can leave in souls which are tender and susceptible to agreeable passions"(APS, 158–59).

Although d'Aubignac here seems to hedge in identifying the customs so responsible for "evil sentiments," he already has revealed them to the readers of his treatise as being related to the child's early incorporation of the disturbing customs of culture. Denouncing the seventeenth-century popularity of the French epic novel as an impressionable site of "fables, marvels, and monsters," he reflects on their earliest pedagogical impact: "And even if we came upon eyewitness accounts enabling us to distinguish the true from the false, we remain

8. Antoine Coypel, *L'excellence de la peinture*, in Nicolas Jouin, ed., *Discours prononcés dans les conferences de l'Académie Royale de Peinture et de Sculpture* (Paris: J. Collombat, 1721), 365.

9. D'Aubignac, "Abbregé de la philosophie des stoïques; avec un eclaircissement general de cette histoire, necessaire à tous ceux qui la voudront lire avec plaisir," included as the preface of *MACARISE, ou LA REYNE des isles fortunées*, 2 vols. (1664; rpt. Geneva: Slatkine, 1979). Hereafter cited as APS.

so preoccupied with the reading of books and the talk of the learned, from the first instructions of our youth, that it would be almost impossible to disabuse ourselves" (APS, 126). Of concern to d'Aubignac is not only the threat of the contemporary epic but also the fictional precedents of Homer and Virgil which were esteemed and disseminated by the learned. The Abbé denounces both the ancients and the moderns for having "smothered the lights of truth with the darkness of fables" (APS, 128–29). According to this line of thought, the novel occludes truth and reason, from the moment of its earliest instruction, with an abusive shroud of "evil sentiment." By this inconstant means, then, the novel always already embodies the seductive Other of impressionable (no doubt, male) youth.

A fascinating aspect of this equation remains its psychoanalytical resonance. D'Aubignac's complaint clearly anticipates the emphasis placed by psychoanalysis on the constitutional role of fantasy in forming the subject. His concern over the impact of fables from the moments of earliest instruction speaks to the limitless mirroring of inconstant memories that haunts the subject from its initial encounter with the specular other. Described by Jean-Baptiste Pontalis as the natural effect of displacement, any scene remembered as apparently significant and different (say, our childhood preoccupation with parents, fables, and books) calls forth, interpellates, some Other forgotten which carries with it the ghostly charge of a signifying effect. The result, so suggests Pontalis, in *Perdre de vue*, is that "we do not have memories *of* childhood but only memories *on* our childhood, which do not arise out of the past but are formed on the run; our memory is a retroactive fiction, retroactively anticipatory, which belongs with no need of sanction to the realm of *Fantasy*."[10] Enshrouded in the scopic fabrics of fiction, hallucination, sexuality, and the body, fantasy constitutes, haunts, and disturbs the unwilling subject. Recalling d'Aubignac's youthful example of reason's uneasy dependence on the two-sided mirror, the subject thus stands split in the realm of fantasy: one observes both from within and from without; one sees oneself and one is seen by oneself observing the retroactive hallucination of oneself. While the subject may well remain uncertain about the actual content of fantasy, one senses strongly its call as an enigmatic signifier. In the words of Jean Laplanche, "we have to place considerable stress on the

10. J.-B. Pontalis, *Perdre de vue* (Paris: Gallimard, 1988), 289.

possibility that the signifier may be *designified,* or lose what it signifies, without thereby losing its power to signify *to.*"[11] This ghostly
summons of the signifier *to the subject* inscribes the self as always
already caught *within* fantasy even though a stoic subject might still
try to think, read, reason, or remember alongside of it. It is thus *on* this
axis of the split screen of memory that the stoic picks up along the way
the kinds of confusing imprints of fiction and learned conversation of
which "it is almost impossible to disabuse ourselves."

THE PRISON HOUSE OF FLESH

Being itself caught in the web of fantasy, d'Aubignac's stoic attack on
the novel functions to sustain the fictional project that it critiques.
Scholars familiar with the literary work of d'Aubignac will certainly
appreciate the unsettling irony of his authorship of three clearly iden-
tifiable novels and numerous literary portraits. Paradoxically, his treatise on stoicism even serves as part of the 214-page, retrospective preface to one of these novels, an incomplete two-volume epic fiction of
over 1,400 pages, *Macarise or the Queen of the Fortunate Isles. An
Allegorical History containing the Moral Philosophy of the Stoics
under the Veil of many agreeable Adventures in the form of the Novel*
(1664).[12] Adding to this irony is the fact that d'Aubignac conceived this
project during his service in the early 1630s as the tutor of the nephew
of Richelieu, Jean-Armand de Maillé-Brézé, whose written portrait
provides the framework for an additional prefatorial text, "Discourse
containing the character of those who will favorably judge this Story,
and take advantage of the truths it teaches" (appended to APS.) This
text also provides further details of the pedagogical imperative of *Macarise.* It is in view of "the reading of this Philosophy, the pleasures it
can give and the fruits one must gather from it" (APS, 207) that d'Aubignac constructs his fictional narrative for the benefit of "reasonable
minds, the learned of society, and virtuous Princes" (APS, 207). Although this novel failed to receive critical acclaim when it was published in the 1660s, its detailed and often juicy tableaus of the para-

11. Jean Laplanche, *New Foundations for Psychoanalysis,* trans. David Macey (Oxford: Basil Blackwell, 1989), 45.
12. *Macarise* was published in two volumes. Citations of Volume 1 are from the
Slatkine reprint, op. cit., hereafter cited as MacI; due to a printer's error, this volume
contains two sets of pages numbered 304–80 (instead of 404–80) which I note as 304–80a
and 304–80b. Citations of Volume 2 are from *Macarise, ou la Reyne des isles fortunées.
Second Volume* (Paris: Jacques Du Brueil, 1664), hereafter cited as MacII.

doxes of French stoicism might well have garnered it more serious attention in the age of Richelieu.

The allegorical narrative of *Macarise* relates the epic quest of the flawed hero, Arianax ("Weak King"), for the incomparable beauty, Macarise ("the complete image of the Stoic Philosophy"), who rules as Queen of the Fortunate Isles ("Bliss").[13] The novel documents how Arianax, accompanied by his wiser twin brother, Dinazel ("the good spirit of Arianax"), successfully traverses two of the three cleansing stages of stoic "Wisdom." The first, from birth to the moment he is love-struck by the beauty of Macarise, includes his successful struggle against Doxane ("Opinion"—source of all passion) who rules the Empire des Mores ("Insane"). The second involves the wars waged by Arianax against the enemies of Macarise, the most significant being his combat of the artifice and violence of Cinais ("Passion"). The Preface also promises an unpublished account of the third stage, Arianax's successful ascent of the "Inaccessible Mountain" which permits his marriage to Macarise "by a form of Apotheosis." Each of these stages involves struggles against seductive portraits, paintings, fables, artifices, spectacles, figures, and bodies—all being cast as formidable enemies of Reason. While the overall historical significance of these adventures could be read to refer to the complexity of d'Aubignac's ambivalence about the French court's centralization of precious games of theatre and artifice, the novel's philosophical aim is the more one-dimensional, allegorical rule of reason over passion, as exemplified by the promise of the philosophical out-of-body marriage of Arianax and Macarise "by a form of Apotheosis."[14]

That the marriage of Macarise is forecast as culminating only in a climax of heavenly abstinence leaves intact both the logical relation of reason over passion as well as the stoic dependence on the corporeal truth of the hymen. This sacred act of the preservation of female plenitude reproduces an important topos of the baroque representation of woman which Walter Benjamin outlined as early as 1924 in *The Origin of German Tragic Drama*. Reflecting on the pressures placed on the

13. See Thomas DiPiero's discussion of the epic quest in the novel, *Dangerous Truths and Criminal Passions: The Evolution of the French Novel, 1569–1791* (Stanford: Stanford University Press, 1992), 90–132, and Georges Van Den Abbeele's analysis of travel in early-modern French philosophy, *Travel as Metaphor from Montaigne to Rousseau* (Minneapolis: University of Minnesota Press, 1992).

14. I analyze d'Aubignac's contradictory attitudes about French neoclassicism in *Theatrical Legitimation: Allegories of Genius in Seventeenth-Century England and France* (New York and Oxford: Oxford University Press, 1987), 157–97.

confidence of sovereignty by the unpredictability of historical accident, Benjamin comments on the dramatic tyrant's tendency to replace these accidents with "the iron constitution of the laws of nature." He stresses how this fictional representation corresponds to the
technique of stoic philosophy which "aims to establish a correspond-
ing fortification against a state of emergency in the soul, the rule of
emotions."[15] To do so, Benjamin suggests, stoicism seeks to establish
new, antihistorical creations the result of which for woman is the
privileged assertion of her chastity. Through chastity, the hallmark of
domestic devotion is supplemented, or even replaced, by the ideal of
physical asceticism.

I should add that this end of physical asceticism comes as no surprise to the reader of *Macarise* who faces it from the earliest moments
of the novel. Book One is highlighted by an account of the death of
Clearte (the figure of Zeno) to whom Macarise is indebted for freeing
her from captivity on an "invisible island." When Clearte sets off to
save yet another princess, following the liberation of Macarise, he falls
prey to the beneficence of the tyrant Olonte who orders Clearte to
sacrifice his life to the gods as the ultimate repayment of the tyrant's
boundless generosity. Clearte accepts this deadly challenge with a dec-
laration of complete asceticism: "One must denude those who are
born of all those veils of flesh enveloping them, our death is a second
birth, and we must not love our bodies" (MacI, 57). Then, placed on the
altar of sacrifice, Clearte accepts Olonte's offer to perform his final
liberty by publicly declaring for whom he wishes to die. Slicing his
finger on the sword of the executioner, he first writes two words on the
altar with blood flowing from his castrating wound, "FOR MA-
CARISE," and then declares, "It is to her that I have . . . dedicated my
life, and it is only to her that I consecrate my death" (MacI, 67). With
this elegant act, whose depiction on the frontispiece of the novel dedi-
cates the text to the stoic principles embodied by Macarise, Clearte
presents the spectator with a tableau of his loyalty to the Queen of
"Bliss." He transforms his body into blood, the sign of pure love. By
thus rehearsing the condition of his death through a secular staging of
the act of corporeal transformation, Clearte fulfills in spirit, word, and
action the stoic maxim of Montaigne: to philosophize is to learn *how*

15. Walter Benjamin, *The Origin of German Tragic Drama*, trans. John Osborne
(London: NLB, 1977), 73.

to die. Or, as d'Aubignac restates it in *Macarise:* "To learn how to die is no longer to submit to this prison of flesh" (MacII, 179).

The novel's lengthy exposition of the subsequent response of Macarise to the loss of Clearte is no less performative of "a profound meditation on the most just conformity of things with their representation" (what d'Aubignac describes as his novel's stoic effect) (MacI, 166). It too is marked by signs of bodily transformation. Rather than mourn the death of Clearte, Macarise refuses to be touched by the depth of her loss and forecloses the unpredictable paths of passionate mourning: "I know well what I lose with the death of Clearte; but do you wish that my soul should be troubled for it? Is it necessary that the merit of this Prince, which completely fills my mind, should disquiet my heart with unruly motions?" (MacI, 85–86). By thus denying the pathos of loss, Macarise here assumes yet another ascetic posture, the neoclassical one of Melancholia who stands, like a Virgin, as a classical icon of passion's submission to the powers of reason. Rather than succumbing to the passion of loss, Macarise envelops the disquiet of Thanatos in the reasoned nobility of ascetic Eros. She thus conforms to what Buci-Glucksmann subtly understands as the contradictory law of the baroque: "to produce *effects* that create *beings* and engender *affects*" (49). The seamlessness of Macarise's steadfast denial of her loss so effects Calistrate, the Head of her School, that he describes Macarise to Arianax as a being Other than the persona of her sex: "She was nevertheless so prudent in her indifference to her feelings that one could note neither the weakness of woman nor the callousness of Barbarians" (MacI, 82–83). Bearing the signs of neither woman nor monster, of neither the weakness of "charms" nor the callousness of "audacity," Macarise stands firm, already at this early stage of the novel, as a dependable being, emblematic of ascetic indifference to the passions. That is, she embodies the effects of divine melancholy, which Clearte recommends as "what makes great men and without which there would be no true Heroes nor a perfect Sage" (MacII, 774).

But while the novel is clearly imprinted by this motto of ascetic perfection, d'Aubignac's narrative fortification against the soul's state of emergency is hardly seamless. Significant blemishes mar the psychic armor of the Virgin-Melancholic who is renowned in the novel for the steadiness of her reasoned incorporations of loss and lust. They surface frequently in relation to her dialogues with Arianax, the dynamics of which foretell the psychoanalytic session. That is, the hero's

enigmatic tales of trauma and seduction are propelled by his transference of passion onto his reasonable and passive interlocutor. For her
part, Macarise too shows vulnerable signs of transference when the
narrative relates the subliminal effect of his physical presence:

> Macarise, who noted in the appearance of Arianax some traits of a
> beautiful Idea she had had for a long time in her mind, and who nev-
> ertheless still endeavored to bring to consciousness some likeness to
> achieve knowledge of what it was she imagined, did not want to allow
> him to leave out any detail of his story, not only for the pleasure she
> received in listening to him speak with such grace, but also with the
> hope of discovering what was troubling her. [MacI, 367–68a]

Or more accurately, this account of the healer's discomfort speaks
more to the process of counter-transference. That is, Macarise displays
signs of the kind of passionate interference of interpretation noted by
Lacan as characteristic of the analyst.[16] At best, counter-transference
merely marks interpretation with the signs of the analyst's censorial
prejudice. At worst, it can lead to traumatic realizations like those of
Macarise whom the narrator says is encased in something more than a
reasonably contained history:

> Arianax presented his tale with such grace that one esteemed his elo-
> quence no less than his valor, and the Queen [was left] with a soul full of
> an infinity of entirely new thoughts, and agitated by many agreeable
> movements, but which she believed to prepare for her an engagement
> she had never known. [MacI, 369–70b]

The engagement, being that of love, subjects Macarise, not to mention her readers, to a state mediated for others throughout the novel by
the vicissitudes of desire and the phantoms of betrayal. This becomes
especially evident in Volume 2 when the Queen is awakened with a
start from a sensual dream just as she imagines Arianax putting his lips
to her hand (MacII, 98–100).

Especially fascinating is how frequently this novel sets loose in
print the very phantasms of bodily pleasure said by the author to counter any project of philosophical control, those pleasures of the flesh
that charm men "as if a sheet of frozen water held in front of the face."
D'Aubignac even reveals that artistic necessity requires him to orna-
ment the narrative of *Macarise* with numerous actions of body and
soul that remain inconsequential to his stoic purpose. In his prefatorial

16. Jacques Lacan, "L'intervention sur le transfert," in *Écrits* (Paris: Seuil, 1966),
215–26.

remarks, he admits freely to the stylistic excess of *Macarise* in which there remain "many minor subjects ["petites actions"] which it is absolutely necessary to convey for the beauty of the novel, which are hardly necessary to explain since they have no relation to the secret intelligence of this Philosophy. I here include no examples because it will not be at all difficult to see them in the text" (APS, 173–74). Notable in this nonchalant disclosure is the trusting reemergence of the very scopic vocabulary of representation which stood earlier to d'Aubignac as a figure of those many troubling phantasms embodied during the instructions of youth. What is merely supplemental to the stoic soul of the novel is now thought to be not only easy to see but also simple to look beyond. The author seems to have warmed up to the ornamental attributes of the mind whose embodiments in flesh and figure are said in d'Aubignac's earlier writings to freeze the most thoughtful reader in the agonizing mirror of libidinal self-torment.

Equally striking to this reader of *Macarise* is how its many "petites actions" consist of numerous and lengthy accounts of the hero's absorption in activities which are primarily scopic in nature. The novel is replete with Arianax's visual accounts of cabinets, paintings, sculptures, columns, ceilings, ballets, galleries, devices, portraits, inscriptions, sonnets, spectacles, monsters, and victims. Indeed, the hero's scattered and dizzying visions are much more significant to the narrative structure of the novel than are the accounts of his more conventionally heroic acts. Sensations of dizziness, fascination, paralysis, and arrest wrought by these multiples of perspective are what lend the "petites actions" an emotive life of their own—one that permeates and unsettles the reasonable constraints of this text's many stoic fortifications.

But first to the kind of counter-example that frames the "petites actions" throughout the novel. Ironically, the novel's most frivolous and blatantly pornographic scenario actually affirms d'Aubignac's confidence in his narrative's control over its specular breach. I am thinking of a lewd mise en scène, early in Book Two, that disrupts Arianax and Dinazel's dialogue on the dangerous appeal of the visual phantasmagoria in the court of Agatide ("The Appearance of False Gains"). Their apprehension of the compelling monstrosities featured in Agatide's collection of grotesque statues and paintings is brought to life by the piercing cries of a woman in distress. Following a search of many labyrinthine chambers, the two courtiers discover the source of these cries at the end of a long gallery where: "We saw . . . a young

woman almost completely nude, bound with irons and confined behind bars" (MacI, 187). Their subsequent motions dramatize the specular strategy typical of d'Aubignac's fictional style. "We withdrew our
torches in order not to offend with our eyes the modesty/shame (*la
pudeur*) of this beautiful captive." While seeming to remove the stoic
voyeurs from the passions of this sight, the narrative actually reveals
its strategy of displacing responsibility from the specular violence of
voyeurism onto the corporeal shame of "this beautiful captive." Two
subsequent passages contribute to the structural stability of such displacement. The first is a telling description of the woman's liberation:

> We found the clothes of this prisoner, I took them and threw them on
> her so that I could approach her without doing her violence; and break-
> ing without difficulty the shackles binding her feet and hands, we gave
> her time to dress as well as she could; and as soon as she was in a state
> enabling her to suffer the light without blushing, we led her to our
> apartment. [MacI, 190]

Here the hero's repetitive insistence on his empathetic concern with
the victim's shame clearly displaces any critical reflection on his specular fascination with her discarded garments and state of undress.[17]
This critical indifference to the scopophiliac compulsion is fore-
grounded in the second example, a prior passage in which Arianax
sneaks a second, more encompassing look at the bound woman "almost completely nude." Although the novelist relies on this account
to reveal the range of Arianax's powers of critical interrogation, d'Aubignac manipulates the narrative to displace the protagonist's more
purposeful gaze as the source of any philosophical concern:

> While she talked I discerned little by little the features of her face, even
> though the light was far distanced from her, and I saw there such beauty
> sparkling among the shadows surrounding her that I was able to make
> the decision to serve her, even if her plight had not excited my compas-
> sion. [MacI, 188]

The recipient of critical suspicion remains to be the shameful woman
whose fallen state fails to excite male (com)passion. But it is in keeping

17. In *Fictions of Feminine Desire: Disclosures of Heloise* (Lincoln: University of
Nebraska Press, 1982), Peggy Kamuf notes, in the context of Abelard's analogy of the
black bride, the additional importance of the female victim's removal to the private
space of the apartment: "The cloistering of woman, by removing her from circulation in
a public domain, sets up a freely mobile masculine desire as the noncontradictory self-
referential discourse of meaningful distinction" (44).

with the stoic agenda of this novel, to return to my introductory claims about the role of gender difference, that her fall also functions as the engine of female redemption. For her release from bondage depends on the same voyeuristic relation that holds her in chains. What persuades Arianax to free her is the passionate match of her perceived beauty to the masculinist conventions of his voyeuristic gaze. Her sparkling beauty is objectified as a passive trait awaiting incorporation and acknowledgment by the active subject who remains empowered by the epistemic virtues of sight and discernment.

While this brief scene may appear to present nothing more than a seemingly insignificant "petite action," its emblematic stature deserves further commentary. For the episode narrativizes a relation consistent throughout *Macarise* in which woman's frightful, fallen flesh depends for redemption on the benevolence of the phallic hero whose actions are contingent on his ability to see beauty, and trouble, for what they are. (This is a typical relation of the neoclassical genre of epic fantasy novels.) The male hero's strongest attribute—his detached, perspectival gaze—corresponds precisely to the rationalized system of scopic disavowal that transforms the "petites actions" of difference into "the beauty of the Novel."[18] In d'Aubignac's plain words: "It will not be difficult to see them." Consistent with both examples is how beauty, passion, and flesh are positioned as phenomena of figural substance, of body, which are Other, external as well as threatening, to the rationalist phallocentric subject. For his part, the phallic subject relies on perspectival prowess either to try to hold passion at an appropriate distance, that is, to externalize it, or to attempt to render it neutral through a procedure of specular internalization in which female shame comes to signify phallic strength.

A striking example of externalization is provided by Arianax's description, in Book 3, of the image of Cinais ("Passion") who attempts to stage his seduction in her Closet of Pretty Passions. His physical description of Cinais is delayed by twenty ornamental pages in which he catalogues the Closet's artwork. In phantasmatic detail, Arianax describes a vast collection of images depicting the history of Western seduction and eroticism, from the taboo images of Diana to the forbid-

---

18. In *Subjectivity and Subjugation in Seventeenth-Century Drama and Prose,* Greenberg analyzes a corollary ocular construct in *La Princesse de Clèves:* "What is being reproduced in the appeal of/to the image is an ideology of sexual difference where the woman is looked at, upon, and seen to figure for the male viewer that difference that corroborates his own sexuality as superiority" (192).

den tragedy of Phèdre. The readers of this sequence receive nothing less than a comprehensive overview of the masculinist history of the passions which has been internalized through books and fables since childhood. Then, somewhat abruptly, the narrative shifts its attention from the images of forbidden love to project their composite, retrospective fantasy directly onto the hero's written portrait of Cinais:

> She was dressed in a gown of silver fabric with a green ground as light as it was delicately crafted; part of her hair hung from the side in great shapely curls gracing her shoulders and her largely exposed breasts, and the rest formed a coiffure adorned with small ribbons of green satin full of many precious stones which embellished her with their brilliance, instead of weighing her down. The rest of her costume was made of precious and loose fabrics common enough in Morea [*dans la Morée*], which serve neither to protect the body nor to veil shame, and which permit a woman to contribute almost nothing to the adulterous complicity of her voluptuous softness that she does not display to the public, who are truly incapable of swearing that she is not nude when she is dressed. [MacI, 336b]

"Neither to protect the body nor to veil shame." Once again the fault lies with the alienating bearer of shame rather than with the gazing fetishist who does not miss a hair, a ribbon, or a breast. The danger of her display, moreover, is to render uncertain the empirical constancy of male spectatorship: to make the viewer incapable of swearing that she is not nude when she is dressed. In the face of such danger, Arianax guards himself with the fetishistic defense of ocular authority allowing him to know a pornographic woman when he sees one. His confident voyeurism can lead only to a negative assessment of Passion.

DISAVOWED MORES

While this scene exemplifies Arianax's fetishistic reordering of the physical threat of Cinais, the narrator provides, at the outset of the novel, an even clearer picture of the phallic subject's embodiment of the Other. Of interest are two columns adorning the Temple of Clearte, the description of which provides the allegorical ballast of the novel:

> In the middle were two Heroes with completely different bearings and countenances. One was the valiant Scenapion so famous for the victories he had won in Africa; he appeared arrayed with a scarlet coat of arms and a fierce and bellicose disposition; he was kicking over a woman with tawny, black skin and a lion on which she appeared to have

been mounted; and with the right hand he was raising a consul's ax as if he wanted to beat the vanquished ones with it. And the other was the Prince Luziel, dressed in a long Roman robe, sporting soft eyes, a face with a tranquil countenance, and a body of very moderate carriage. He was shown trampling under foot serpents which seemed to respect him and shrink from his presence. Arianax already had become pregnant with the desire to imitate these illustrious persons whose commemoration had been proposed for public instruction. [MacI, 16–17]

From the outset of the novel, Arianax incorporates these images as the signifiers of his noble quest. Both ideals stand tall as victors of the Other who is commonly figured as the monstrous female. The first column depicts the woman with tawny, black skin and her African lion who cowers subdued at Scenapion's feet. Foretelling the novel's later scene of bondage which I discuss above, the conqueror stands poised with his weapon as if he *wanted* to beat his victims. Similarly, the second column represents the moderate Roman, whose mere presence is forceful enough to drive out evil serpents. That this tamer of snakes bears a tranquil countenance with mellow eyes establishes a striking contrast to that mythological figure of evil here alluded to—the paragon of apotropaic serpents, the Gorgon Medusa, whose deadly look was neutralized by the subtle wiles of her spoiler, the moderate Perseus.[19]

Ironically, admiration of these images commemorated by public instruction is what subjects Arianax to the same kinds of destabilization that d'Aubignac criticizes as the negative fruits of the novel. For the hero's mimetic incorporation of the above images of monstrous women can be said to rise up against him and the narrative's stoic control of reason over passion, just as the purposefully seductive image of Cinais is susceptible to its enfeebling fetishization by Arianax. As I have suggested above, specular reflections and visual incorporations are always already divided in themselves. Although a detailed analysis of the many instances of such destabilization is beyond the scope of this article, brief consideration of two additional examples should clarify the narrative's in-difference to the orderly shackles of stoic reason, not to mention the ocular complexity of the many encrypted phantoms fueling this resistance.

Visualize, if you will, the composite fantasies of two monsters that threaten the tranquility of Arianax in Books 2 and 3. The first is a

19. In reading Derek Jarman's film, *Caravaggio,* in *Like a Film: Ideological Fantasy on Screen, Camera, and Canvas* (London and New York: Routledge, 1993), I provide an overview of the critical implications of the Medusa myth (143–54).

specter of popular culture nurtured by Agatide to disturb her imprisoned guests. It is compared to the Chimera, a

> monstrous figure composed of a lion's head, a goat's belly, and a ser-
> pent's tail, which the vulgar took as a fiction of the ancient Poets and
> [which] has given its name to all of the imaginations of the human
> spirit. And, so you can be assured that we are well informed of every-
> thing, this Chimera of Lycia was born in Africa. [MacI, 184–85]

The second is a similar monster, named Bascanin ("Envy"). It is sent in
Book 3 by Agatide to haunt Macarise's kingdom:

> One sees there none more terrible than . . . [Bascanin] which they con-
> sider to be the cross of a boar and a lioness. . . . It is taller than most
> boars and much faster than lions; it sports eyes whose burning fire
> makes one tremble, and among its sharp teeth, like those of its mother,
> it has tusks which can be seen to emerge out above its head and which
> are almost always stained with blood. . . . This then is what corrupt
> nature has produced through a mixture of the black and melancholic
> fury of the boar and the inflamed rage of the lioness. [MacI, 372–75b]

While it is difficult to say precisely what these monsters signify, it is
easier to note their composite resemblance to the monstrous figures
held at bay by the heroes Scenapion and Luziel. From the combination
of lion and serpent to the boar/lion who sports a disturbing gaze and a
bloody headdress of phallic appendages, those memorable figures frozen in stone to support the Temple of Clearte here come brazenly to
life. Being merely supplemental to the aim of the narrative, they spring
forth as "petites actions" in the form of hallucinations, as it were, of
the monsters of passionate intensity which have been eclipsed by phallic prowess and encrypted deep in the cultural depositories of vulgar
opinion, literary tradition, and public instruction. These are the kinds
of "petites sensations," to turn to a phrase coined by Jean-François
Lyotard, that "remain hidden in ordinary perception which is con-
strained by the hegemony of the habitual and classical manner of looking. They are accessible . . . only at the price of an interior ascesis that
clears the perceptive and mental field of prejudices inscribed in vision
itself."[20]

Bearing further witness to the sensational side of stoic incorpora-

20. Jean-François Lyotard, *L'Inhumain. Causeries sur le temps* (Paris: Galilée, 1988),
113. See also Marie-Hélène Huet's discussion of the linguistic excess of seventeenth-
century monstrosity in *Monstrous Imagination* (Cambridge: Harvard University Press,
1993), 36–55.

tion is the irony that the ascetic features of Melancholy embodied by Macarise here haunt her kingdom in the passionate guise of the fury, Bascanin. Indeed, these and other horrific figures surface frequently in the novel as aggressive phantoms of d'Aubignac's stoic foreclosure of the fantastic appeal of his earliest instructions. Consider, finally, how frequently the figures of Otherness surface in *Macarise* as specters of Africa and Africans that continually threaten the philosophical calm of Western stoicism. The novel projects a curiously anxious familiarity with perceptions of the cultural difference of Africa, from the clothes of Cinais, "common enough 'dans la Morée'" and the "woman with tawny, black skin," to the apotropaic specter of Lycia who "was born in Africa." These references certainly seem to belie two important claims made by d'Aubignac in his prefatorial material. The first concerns his fictional disclaimer regarding his "Empire des Mores," the land of Opinion: "One must note that these MORES are not those peoples of Africa who bear this name, even though I stage my Theatre of Adventures there, for it is fortunate that this word signifies Insane in Greek" (APS, 32). However hollow it might ring in the novel, this awkward disclaimer sustains another crucial prefatorial claim regarding the universal appeal of stoicism:

> This so salutary Philosophy could have been examined in the diverse places in the World which it has rendered famous by its presence, and under the different visages which it has worn among those who have welcomed it. I could have sought it in India where the Brahmans have respected it in their lofty speculations and mysterious practices; in Ethiopia where the Gymnosophists have served it through their general detachment from all things; in Egypt where the Priests of Memphis conserved it in all the sacred Enigmas of which they were the Trustees; in Italy where Pythagoras enriched it, and circulated it in so many ingenious symbols; in the Gallic lands where our ancient Druids maintained it mixed with the rules of Religion; in Persia, in Africa, and in the other Lands which it favored with its lights. [APS, 15–16]

From the outset, d'Aubignac grounds the success of his allegory on claims of its natural universality. Stoicism is said to have permeated the spirit of religion and belief across the globe, from the Brahmans to the Pythagoreans, from the Egyptians to the Druids. The fantasy of "the secret intelligence of this Philosophy" is represented, then, as universally knowable and translatable into indigenous philosophical practices. Indeed, a crucial principle of this philosophy holds that "all men are born with a good inclination toward virtue which is more

natural to us than vice" (APS, 42). This maxim of a universal inclination toward stoicism is based, then, on the negation or foreclusion of
the possibility of incommensurable radical difference, of an Other of
stoicism.

Still, what the novel makes demonstrably clear is the cost of stoicism's incorporation of and by the African Other whose native residue
haunts reason's control over enigma. This residue is evident in d'Aubignac's vehement denial of the resemblance of the popular notion of
Africa to his Empire des Mores as well as the curious absence in his
catalogue of stoic utopias of any reference to the New World, that
irretrievably Other place, so d'Aubignac writes in 1627, "where Satan
has seen his greatest days and reigned for so many centuries."[21] But
always in the wake of their disavowal and foreclusion, the composite
figures of Africans, and perhaps New World Natives, return forcefully
to the foreground of *Macarise* as specters of the body monstrous. These
serve as ocular manifestations of the Other that always already divides
stoic reason and its philosophical antibodies "in-difference."

There still remain other crucial narratives to analyze in *Macarise*,
especially as they regard the body's continual disturbance of the cer-
tainties of stoic reason, and the tendency of stoicism to mark its internal disturbances as corporeally other, as woman, as color. Readers familiar with the novel might recall the "petite action" of Mimelithe's
repeated attempts to seduce her half-brother, Arianax. It is not coincidental that these and similar female seductions are rebuffed consistently by abrupt narrative interruptions, thus firmly situating sexuality in the dual Freudian realm of hallucination and paranoia. Add to
this the enigmatic revelation made by Arianax that he too is on-
tologically polluted by his status as a bastard twin. Further complicating the Oedipal trajectory I've yet to trace, there's the predictable result
of this dual stain, a matricide at birth whose mournful signifier almost
eclipses the trace of Arianax's own African lineage—on his father's
side. Doesn't this mixed blood spoil forever the stoic—can't we now
say "colonial"—divisions of inner and outer which are still so dear to
so many adherents of the Republic and its extreme phallocrat, Le Pen?
All of these traces point to a kind of internal division far too strong to
remain confined to the reasonable allegory of stoic antibodies.

These enigmatic divisions are figured with particular rhetorical

21. D'Aubignac, *Des satyres, brutes, monstres, et demons, de leur nature et adoration*
(Paris: Nicolas Buon, 1627), 163.

force in an engraved illustration of the novel with whose description I conclude. On the floor in the background of a woman's cabinet lies a discarded book, already devoured or still to be rediscovered, the material sign of retroactive fantasies yet to be spun. The foreground is marked by the enigmatic gesture of a Moor, of all people, who designates, frames, interrupts, or explains the honor paid here by Arianax to the body of his female guardian. Were I to have been the binder of d'Aubignac's novel who was responsible for positioning the engravings, I would have inserted this one in close proximity to a poignantly transferential moment. This is when Arianax concludes the report of his exchange with Doxane ("Opinion") by making a telling confession to Macarise, the Queen of "Bliss":

> This was just about the conversation we had, and of which it is discomforting to report all of the particularities. [MacI, 351b]

BENJAMIN SEMPLE

The Male Psyche and the Female Sacred Body in Marie de France and Christine de Pizan

To study the sacred body in the Middle Ages is to run the risk of accepting at face value the prevailing ideology of the period. In the Middle Ages, the sacred body is often simply the denial of the profane body, and the profane body is the woman's body. The concept of the sacred body can lead us into one of those binarisms with which medieval Christianity was filled: body and soul, dead and living, damned and saved, letter and spirit, profane and sacred. And female and male. In most instances, the dividing line between the sacred body and the profane body ran between the male and the female for "the worst of the body and of sexuality was the female body"[1]: women were excluded from the priesthood, there were fewer female than male saints, the female body was invested with taboos, and God, while neither male nor female in theory, is typically rendered in the Christian imaginary as a man. Under Christianity, the sexual, which had played an integral role in pagan religions, became the sign of human debasement: "The very qualities for which woman once had been considered sacred now became the reason for which she was degraded."[2]

Christian theologians perceived woman as a threat, along with all that she represented. In the story of the Fall of Adam and Eve, the role of temptress of man had been assigned to Eve, who in turn had caused Adam to sin. In Genesis, Adam had not sinned because of the direct

1. Jacques Legoff, *The Medieval Imagination*, trans. Arthur Goldhammer (Chicago: University of Chicago Press, 1980), 83.
2. Nancy Qualls-Corbett, *The Sacred Prostitute* (Toronto: Inner City Books, 1988), 43.

YFS 86, *Corps Mystique, Corps Sacré: Textual Transfigurations of the Body from the Middle Ages to the Seventeenth Century*, ed. Françoise Jaouën and Benjamin Semple, © 1994 by Yale University.

temptation of the serpent, like Eve, but had followed the woman. This was a point that was not lost on Biblical commentators and theologians. Augustine suggested that the woman had been susceptible to the serpent's temptation because she was still undergoing instruction from the man and her moral education had not yet been finished:

> Perhaps the woman had not yet received the gift of the knowledge of God, but under the direction and tutelage of her husband she was to acquire it gradually.[3]

The direction of sin was from woman to man, not from man to woman. Furthermore, Augustine's statement granted that women were inherently less virtuous than men, and that men were to be entrusted with their education. The sin introduced through Eve, through an unruly female body subject to the appeal of sense (the tree was "good for food and . . . a delight to the eyes" [Genesis 3:6]), was a defeat of mind by body so grievous that it introduced sin into the entire community and to all the sons and daughters of the first couple.

The account of the Fall in Genesis stressed the irony of the event. Adam and Eve hoped to gain additional knowledge: they ate of a tree that promised "*knowledge* of good and evil." But rather than gain knowledge, they lost innocence. The only "knowledge" they gained, as Augustine showed, was a bodily experience, the feeling of sexual desire: they became aware, said Augustine, following Paul, of "a law in their members" at war with the "law of their mind."[4] This notion that sexual desire can constitute no knowledge, that there is nothing to be learned about it as an experience, is of great importance for the early and medieval Christian attitude toward sex. As a doctrinal matter, sexual desire can be examined in intellectual terms, provided that one remembers its connection to original sin; but the actual feeling, a bodily experience, cannot be a subject of investigation. The medieval church gave primarily negative information about sexuality to its flock.[5]

Under such circumstances, the chief focus of men writing about

3. Augustine, *The Literal Meaning of Genesis*, trans. John Hammond Taylor (New York: Newman Press, 1982), Ancient Christian Writers 42, vol. 2, 175.

4. Cf. Augustine, *Literal Meaning of Genesis*, 165: "Even in its punishment the rational soul gave evidence of its innate nobility when it blushed because of the animal movement of the members of its body." For Paul's expression, see Romans 7: 23.

5. See, for example, the advice offered by Adam de Perseigne to the countess of Perche, discussed by Georges Duby, *Que sait-on de l'amour au 12e siècle?* (Oxford: Oxford University Press, 1983), 9–10.

women became women's effect on male sexuality, and they were valued or condemned by the community based on whether they aroused or quieted male desire. For example, in looking at medieval saints, we find two models of sanctity, one for men and one for women.[6] The male model includes the control of sexual desire, often as a first step. But it proceeds through a series of renunciations afterwards. In the *Vie de saint Alexis*[7], for example, Alexis undergoes a series of trials that result in abandonment of sex (he leaves his wife), abandonment of worldly power and wealth (he forsakes his social position and gives away his money), abandonment of family (he replaces familial love with Christian *caritas*), and abandonment ultimately even of the narcissistic pleasure of being worshiped during his own lifetime (when he is discovered as a holy man prematurely, he flees the people who have recognized him). Alexis's many-layered renunciation recalls the model of Christ and resembles the temptations Christ undergoes at the hands of the devil (Matt. 4:1–11; Luke 4:1–13), temptations which are both temporal and spiritual and involve the soul more than the body.

The male saint's life represents a complete elimination of the aggressive impulses such as sexual desire or striving for power that can be seen to threaten social stability. Any society requires limits on expressions of desire, especially when desire threatens to erupt in conflict, leading to internal strife. In medieval hagiographical texts, the control of such desires (beginning with the sexual, but including the thirst for wealth or power) was incarnated chiefly in the male saint.

The model for female saints differs from that of men. While a great deal of value is attached to male control of desire, female desire is not a threat to the community. But chastity is still enjoined on women saints. They reinforce the male renunciation of desire by maintaining their own chastity. Men control their sexual desire and women help them to do it, largely through models of comportment prepared for them by men, in accordance with the notion of Adam educating Eve. This is not to say that female desire is not sometimes displayed. For example, in the *Vie de sainte Marie l'Egyptienne*[8], a saint's life from

6. On male and female sanctity, see especially Brigitte Cazelles, *The Lady as Saint* (Philadelphia: University of Pennsylvania Press, 1991); idem, *Le Corps de sainteté* (Geneva: Droz, 1982); Phillis Johnson and Brigitte Cazelles, *Le Vain Siecle Guerpir: A Literary Approach to Sainthood through Old French Hagiography of the Twelfth Century* (Chapel Hill: University of North Carolina Press, 1979).

7. *La Vie de Saint Alexis*, ed. Christopher Storey (Geneva: Droz, 1968).

8. All of my remarks about the *Vie de sainte Marie l'Egyptienne* refer to the T version. For the edition, see *La Vie de sainte Marie l'Egyptienne*, ed. Peter Dembowski (Geneva: Droz, 1977).

the twelfth century, the heroine, Mary, leads a life of unbridled lust. She leaves her family, disobeying her father, whose disapproval is, significantly, voiced through her mother (suggesting that the proper type of woman is one who echoes male authority and teaching) and goes to Alexandria, where she becomes a prostitute. She works there for a number of years, seducing every young man who comes within sight of her. Indeed, her beauty is especially bewitching, and no young man seems capable of resisting it. This is an important detail, since it shows that only the disappearance of Mary's body can control male desire: her irresistible beauty makes removal of her body from the community necessary. While the text makes some small reference to Mary's desire, the preoccupation is not with her experience of desire, but with the way she manages her body.

After years of life as a prostitute in Alexandria, Mary makes her way to Jerusalem aboard a ship of pilgrims. Her presence on this ship completely disrupts the holy mission and shows how vulnerable the sacred is to the profane. When Mary's body (for we have to speak of Mary's body here: that is the disruptive force) enters this ship on its sacred mission, the pilgrims fall under her charms. The entire ship is infected by the sexual contagion, and Mary pays for her passage by sleeping with as many pilgrims as possible.

When Mary arrives in Jerusalem, she continues her ways, and becomes a prostitute now in the holiest of cities. Her conversion, however, is soon at hand. On the day of the feast of the Exaltation of the Holy Cross, she joins a group of pilgrims heading for the temple where mass is to be celebrated. She keeps trying to approach the temple, but is continually thrust back by the press of the crowds. At first she takes this for coincidence, but finally she has a vision of angelic knights guarding the approach to the temple. Reminiscent of the angels that God posted at the entry to the Garden of Paradise, these knights suggest the exclusion of Mary as a "second Eve" from the temple, which is thus posited as a second Paradise. At this point, Mary converts: she directs herself to a statue of the Virgin Mary outside the temple. She addresses a long prayer to the Virgin Mary, recognizing and confessing her sin. She is then permitted to enter the temple, where she hears mass. Returning to the statue, she now seeks guidance from the Virgin. The Virgin's instructions are that Mary should go to the monastery of Saint John, where she will take communion, and then go into the wilderness, where her penance is to be performed.

Mary follows the Virgin's instructions. She spends more than forty years in the wilderness, surviving on nothing but three loaves of bread, a penance that underscores her body more than her soul. When her life is almost completed, she is discovered by an exemplary monk named Zosimas. He recognizes her for the saintly creature she is and returns to her in a year to grant her communion, after which she goes into the wilderness to die. Zosimas returns after yet another year to recover her body and bury it.

The life of Mary of Egypt, while colorful, is not unique. Mary is one of a cluster of female saints—including Thais, Affra, Pelagia, and the archetype herself, Mary Magdalen—who lead lives of prostitution and then convert to lead lives of utter devotion to God. The message of such lives is that the chief contribution of women in the arena of sanctity lies not so much in control of their own body as in control of the effect of that body on men. Mary of Egypt achieves her sanctity chiefly through identification with the Virgin. It is noteworthy that in the *Vie de sainte Marie l'Egyptienne*, the saint's body is the center of the hagiographer's preoccupations: just as she was irresistibly beautiful before her conversion so, during her life in the desert, she becomes hideously ugly.[9] She neutralizes the very body that presented a danger to the community. Furthermore, the price of her entry into the temple—the point at which the female body crosses over into sacred space—is utter devotion to and identification with the Virgin, and renunciation of sexual behavior. Cazelles has described the effect of Mary of Egypt's body as "talismanic" ("Modèle ou mirage," 15): Mary's body protects the male body (the narrative is specifically directed toward "lords" in the opening verse) against desire by removing itself from sight and mind as an object of male desire.

The story of Mary of Egypt shows how central female chastity was to the female saint, to the point that Cazelles has stated that the female saint cannot really be taken as paradigmatic of the notion of sanctity in the Middle Ages and needs to be treated as a particular case (*Corps de sainteté*, 21). Other scholars have pointed out that the female saint is presented essentially as an aberration because she has adopted a virile virtue, one usually associated with men, and which the female saint only assumes in the most unusual of circumstances.[10] Furthermore,

9. On this transformation and on the binary nature of the saint's existence, see especially Brigitte Cazelles, "Modèle ou mirage: Marie l'Egyptienne," *The French Review* 53 (October 1979): 13–22.

10. See Margaret R. Miles, *Carnal Knowing: Female Nakedness and Religious Meaning in the Christian West* (Boston: Beacon Press, 1989), especially "Becoming Male," 53–77.

the all-important role of witness is usually played by a man. The sex of the witness is as instructive as that of the saint: witnesses are the necessary link between the saint and society. Revelation is an epistemological event and can only occur if there is someone to receive it. The fact that it is usually a man who recognizes the saint underscores the idea that rational, logical, interpretive processes remain in the hands of men. The female saint has in effect attained a virtue that only a man would recognize.

The life of Mary of Egypt provides several interesting examples of how the theme of female sanctity, while it appears to elevate women, can actually reinforce Church teaching about women. When Zosimas first encounters Mary, there is a scene in which both saints rival each other in humility, trying to decide who will bless the other first: Mary's argument is that Zosimas should bless her first since as a priest he has the miraculous power of consecrating the host and presiding over transubstantiation.[11] Here masculine spiritual power is linked to a male priestly prerogative. Mary's sanctity is achieved only at the price of an extraordinary feat of penance, while Zosimas's right to bless her is presented by the saint herself (who is now, let us not forget, a role model for female piety) as a power related to his ecclesiastical position. Again, later in the narrative, when Zosimas blesses the host, he explains what the bread signifies. Mary immediately chimes in to explain the significance of the wine, and Zosimas recoils in surprise. The surprise of the monk seems to be a reaction to a piece of knowledge not that one would not expect a saint to possess, but that one would not expect a woman to possess (especially since knowledge of the Eucharist is a priestly, i.e. male, kind of knowledge). Zosimas's surprise is a compliment to Mary, but an implicit judgment of other women: Mary's knowledge is defined as extraordinary when compared to what Zosimas expects a woman to know. Finally, the Eucharist itself plays a significant role in lives like those of Mary of Egypt or in the Old French Mary Magdalen.[12] The woman's joining with Christ through the Eu-

11. On the role of the Eucharist as a means of increasing the prestige of the priest-hood, see Miri Rubin, *Corpus Christi: The Eucharist in Late Medieval Culture* (Cambridge: Cambridge University Press, 1991), 12ff. By alluding to Zosimas's ability to participate in the rite, Mary underscores a form of authority that can only be granted institutionally.

12. For a scene of Mary Magdalen receiving the Host, see "De la Madelaine: vie anonyme de Marie-Madeleine en prose française de la fin du XIIe siècle: édition critique," ed. Cindy Corcoran et al., *Zeitschrift für romanische Philologie* 98.1 (1982): 35–36.

charist is her chief way of uniting with Christ; men, on the other hand, tend to unite with him by becoming him in the classic tradition of the *imitatio Christi*, i.e. by adopting his behaviors.

The *Vie de sainte Marie l'Egyptienne* demonstrates how lives of women saints, while they do offer models of female sanctity, also subtly undermine women in a more general way. As Cazelles states: "In short, woman is, by instinct and nature, more inclined to succumb to the sins of the flesh, whereas man, whose very name (*vir*) evokes physical (*vis*) and mental (*virtus*) strength and who possesses rational and logical abilities, evolves in the world of ideas" (*Lady as Saint*, 48). In the remainder of this essay, I will look at examples of portrayals of women taken from works written by women. These works show how women created a space in which they could be examined as creatures both experiencing (and controlling) sexual desire and as doing so according to inherent concern for the community, not simply as a response to male control. Furthermore, the women achieve their transformation of society through using their body with obvious intelligence and ethical concern: this shows that at least some women were aware that sexual desire did not have to play a purely negative function, that women's bodies did not have to be removed from male society. While it would be unreasonable to expect these women to have utterly overthrown the models of their society, their texts offer strong evidence that women did not passively accept the exclusion of the female body by the ideological "sacred" body; in their own writings they sought to grant the female body its own sacred status independently of Christian models or through their transformation.

THE HEALING FEMALE BODY

The Christian tradition that I have sketched demonstrates that the direction of teaching was from male to female. The moral code is embodied in the male; the woman, more associated with the body, is under the tutelage of the male. In Christianity, morality is not only a code separate from the individual. Christianity places great emphasis on the internalization of this code and on its actualization in a human being: the Christ or Logos. This is the internalization of which Paul speaks in II Corinthians 3:3 when he uses the metaphor of a law written not on stone tablets but on "tablets of human hearts." The ethics of Christianity are passed on from one human being to another: they are not simply listed in writing but need to be deduced by the receiver of revelation from the actions of the Logos. This makes the individual who can incarnate the teachings of the community of extreme importance and explains in part the development of the cult of saints. It also shows why the inability to represent women in certain ways led to the notion that they could impart no knowledge to the community. To be incapable of incarnating the Christian word and transmitting it to another made one less than fully human.

The Logos is sometimes construed as a purely intellectual principle. But as presented in the Gospels, i.e., as the second person of the Trinity, the Logos is a principle of moral action as well. One of the chief functions of the Logos is that of teaching. The Logos educates—leads forth—that which is inside the human being. Christ is a teacher who instructs his disciples, a word which etymologically means students. The teaching he conveys is not merely intellectual. It is hard to grasp, difficult to implement, and often seemingly contrary to everyday logic.[13] In spite of this, the Logos commands that, to the extent possible, the example of the Logos be imitated. This teaching function was largely denied to medieval women. But in the *Lays* of Marie de France (a collection of short narrative poems dating from the third quarter of the twelfth century), we begin to find the development of the presentation of the woman as Logos. When the woman becomes the Logos, an additional element is added to the teaching. The one thing Christ could not teach his disciples was the wisdom of the body. Christ is not a sexual creature: Christianity, as illustrated by Augustine's reading of the Fall, does not allow for reason and sexual desire to unite. The Logos did not ever experience sexual desire: Christ was born of a Virgin mother. Christianity denied that either he or his mother had been tainted by sexual desire.

There is a language of emotions similar to spoken language. Erotic love is not simply felt: one learns how to feel it. Affects are trained and conditioned: Freud referred to this as "psychical working over."[14] Comportments are ritualized and codified. Marie de France shows us this knowledge about love in the *Lays*. When the direction of transmission of teaching moves from the woman to the man, sexual initiation becomes a part of the teaching; sexual initiation does not consist en-

13. See Diana Culbertson, *The Poetics of Revelation: Recognition and the Narrative Tradition*, Studies in American Biblical Hermeneutics 4 (Macon, Georgia: Mercer University Press, 1989), 23.

14. See J. Laplanche and J.-B. Pontalis, eds., *The Language of Psychoanalysis*, trans. Donald Nicholson-Smith (New York: W. W. Norton, 1973), 365–67.

tirely or even primarily of the physical act of sex, but of the entire range of feelings and affects that surround the experience of erotic love. When erotic love is posited as knowledge, the concept of knowledge begins to embrace an aspect of somatic and psychological experience that had formerly been thought to lie outside of knowledge.

It is noteworthy that many clerics continued to ridicule the idea that erotic love as it is represented in the courtly tradition can have any status as knowledge, suggesting both their adherence to the authority of the Church and the threat that this new view of love posed. The clerics who do examine sexual desire usually conform to some version of the following dictum, offered by Reason in the *Romance of the Rose:* "If you follow [Love], he will follow you; if you flee, he will flee."[15] There is no learning to be had in erotic love; it is simply an experience to be avoided. If not avoided, it contaminates. The idea that the experience of love could be a learning experience was a novel one for Christianity. I am not speaking here of the intellectual or doctrinal knowledge of sexuality: this had been intensively examined, especially by Augustine, and had of course thoroughly connected sexual desire with sin. Rather, I am referring to the fact that sexual life in its myriad expressions—from the basest desire to the most spiritual forms of love—is, as a lived experience, learned behavior.

At the beginning of her *Lays,* in the first line of the *Prologue,* Marie de France announces her intention to convey a teaching to her audience:

> Ki Deus a duné escience
> E de parler bone eloquence
> Ne s'en deit taisir ne celer
> Ainz se deit voluntiers mustrer. [1–4]

> Anyone who has received from God the gift of knowledge and true eloquence has a duty not to remain silent: rather one should be happy to reveal such talents. [41][16]

The word "knowledge" in the first line is meant to catch our attention: Marie predicates of herself, a woman, attributes normally associated with men. Even more surprising, when we consider the content of the

15. Guillaume de Lorris and Jean de Meun, *The Romance of the Rose,* trans. Charles Dahlberg (Hanover, New Hampshire: University Press of New England, 1983), 95.

16. Old French quotations are from *Les Lais de Marie de France,* ed. Jean Rychner (Paris: Champion, 1983). English translations are from *The Lays of Marie de France,* trans. Glyn S. Burgess and Keith Busby (London: Penguin, 1986).

Lays, is the allusion to a moral imperative that drives the writer to reveal what she knows because it can contribute to the public good: this is a Christian ethos of testimony ("let your light shine before others") applied to a subject matter Christianity associated with sin. Unlike Mary of Egypt, who actualizes the male model of a woman who facilitates male sexual renunciation, Marie de France does not present the female body in the same self-negating way. Here we enter a world of erotic love where sexual chastity is not a prerequisite for moral behavior. To make a comparison which can only be anachronistic: Marie is one of the founders of psychoanalytic thought, of the recognition that the desires felt in the body can be civilized and reconciled with society, and need not destroy society. One of the main themes of the *Lays* will be how sexual desire can result in communal good. One of the chief virtues taught in the *Lays* is not elimination of the experience of sexual desire, but something more like sublimation—although sublimation usually means a complete deviation of the initially sexual aim of the instinct[17]—whereas Marie de France's *Lays* accord satisfaction to the instinct while establishing some parameters within which satisfaction is to be found. As a whole, the *Lays* tend to show either how erotic love can support social tranquility or how it can disrupt it. At times, some of the renunciations of Marie de France's heroines may be distasteful to modern readers. It is important, however, to bear in mind the historical context in which she was writing: Christianity saw sexual desire as inherently at odds with the community. This belief was the basis of the exclusion of women from many social and political activities. Improving the lot of women had a direct link to demonstrating that sexual behavior was not incompatible with a stable social order, on condition that education was provided.

While in the medieval Christian tradition women are given much of the responsibility for arousing male desire, they are not credited with knowing anything about desire. In the *Lays,* however, women are not simply passive objects of male desire that have to be removed from sight and mind; rather, they hold the key to greater knowledge about erotic life. It is unfortunate, since the wisdom of Marie de France emerges most forcefully when the *Lays* are treated as a whole, that it is impossible to discuss all of the *Lays* here. I will limit myself to an analysis of the first of the *Lays, Guigemar.*[18]

17. See *The Language of Psychoanalysis,* 431–33.
18. On the body in this lay, see especially Stephen G. Nichols, "Deflections of the Body in the Old French Lay," *Stanford French Review* 14.1–2 (1990): 28–33.

In *Guigemar*, the female body is gifted with healing and talismanic qualities. At the beginning of the lay, Guigemar is presented as a man incapable of loving. He is beautiful, chivalric, and admired by the young women of the country where he resides. But like Narcissus, he is completely uninterested in love. Marie de France attributes this to a mistake of Nature:

> De tant i out mespris Nature
> Ke unc de nule amur n'out cure. [57-58]

> But Nature had done him such a grievous wrong that he never displayed the slightest interest in love. [44]

Significantly, Guigemar is at the home of his parents when the event occurs that compels him to love. There is a suggestion here that family dynamics may contribute to Guigemar's problem. The event that drives him to love occurs during the hunt, an activity associated with the nobility, with erotic conquest, but also with moments of tragic male sexual discovery (Narcissus is a hunter, as is Adonis). Unlike Narcissus or Adonis, however, Guigemar receives a wound from a woman that obliges him to seek a cure from a woman. He shoots an arrow at a hind. The arrow rebounds off the hind and strikes him in the thigh. The hind, wounded herself, speaks and tells him that he will only be cured of this wound by the woman who will suffer as much for him as he will suffer for her.

Guigemar binds the wound. Then he sees a ship in a nearby harbor, ready to sail. He embarks and is taken to a faraway land. He comes to a city where there lives an old lord who keeps his wife imprisoned in a room he has had constructed specifically for her since "he was exceedingly jealous, as befitted his nature, for all old men are jealous and hate to be cuckolded" (46). The only passage to the Lady's room is through a chapel; the chapel is guarded by a castrated priest. Fortunately for Guigemar, it is also possible to approach the castle from the sea, where the Lady, walking in her garden, spies the ship.

Everything about the environment of the Lady suggests an attempt to control female sexuality and to imprison the female body, all of this, significantly, through the presence of religion. As the only way of entry to the Lady's room, the chapel is portrayed as a command post over which the castrated priest presides. The castrated priest is the only male allowed near the Lady: "He had lost his lower members, otherwise he would not have been trusted" (46). But the Lady's body possesses miraculous healing powers for Guigemar. When she and her servant, a maiden, find Guigemar unconscious on the ship, the Lady lays her hand upon his heart, and he awakens. The wound in his thigh is soon healed, but it is replaced by another wound, this one more metaphorical: a wound in the heart for, as the narrator says, "Love is an invisible wound inside the body, and since it has its source in Nature, it is a long-lasting ill" (49). The movement from the outer wound to the inner wound moves us from the body to the psyche. Here is where the more serious wound needs to be healed, and where Nature's accident has occurred. This wound cannot be healed simply by the Lady's body: it requires an engagement on the part of Guigemar. Love induces him to a self-revelation accompanied by a risk of rejection since, being an invisible and internal wound, it can only be healed if it is made known through speech: "He was afraid that, if he spoke to her of his emotions, she would hate him and send him away. But he who does not let his infirmity be known can scarcely expect to receive a cure" (49).

One of the striking aspects of the love that transpires between Guigemar and the Lady is the power differential that exists between the two. Guigemar is weak, and described as "a stranger from a foreign land" (49). Because he is under the Lady's power, yet needs her love, he is placed in the position of having to ask for it. The social setting in which Marie de France portrays the love match can provide an interesting commentary on the relation between power and the level of psychical working over to which one will submit oneself. Change can be effected through a desire to change from within or an obligation to change imposed from without. To be in a position of power frequently means that one can choose not to change and can rather force the weaker party to conform to one's wishes. Stripped of his social context and wounded, Guigemar is pushed to an effort that he might not otherwise have made.

Guigemar is weak when he has to ask the Lady for her love. He recognizes the Lady as the owner of something that he needs. In the movement from desire to expressing desire in language, love is elevated from the purely sensual to the affective. The Lady's body becomes not the absolute goal but the means by which change is wrought.

The psychoanalyst Karen Horney proposed that a major narcissistic wound is inflicted on men when they are separated from the mother.[19] Their fear is that the separation is due to a rejection by the mother (rather than being a forced separation enjoined by the father). It may be

19. Karen Horney, "The Dread of Woman," in *Feminine Psychology* (New York: Norton, 1967), 133–46.

that the threat of castration is a more palatable way of construing the separation from the mother for the child (i.e. the mother did not reject the son, rather the father forced the son to separate from her), and that the need to cling to this fantasy contributes to male competition for women. By reliving an experience of dependence in which he is forced to confront the narcissistic wound of fear of rejection by the Lady, Guigemar is freed from the need to live out the fantasy of jealously possessing her and guarding her from other men. Guigemar's experience would thus bear the traits of a transference. This is an experience that only the love experience can procure him, and it points to the Lady's role as a healer. Let's note here that the Church position, which denies to such experience any social value, would preclude such a psychological event. The Lady is a healer in two separate instances. First, she heals the physical wound; but this is represented as the more easily healed wound. Then she heals the psychical wound: the second healing requires an active engagement and a psychic risk on Guigemar's part.

In a paper entitled "On the Universal Tendency to Debasement in the Sphere of Love,"[20] Freud examined the problem of what he termed "psychical impotency": the inability for a man to achieve arousal with a woman whom he respected (for any of a number of qualities) or adored. He distinguished between two currents, the sensual and the affectionate. Freud proposed that both currents are brought together, ideally, in erotic love. The problem arises when the currents are separated, usually as a strategy for resolving the Oedipal situation: the mother is elevated to the status of saintliness; the man ends up loving only women for whom he can feel no sexual desire, or desiring women whom he cannot respect. This situation is regarded by Horney as

> a way of averting the soreness of the narcissistic scar. . . . If a man does not desire any woman who is his equal or even his superior, may it not be that he is protecting his threatened self-regard in accordance with that most useful principle of sour grapes? From the prostitute or the woman of easy virtue one need fear no rejection, and no demands in the sexual, ethical or intellectual sphere. [46]

Referring to the son's perceived rejection by the mother, Horney locates the tendency to debasement as described by Freud in the same

20. Sigmund Freud, "On the Universal Tendency to Debasement in the Sphere of Love," *The Standard Edition of the Complete Psychological Works of Sigmund Freud,* ed. James Strachey (London: Hogarth, 1957), vol. 11, 179–90.

narcissistic wound that led to the avoidance of a situation of dependency on the woman. Freud's notion of two currents, which make the traditional split between Madonna, on the one hand, and prostitute, on the other, describes the situation I examined above in the *Vie de sainte Marie l'Egyptienne*. Here the woman was first prostitute, then virgin: particularly significant is the way in which Mary of Egypt's capacity to be one or the other was attached to her body. Furthermore, the split either reduces the woman to a body (the sensual current) or disembodies her (the affectionate current). The problem is bringing the two halves of women together, seeing the ethical and intellectual qualities in conjunction with the sexual. This is what is accomplished in *Guigemar*. The role of power is crucial. Psychical conflict is difficult to face, and even more difficult to resolve. The fact that the Lady has power over Guigemar is central to his undergoing the "cure." Marie de France recognizes the role that power plays in this resolution, and why Guigemar can only be cured in this "Other World" where the power structure is reversed. The love match between Guigemar and the Lady has therapeutic qualities, and her body is now not tabooed, but magical; not wretched, but sacred.

The later events of *Guigemar* are instructive because of the transformative effects of Guigemar's successful apprenticeship in love on the society to which he returns. The love match between Guigemar and the Lady occurs in what has often been termed the "Other World," a standard feature in Celtic mythology. This is the land into which Guigemar voyaged in the boat after his wounding. The Other World is a land of magic and often, in Old French romance, the place where erotic love is born. While Guigemar and his Lady are together in her room, they exchange tokens: she ties a knot in his shirt which only she can undo, and he gives her a belt which she places around her loins. When the lovers are finally discovered by the jealous husband, Guigemar has to flee, to his despair, in the ship that brought him. Unbeknownst to him, the Lady later escapes from her room, boards the ship which has returned for her, and crosses the water. There, on the same side of the water as Guigemar, she is captured by a baron named Meriaduc. The same situation in which she formerly found herself is replicated: Meriaduc makes her his prisoner. He falls in love with her, but when she tells him she is pledged to another, he angrily tries to take her by force. He is, however, prevented by the belt, which he is unable to remove.

Guigemar comes to Meriaduc's castle for a tournament. There, in a scene of recognition, the Lady unties his shirt (although the scene in which he removes her belt is absent from the lay, and demonstrates a certain suggestive reserve on Marie de France's part). Meriaduc refuses to give up the Lady. Guigemar is forced to storm Meriaduc's castle, kill Meriaduc, and win back the Lady. Because Guigemar learned about love in the Other World where the Lady lived, he is prepared to transform the world in which he lives, abolishing the replication of hostile male jealousy that the Lady suffered in her former relationship. Reaching a more satisfactory resolution of the Oedipal situation proves to be good not only for Guigemar, but also for the Lady, since it leads to a dissipation of male jealousy.

The Lady of *Guigemar* effects a redefinition of the female body. The desire for the female body no longer has to be driven from male consciousness, but becomes a focal point around which healing can occur. This notion of the female body as a healing body occurs throughout courtly literature. The lay of *Guigemar* presents the female body not as taboo but as sacred, not as an object that can only protect through being removed from society, but as an object that can transform. Most importantly, the *Lays* make of questions of sexual desire and erotic love a realm of learning. Whereas Christian thought could not accept the notion of the experience of erotic love as a matter in which teaching could occur, the rise of courtly love in the twelfth century does precisely that. As middle zone between body and intellect, psyche becomes the site of a new kind of wisdom.

CHRISTINE DE PIZAN'S *LIVRE DE LA CITÉ DES DAMES*[21]

One feature of Marie de France's *Lays* that emerges from the above discussion is the importance of architectural spaces, constructed and owned by men, in which women are housed. Guigemar wooed his Lady in the room her husband had constructed for her, and Meriaduc later imprisoned her in his castle. Medieval courtly literature is replete with images of women being saved from dungeons and towers. The husband's tower or castle was a literal place of imprisonment, but also a symbolic expression of the fundamental distrust in which men held women. In the lives of female saints, architectural spaces have an important symbolic value. In the *Vie de sainte Marie l'Egyptienne*, examined at the beginning of this paper, the threshold of the temple is the point beyond which Marie cannot pass without renouncing female

21. *The Livre de la Cité des Dames*, ed. Maureen Cheney Curnow (PhD diss., Vanderbilt University, 1975), 2 vols. English translations are my own.

desire and without agreeing not to arouse male desire. Only after she prays to the Virgin and essentially accepts to model herself on the Virgin is she allowed to enter into the Temple. In other saints lives, for example in the life of Thais, the saint is enclosed in a stone cell. Part of the value of this cell is that it disguises her from view, thus neutralizing the effect of her body on the male viewer. In the lives of transvestite saints such as Euphrosyna or Marina, there is an emphasis on cross-dressing as a means of disguise. All of these removals of the female saint from view emphasize her role in maintaining social order by refraining from arousing male desire.

In courtly love romances, the imprisonment arises from possessive male jealousy, but it still figures a basic mistrust of women's sexuality: in the *Lays*, for example, the husband is frequently much older, clearly not a courtly lover, controlling the lady and openly hostile to her. The symbol of the castle as the courtly lady's prison reached its apogee in the *Romance of the Rose*. Here, the lover's approach to the Rose was metaphorically figured as the storming and assault of, and entry into, the Castle of Jealousy. While the construction of this structure is consigned to a female allegorical figure (Jalousie), its association with a typical husbandly passion in the courtly scenario, as well as the presence in the *Romance* of a male character called Le Jaloux, certainly suggest that the structure is linked to the masculine and perhaps even to the presence of a husband or father (who is never named, however).

For Christine de Pizan, the *Romance of the Rose* was the archetypal misogynist text. I have described above the way in which the male psyche, because of medieval Christianity's incapacity to deal with matters of sexual desire, distributed women into the categories of virgins or prostitutes (or both, as in the stories of saints like Mary of Egypt). This split was damaging to women for a number of obvious reasons. First of all, it was out of their control: it represented a male characterization of women which was all the more difficult to change because it was rooted in unconscious beliefs as opposed to being rooted only in conscious practices. Second, it was impossible to change the man because, given the social power structures, a woman had no power over a man to oblige him to change: the inner psychic journey this would have required is difficult, and there is a powerful resistance to psychical working over.[22] Finally, there was no true estimation of the woman even if she was assigned the "virgin" position because she thus became a saint on the backs of other women, by transcending what was

22. The process by which "somatic sexual tension . . . is turned into affect," *The Language of Psychoanalysis*, 366.

seen to be her womanly nature. She became a saint by implicitly condemning the basic nature of other women who were not like her.

The third part of Christine de Pizan's *Livre de la Cité des Dames* consists entirely of female saints, virgins for the most part.[23] At first, we may be led, by the emphasis on virginity, to believe that Christine was duped by the prevailing ideology of the period and that she accepted the split between prostitute and virgin, identified with the virgin (much as did Mary of Egypt when she prayed before the statue of the Virgin Mary), and condemned other women who were not chaste. This initial impression is false for two reasons.

First, the *Cité* consists of three parts (not just one). Christine makes abundantly clear that all the women included in the *Cité* are an integral part of it. In the other two parts, chastity is not a prerequisite for inclusion or even the primary consideration, since a woman's inclusion is based on her political, intellectual, and moral achievements. The first woman's story to be told in the *Cité* explicitly flaunts what is largely considered to be the foundational law of human society: Semiramis, queen of Babylon, the first stone of the *Cité*'s foundation, was known for having committed incest with her son. Dante, a major vernacular authority figure for the late Middle Ages, had placed her in the *Inferno* for this transgression.[24]

The second reason indicating that Christine was not duped by her culture is that even the third part of the *Cité* does not consist exclusively of virgins, only primarily of virgins. Saint Affra, a penitent saint whose life resembled that of Mary of Egypt, makes a discreet but significant appearance. Christine, however, while alluding to Affra's life as a prostitute, focuses on Affra's resistance to male authority and sexual aggression, on her spiritual rather than her physical virginity.

The portrait of women that emerges from the *Cité* has to be taken as a continuum. The organization of the *Cité* into three parts is trinitarian: three equal persons within one godhead. The paradox is that the

23. On virginity in the *Cité des Dames*, see the seminal article by Christine Reno, "Virginity as an Ideal in Christine de Pizan's *Cité des Dames*," in Diane Bornstein, ed., *Ideals for Women in the Works of Christine de Pizan* (Detroit, Michigan: Michigan Consortium for Medieval and Early Modern Studies, 1981), 69–90. Reno's article makes a number of significant points, most notably that virginity has a positive value in Christine's *Cité* because it "implies . . . the sort of freedom from any sort of involvement with men that might hamper woman's pursuit of her particular goals" (70) and that the metaphor of the city is a figure for female bodily integrity (79–82), as opposed to Jean de Meun's Castle of Jealousy in the *Roman de la Rose*.

24. Dante, *The Divine Comedy*, ed. and trans. Charles S. Singleton (Princeton: Princeton University Press, 1975), vol.1, *Inferno*, 51.

virgin saints represent the pinnacle of the *Cité*, yet they are equivalent to the other women as well: superiors among equals.

A different allegorical figure presides over each of the *Cité*'s three parts. In part three, this figure is Justice. Psychoanalytic theory can offer insights into why sexual behavior was connected to justice in the third part of the City, but it can do so only partially because of the inherent bias of the Oedipal story. The taboo that separates the son from the mother, the injunction against incest, is generally taken as the foundational law of culture. It is the law of laws, the understanding upon which all moral behavior is based. For this reason, Freud equated God the Father with the Oedipal father.[25] Circumcision was a symbolic castration in commemoration of the father's law.

Certainly the castration threat hovers over the third part of the *Cité*, where sexual aggression towards women is continually thwarted by divine intervention. But to attribute the threat wholly to God the Father ignores the fact that resistance to sexual aggression is also the work of each of the female saints. Saint Christine in particular, Christine de Pizan's namesake, symbolically castrates one of her persecutors (by blinding him with her severed tongue) when he refuses to cease his torments.[26] Here it is clear that the saint has taken castration into her own hands.

Christine de Pizan may be asking us to consider the mother as castrator, although Maureen Quilligan's analysis demonstrates as well that Christine is overturning the fundamental effect of the incest taboo on women, which is to control female desire (69–84). Certainly this gesture of posing the mother as castrator or desiring subject reempowers the mother by granting her the same ultimate force as the father and by actualizing her desire in the most fully transgressive way possible. But there is an ethical question here as well. It is the question of power: the power to transgress a law. The power to transgress a law represents freedom to obey the law as a conscious choice. If obedience

25. On Freud's description of God, and on his intuitions and limits in this regard, see W. W. Meissner, *Psychoanalysis and Religious Experience* (New Haven: Yale University Press, 1984), especially 129–59.

26. On Saint Christine and the relation between the severed tongue, Oedipal relations, spiritual and physical blindness, and the female voice, see Maureen Quilligan, *The Allegory of Female Authority: Christine de Pizan's Cité des Dames* (Ithaca, New York: Cornell University Press, 1991), 212–34. See also the important article by Kevin Brownlee, "Martyrdom and the Female Voice: Saint Christine in the *Cité des Dames*" in *Images of Sainthood in Medieval Europe*, ed. Renate Blumenfeld Kosinski and Timea Szell (Ithaca, New York: Cornell University Press, 1991), 115–35.

is compelled, the individual's ability to act in accordance with internal mandates is infringed on. At best, the nature of ethical action becomes ambiguous: is obedience freely granted or imposed? At worst, it becomes simple compliance through fear or force. By showing us at the beginning of the *Cité* that women *can* transgress the law, Christine reminds us that they obey it out of concern, not submission. Here, instead of reading Christine through Freud, we can read Freud through Christine, reversing the direction of the transmission of knowledge, making the teaching proceed from woman to man: the implication of the incest taboo as described when the father imposes the law is that the mother would not impose it, either because she is without power to do so or perhaps, even more importantly, because she is not ethically capable of doing so.

This takes us to the heart of the question of justice. Much scholarship has focused on Christine's representation of women's intellectual contributions in the *Cité*. This is a crucial part of her message. But as I stated before, the Logos in the Middle Ages was more than an intellectual principle. It united the spheres of intellect and ethics. One of the principle criticisms that had been leveled against women from early Christianity on is not only that they were less intelligent than men, but also that they were not as ethical as men. Christine is in the process of readapting the Logos to the feminine. In the third part of the *Cité*, virginity is assumed, not imposed. In case after case, the female saints assume their virginity in the face of sexual, political, and ethical aggression (by "ethical" aggression, I refer to the attempt to impose values on the saint).

The virgin, for Christine de Pizan, is not the victim of the imposed chastity of a female saint like Mary of Egypt. The virgin represents the part of the mother that withholds her body and who will do so when necessary. *All* the women in the *Cité* are part of the allegorical city, and many of these women do engage in sexual activity, some even making extraordinary sacrifices of their body to the community (the story of the Sabine women is illustrative in this respect: it illustrates a concern for community even in the face of male acts of sexual or physical aggression). The virgins therefore are not the woman in her entirety, but the part that retains the right to refuse her body—and does so—to the son. This refusal can be gentle or harsh. Freudian theory presumes that the mother might not relinquish the son. There are reasons why the mother might be reluctant to do so. But there are also reasons, ethical ones, why she would: in particular, her concern for the growth of the individual, for separation and individuation.

The constant imprisonment of women in courtly literature suggests that the fidelity of women could only be guaranteed through surveillance and force. Here again, women's ethical nature was undermined: when obedience to a social law is compelled, the person who is subject to force loses the right to grant what he or she can contribute to the community. By controlling the female body, medieval society took away from women the power to grant it or withhold it when necessary, thereby demonstrating their ethical nature. In Marie de France, we see the female body granted to Guigemar. In Christine de Pizan, we are reminded that the body is given as gift because it can be withheld, and that the body as threat is only considered threatening because the person who directs the body—the woman—has been represented as divested of ethical capability. At the beginning of this paper, I stated that the sacred is worshiped because it is that which is fundamental to the survival of the community. By restoring to the body its status as gift, Christine de Pizan underscores the contribution of women of a body which is sacred.

There is a final reason why virginity is essential to Christine's project in the *Cité*. There is always the danger of reducing the human— and especially the woman—to body. Virginity, when it is assumed, compels the receiver of revelation to acknowledge the transcendent qualities of the woman. Again, it is the capacity of the woman to remove herself from the body by refusing to be reduced to an exclusively sexual being (Freud's sensual current, the prostitute). To illustrate this point let me briefly describe the first three saints' lives in the third part of the *Cité*.

The first three saints' lives related in the *Cité* are the lives of Saints Catherine, Margaret, and Lucy. Taken collectively, these saints' stories give us a striking portrait of how Christine de Pizan viewed virginity as the means by which the woman's transcendent intellectual and ethical qualities could command that they be received by the male viewer/ reader.

The split between virgin and prostitute is a projection of a male psychical conflict onto the woman's body. That body is either an object purely of sensual interest, to use Freud's term, or a body that is beyond any sensual interest, and only gives rise to what Freud calls "the affectionate current."

If we examine the first three saints' lives, we find that in each case the confusion between virgin and prostitute is not assumed by the saint but is in fact shown to reside with the man as a projection. Catherine and Margaret, the first two saints, are both virgins who are the objects of male sexual aggression. Catherine of Alexandria, one of the most respected and beloved of saints in the Middle Ages, is the first saint to be placed into the city by Justice. When she tries to prevent the emperor Maxentius from worshiping idols, she becomes the victim of his unwanted advances. Catherine is, significantly, one of the most teacherly of female saints. She is best known for having debated with and converted fifty philosophers assembled by the emperor. Thus she incarnates the teaching function of the Logos both in word and deed.

Maxentius's desire represents a radical misreading of the saint. For example, when the saint proves through philosophical speech that there is only one God, creator of all things, the text tells us that the emperor did not know what to answer to her speech but that "he wanted to look at her" (979). Here, the man's inability to recognize the saint is linked to his visual apprehension of her body as opposed to his heeding of the spiritual contents of her speech. Later, after Catherine has defeated the fifty philosophers in debate and presided over their martyrdom, the text tells us that "the tyrant Maxentius, who greatly coveted the blessed Catherine because of her beauty, began to flatter her to make her do his bidding" (979). When she rejects his advances, he throws her into prison, where the angels minister to her. The prison is like the enclosures of the jealous husbands of courtly romance but it is miraculously turned into a haven and refuge. The emperor tries to kill Catherine between two wheels equipped with razors, but angels descend and smash the wheels.

Here an important event occurs: the emperor's wife, witness to these events, converts to Christianity and is martyred while Catherine comforts her. The witness, as I mentioned above, is an extremely significant figure in saints' lives since he or she assures the continuum of revelation from the saint to the community. By and large, the role of witness is given to a man in medieval hagiography. The conversion of the emperor's wife, which contrasts so blatantly with her husband's spiritual blindness, shows that the privileged role of witness will be more associated with women in the lives related by Christine.

In terms of the psychoanalytic model, what previously existed as an unconscious projection of male conflict onto the representation of women is here *revealed* as a projection. Catherine is both beautiful and wise. She represents the conflation of the two images of woman that the male psyche represents as a split in the *Vie de sainte Marie l'Egyptienne*. Now, one would expect the conflation of these two images, for a male audience that is striving to keep them apart, to produce considerable anxiety, to provoke a consciousness of the split, or at the very least to command respect for the woman by insisting on a blatant male failure of witnessing from which the male reader finds himself obliged to learn.

The second story, that of Saint Margaret, echoes the pattern of the story of Saint Catherine. Now it is the prefect Olybrius who attempts to force himself on her through marriage. When she refuses, he denounces her as a Christian, and this leads to her martyrdom. To reinforce the theme of illicit male desire, Christine reports at the end of the story of Margaret that "this false Olybrius also had the holy virgin Regina tortured and beheaded . . . because she did not want to submit to him and because she converted many through her preaching" (983). The detail of Regina's preaching is not extraneous: throughout this third part of the *Cité*, Christine will contrast the word—a symbol of women's teaching—with the body—the aspect of the woman that attracts the male persecutor. The persistence of the persecutor demonstrates a refusal to receive revelation (a fault of the will). Revelation consists of the entire trajectory from the positing of the example by the saint to the act of learning by the witness.

In the third story, that of Saint Lucy, the pattern changes. This time, the saint is captured by King Aucejas who has the intention of raping her, but when she begins to preach to him, he is converted, desists, and is "very astonished at her wisdom" (984). He forsakes her body for her speech. She becomes his political and spiritual adviser. When she is leaving for Rome where she is to be martyred, he is despondent. Finally, he accompanies her to Rome and, as her head is being placed on the block, he places his head on the block with her and they are martyred together. In accordance with the teaching function of the Logos, Lucy induces a man to imitate her behavior. But furthermore, the pattern of male desire for the body as opposed to male respect for the woman's wisdom, is reversed. Significantly, the female body acts as lure in this process, suggesting that knowledge of the feminine, rather than excluding sensuality, proceeds through it.

The theologian Paul Tillich wrote of justice:

> Divine love includes the justice which acknowledges and preserves the freedom and the unique character of the beloved. It does justice to man while it drives him toward fulfillment. It neither forces him nor leaves him; it attracts him and lures him toward reunion. But in this process justice not only affirms and lures; it also resists and condemns.[27]

27. Paul Tillich, *Systematic Theology* (Chicago: University of Chicago Press, 1951), 3 vols., vol. 1, 282–83.

Tillich's description of justice is not altogether different from the way the Middle Ages conceived justice. For the Middle Ages, justice had two complementary faces: punishment, usually associated with the Father, and mercy, a quality associated increasingly with the active intervention of the Virgin Mary before the Father from the twelfth century on. Mercy is the part of justice that pleads for the defendant. The justice of the third part of the City both "affirms and lures" the male reader (as in the case of Lucy) but also "resists and condemns" (as in the case of Catherine and Margaret). It is important not to separate these two faces of Justice, to make one "feminine" and the other "masculine": the medieval conception of God is one of a deity in which all oppositions are united.

The mystical vision is always associated with paradox. Paradox is created when seemingly hostile principles or elements are combined to reveal their hidden unity. Dante described this kind of vision at the end of the *Paradiso*. In the Eternal light, he "saw ingathered, bound by love in one single volume, that which is dispersed in leaves throughout the universe" (*Paradiso*, 377). The Logos as understood in the Middle Ages is a revelation of the entire human—intellectual, ethical, bodily—in humanity's most perfected state. It embodies the fundamental paradox of the word made flesh. But the Christian Logos could not include sexuality, and could only include the feminine partially. Christine de Pizan and Marie de France not only show woman as Logos but reveal a side of the Logos that had been obscured. In so doing, they restore to the Logos a part of humanity: the female body as object of desire. The image of humanity that emerges from the *Lays* and the *Cité des Dames*, like the mystical vision, invites us to contemplate the essential paradox of a body which is at once sexual, intellectual, and ethical. It restores the harmony of the biological and the cultural by reintegrating the body as object of desire into the Logos, thus offering us the sacred body.

ABBY ZANGER

Making Sweat:
Sex and the Gender of National
Reproduction in the Marriage
of Louis XIII*

Discussions of the relation of the King's physical, mortal body to his divine, sacred persona have traditionally focused on the death of the monarch. This emphasis is logical given that the politics of dynastic continuity reach a crisis point upon the demise of a ruler. It is thus that the elaborate symbolic displays and nuanced juridical rhetoric produced to justify the permanence of sovereign power in the face of the undeniable evidence of a monarch's mortality motivate the work of Ernst Kantorowicz on the "mystical fiction of the 'King's Two Bodies'" in the Middle Ages and that of Ralph Giesey on the royal funerary ceremony in the Renaissance.[1] These scholars' paradigm-forging studies have also offered the principal lens through which semioticians have examined images of the absolutist monarchy; Louis Marin and Claude Reichler, for example, in studying the representation of Louis XIV's sexuality, focus on the practices and discourses that recuperate the dissolution and decay of the king's body natural in order to reinvest the sacred (and powerful) body of monarchy.[2] Without casting aside a schema which has been so fruitful for our understanding of the

*This essay is dedicated to the memory of Louis Marin.

1. Ernst H. Kantorowicz, *The King's Two Bodies: A Study in Medieval Political Theology* (Princeton, Princeton University Press, 1981) and Ralph E. Giesey, *The Royal Funeral Ceremony in Renaissance France* (Geneva: Droz, 1960).

2. Claude Reichler, "La Jambe du Roi" in *L'Âge libertin* (Paris: Minuit, 1987) and Louis Marin, "Le corps glorieux du Roi et son portrait" and "Le corps pathétique et son médecin: Sur le *Journal de Santé de Louis XIV*," in *La Parole mangée et autres essais théologico-politiques* (Paris: Klincksieck, 1986). Both follow Kantorowicz's formula, focusing on the tension between the king's aging upper body and the iconic sexuality of the leg.

YFS 86, *Corps Mystique, Corps Sacré: Textual Transfigurations of the Body from the Middle Ages to the Seventeenth Century,* ed. Françoise Jaouën and Benjamin Semple, © 1994 by Yale University.

early-modern European sovereign body sacred and profane, I wish to suggest that by uniquely privileging the powerful and compelling paradigm of Kantorowicz and Giesey, moments of a reign in which the king's mortal body may not be at odds with his divine status, but may engage with other dimensions of his own body as well as with other bodies, seem to have slipped out of our focus.

One event that offers an interesting complement and contrast to this emphasis on the monarch's dead or ill body is the representation of sovereignty during marriage. Interestingly, this particular ritual has been neglected by historians of political culture and semioticians of sovereign power. Perhaps this is because the death of a monarch poses a crisis for dynastic continuity, whereas the joining of royal bodies in marriage presents no imminent crisis, but rather union and beginning, a joining of two royal bodies and not a separation. Despite this obvious divergence, there are similarities between royal marriage and the funerary ceremony. For example, the rites of marriage, like those of dying, are both rituals of sanctification within the Catholic church; marriage, like extreme unction, is one of the seven sacraments. In both, furthermore, the mortal and divine dimensions of the royal body are invoked around issues of succession and dynastic continuity; the ceremonies associated with both events are highly choreographed occasions whose rites and discourses of self-legitimation are produced by the state apparatus with the goal of securing dynastic continuity through unperturbed succession. Marriage ceremonies, finally, play out the tension between the sacred investiture of kingship and the profane dimension of sovereignty's self-reproduction. In marriage, however, the tension between sacred and profane is not figured by the adjudication of two dimensions (mortal and divine) of the king's royal body, but by the engagement and fusion of two (at least apparently) different royal bodies, male and female, in the joining of the king and his new bride (and of two nation-states). This fusion, or coming together, of two bodies of different genders (and not just of different ontological or metaphysical statuses), raises a new set of issues about the body natural and the body politic, concerns enmeshed with the nature of the female body (or bodies), political or otherwise.

This essay lays out and explores the issues that emerge in such a shift of emphasis by examining a description of the 1615 Marriage Mass of Louis XIII and the Spanish infanta Anne of Austria. It is not the actual events of the Mass that are of import here, but rather the narrative of those events provided in a text titled *La Royalle Reception de leurs Maiestez tres-chrestiennes en la ville de Bourdeaus, ou le Siecle d'or ramené par les alliances de France et d'Espagne, recueilli par le commandement du Roy.*[3] Published in Bordeaux, two months after the events of the marriage, by a printer appointed by the king, the text collates, and elaborates on, the many shorter, occasional pamphlets also published in this period; it covers not just the reception, but all the events of the alliance from the queen's arrival in France and welcome at the border (where she was exchanged for Louis XIII's sister who married Philip IV) to her journey to meet the court at Bordeaux, and the events that occurred there (audiences with her new family, ceremonial entries, the Marriage Mass, etc.). Given the political stakes of royal alliances, it should be clear that the text considered is not a "real" account of the events (if such an account is ever possible). It should be seen, rather, as an after-effect of the marriage, an official version (a recreation or restaging) of ceremonies several months after their occurrence. It was no coincidence that such a recreation was authored by a Jesuit, François Garasse, a critic of the "reformed religion." For, after generations of religious unrest between French Protestants and Catholics, the alliance was a (somewhat controversial) triumph for the Catholic party. That was because Marie de Medicis, in opting for a marriage with "The Very Catholic King," Philip II, moved away from her husband's policy of religious tolerance and inclusion.[4] Neither should it be seen as coincidental that a writer who would later be best known as the author of *La doctrine curieuse des beaux-esprits de ce temps* (1624), a virulent satire against libertinism, should utilize a wide range of intersecting cultural discourses, not just theological and political, but also medical and pornographic, to inform his reading of the most sacred moment in the marriage, the Mass that sanctified the alliance.[5]

Garasse's text offers a myriad of details about the king and queen during the Mass, information provided about a ceremony that occurred in public, but in a closed-off space, and thus lent itself to report-

3. *La Royalle Reception de leurs Maiestez tres-chrestiennes en la ville de Bourdeaus, ou le Siecle d'or ramené par les alliances de France et d'Espagne, recueilli par le commandement du Roy* [*The Royal Reception of their Very Christian Majesties in the City of Bordeaux, or the Golden Age Restored by the Alliances of France and Spain, collected by commandment of the King*] (Bordeaux: Simon Millanges, 1615), 107–108.

4. According to Ruth Kleinman, the match was seen by the Huguenots as moving toward a "pronouncedly Catholic foreign policy." See her *Anne of Austria, Queen of France* (Columbus: Ohio State University Press, 1985), 14.

5. For an overview of the complex career of Garasse, see the entry under his name in *Biographie Universelle, ancienne et moderne* (Paris: Ch. Delagrave et Cie, 1843–1865), 522–524.

ing. Indeed, Garasse underlines the crowd's eagerness to see the new queen and emphasizes the importance of his own narrative by underlining the difficulty of gaining access to the cathedral: "There were a large number [of people] who entered the Church as early as four o'clock in the morning, not leaving there before seven at night, preferring a fast of the mouth to one of the eyes" (105). The much coveted information Garasse provides those who could not gain access to the closed-off space of the cathedral, or who did not have a clear view once inside, includes particularities about the couple's placement and movements during the various stages of the ceremony, as well as about how they were dressed, the king in "a cape of silver brocade with gold embroidery, laden with precious insignia," and the new queen with "a Gold Crown on her head," wearing "the royal dress of purple velvet strewn with fleurs de lys, and a cape of the same material and decoration, with a long train, lined with ermine." Garasse lists as well those in attendance at the ceremony and summarizes the various speeches made. At the conclusion of this in fact formulaic account of the Mass, Garasse offers the following, rather surprising detail:

> The King looked at her often, laughing: she, although burdened by the weight of the robes and gems, sweating large drops [suant à grosses gouttes], could not contain herself from smiling back at him, & at the Duc de Monte Leone, the ambassador from Spain, with a marvelous grace and majesty. [108–109]

It is this passage that anchors our discussion. Whether a detail meant to demonstrate royal grace under pressure, or perhaps to suggest the new bride is no fairy tale princess, to a twentieth-century sensibility, the "grosses gouttes/large drops of sweat" that Anne of Austria contained no more effectively than her smile during the solemn ceremony seem incongruous, out of place, in the pomp and majesty of the Mass and the respectful discourse of Garasse.

Indeed we might wonder if this short passage is simply an indication of an aesthetic of realism on the part of Garasse, or if it is a component of the symbolic apparatus of Bourbon absolutism. It is more likely to be the latter than the former, since early on in his description, Garasse casts his doubts on the possibility of accurate reporting of state events, noting that:

> The actions and past celebrated acts seem a favorable subject for Publishers [la Presse des Imprimeurs] and the curiosity of the people; neither one nor the other will be idle, because there are appearing, at this

very instant, a good number of little discourses and narrations, French
and Spanish, some marvelously well detailed to content the taste of
those who want to know everything, others mixed with some falsehood
of no consequence, like the size of the medals and other incidents,
which occurred only several days later; either because of the little care
of writers or because of the nature of truth, which is itself slippery
[glissante] and of itself vanishes and disperses in the press of large
assemblies [la presse des grandes assemblées]. [58–59]

Punning on publication and crowds, two kinds of "presse," or pressures that bring out the slipperiness of truth that "vanishes and disperses" in published accounts of state rituals, Garasse takes an ironic
jab at the fantasy of realism. While I shall return to this citation at the
conclusion of my essay, I shall simply propose that we use it now to
assume that Garasse's detail or scene of making sweat is part of the
slippery wetness of the truth or symbolics of his topic, royal marriage.
In what follows, this seemingly insignificant detail will be deciphered
by exploring how, even within the frame of public curiosity about the
new queen, her body, indeed her bodily secretions, come to play a role
in a legitimized official account of royal marriage. The slippery nature
of this role will ultimately return us to the "truth," however sticky,
about the sovereign body politic, now viewed from a new perspective,
one offered by the diffraction off the drops on a new queen's face.

MAKING SWEAT

To understand the nature of Garasse's description of the queen during
the Mass, we first need to decipher the image of the sweating queen.
While Garasse's detail about Anne of Austria's "grosses gouttes"
seems anomalous in the otherwise formal tone of the text, and while it
is a fact that it is not present in earlier or later descriptions of this
marriage,[6] it is likely that making sweat was a traditional (and necessary) part of the choreography of French royal wedding rituals. For
while I have not yet been able to trace sweating queens to French
marriages before that of Louis XIII, my experience reading reports

6. The many occasional pamphlets produced at the time of the marriage do not
mention the sweat. See the LB[36] rubric of the *Catalogue de l'Histoire de France* for the
year 1615 for a list of these sources. Neither does the historian Théodore Godefroy make
reference to sweat either in the account of the marriage he includes in *Ordre des cérémo-
nies observées aux mariages de France et d'Espagne . . .* (Paris: E. Martin, 1627), 57–59.
On the other hand, an almost verbatim synopsis of the passage I shall be discussing was
published in 1617 by the official gazette, *MERCURE FRANÇOIS* vol. 4.

of royal marriages as far back as that of Charles IX to Elizabeth of Hapsburg in 1570, is that these accounts, while they may differ in minor ways, all contain the same recurring elements. I can say with assurance, furthermore, that sweating queens are part of the choreography of the seventeenth-century Bourbon-Hapsburg alliances. During the 1660 wedding of Louis XIV to Marie-Thérèse of Austria, the new queen was also described as sweating, although not during the French wedding Mass, and thus not in front of a myriad of officials and invited nobility as had her aunt. Marie-Thérèse held out until after the Mass, letting loose in a more private venue (but not in private) "at the Queen Mother's quarters," after returning from the Mass "dripping with sweat [toute en eau] because of the weight of her clothing, or her gems and of her large cape. . . ."[7] Despite the repetition of the topos, historians of both infantas (Anne and Marie-Thérèse), such as Ruth Kleinman and Claude Dulong, have attributed these details simply to the enormous weight of the ceremonial clothing worn by the new queens.[8] This reading is not inappropriate. The texts themselves certainly suggest a link between the richness of the French clothing and the sweating of the formerly Spanish (now French) bodies. I would like to argue, however, for a less literal and more semiotic reading of these passages. Indeed we cannot help but note that the king, too, wears heavy clothing during the ceremonial, but he is not described as "tout en eau." On the contrary, no such physiological reaction on the part of the king is depicted in the texts in question. Clearly, sweat in these marriages (and perhaps physicality in general) lies in the domain of the symbolic apparatus of representing queens.

Taking the description of sweaty queens less literally, then, we

7. *La Pompe et Magnificence faite au mariage du Roy et de L'Infante D'Espagne, Ensemble les entretiens qui ont esté faits entre les deux Roys, & les deux Reynes, dans l'Isle de la Conference Et Relation de ce qui s'est passé mesmes apres la Consommation* (Toulouse: Imprimeurs ordinaires du Roy, 1660), 15. I have analyzed this text in my essay "Fashioning the Body Politic: Imagining the Queen in the Marriage of Louis XIV" in *Women and Sovereignty*, ed. Louise Fradenburg (Edinburgh: Edinburgh University Press, 1992), 101–120. Note that while *La Pompe* was officially sanctioned as was Garasse's text, it is not the official account of the marriage festivities. It is, rather, a short occasional pamphlet published both in a city near the events and then in Paris by Jean Promé.

8. Ruth Kleinman's *Anne of Austria . . .* and Claude Dulong's *Anne d'Autriche, Mère de Louis XIV* (Paris: Hachette, 1980), ch. 1. In her *Le mariage du Roi-Soleil* (Paris: Albin Michel, 1986), Dulong does not mention Marie-Thérèse's sweat, although she would surely have read the pamphlet in which it occurs and made the link with the previous marriage on which she also wrote. See chapter 12 in which she describes the Marriage Mass.

might wonder if the sweat signifies something important and necessary about Spanish-Hapsburg princesses who would be French queens,
something that demonstrates a Hapsburg infanta's worth to the Bourbon dynasty, while also making her interesting to the eager readers of
these texts. In that sense, Anne of Austria's large, almost luscious
drops of sweat ("grosses gouttes," not droplets or "gouttelettes") might
be likened to another item adorning her face, that is, her amorous
smile. Since smiles along with gazes were an important topos in courtly
romance, we might thus make the link between adorning sweat and
sexual desire. Indeed this connection was available in seventeenth-
century erotica. For example, the 1610 best seller *Erotomania or
A Treatise Discoursing of the Essence, Causes, Symptomes, Prog-
nosticks, and Cure of Love or Erotic Melancholy* by Jacques Ferrand
recounts the effects on a man of seeing the woman he loved: "As soon as
she but entered into the Chamber, his colour changed, his speech was
stopped, his lookes were smiling and pleasant, or else . . . his face
burned, and hee was all in a sweat, his Pulse beat very disorderly . . . he
grew pale, amazed, astonished often. . . ."[9] When Ferrand remarks that
the symptoms his melancholy lover exhibits are like those described
by Sappho in her *Sonnet 31*,[10] it becomes apparent that although he
takes the example of the male lover, the libido that sweat indicates is
not limited to the male, but might also be a characteristic of the female. That fact, too, was a commonality of contemporary erotic literature. In his *Conjugal love; or Pleasures of the Marriage Bed Considered* (1687), Nicolas Venette devotes an entire chapter to the subject of
the libidinous woman. In this chapter ("The Signs of a Woman who is
of hot Constitution, and naturally prone to the Act of Copulation"),
Venette argues one can identify ardent women by their sweet smelling
sweat.[11] While Venette's book postdates Garasse's description of Anne
of Austria's sweat, it seems likely that Garasse would have been aware
more generally of contemporary erotic writings and their precedents.

9. The work was first published in Toulouse in 1610 (in Paris in 1623) under the title
*De la maladie d'amour, ou Mélancolie érotique. . . l'essence, les causes, les signes et les
remèdes de ce mal fantastique.* I cite from the reprint of the 1645 Oxford translation
(Syracuse: Syracuse University Press, 1990), 113.

10. Ferrand's example is taken from the story of Antiochus as told in Plutarch's *Life
of Demetrius.* See *Plutarch's Lives,* trans. Bernadotte Perrin (Cambridge: Harvard University Press, 1959), vol. 9, 93.

11. The work was first published in Amsterdam under the title *Tableau de l'Amour
considéré dans l'état du mariage.* I quote from the reprint of the 1750 London edition
(New York: Garland, 1984), 56–58.

Indeed, the association between sweat and ripeness did not originate in early-modern erotic writings, but dates back to antiquity.[12] Furthermore, one of Garasse's early pamphlets, *L'anti Joseph*, published the same year as *La Royalle Reception*, exhibits familiarity with the libertine discourses it attacks.

So we might say at this point that Anne of Austria was not just described as adorned by French ceremonial clothing during the Mass in Bordeaux in October 1615, but also by her sweet, sweaty, libidinous desire for her new husband.[13] Such adornment was not gratuitous titillation. In underlining the new queen's libido and her ripeness for the picking, the description not only piqued reader interest, but also underlined the availability of the new queen for what would be her major role in state building: procreation, reproducing and thus ensuring the continuation of the Bourbon lineage.[14] Indeed writers on sexuality (authors both of scientific and of the pseudoscientific texts to which I have alluded) generally attributed generative powers to wet heat in both men and women.[15]

12. See, for example, Virgil's *Eclogue IV* which utilizes the image of dewy honey sweat on oaks to link the fertility of the fields with peace in a text written at the time of an important marriage treaty. *The Eclogues*, trans. Guy Lee (London: Penguin Books, 1984), 57.

13. If the sweat on the body of the infanta queen in the 1660 marriage is not as luscious and does not occur during the mass, but in the relative privacy of the queen mother's quarters, it may be simply a question of expectations about the taste of the readership. Indeed in 1615 the reigning aesthetic would have highlighted baroque details which drew attention to the processes of the body, while in 1660 taste would have favored classical simplicity and a Horatian ideology of hidden art. That may be why Nicolas Boileau, in the translation of Longinus's *Treatise on the Sublime*, translated the Greek "a cold sweat " into "a shiver seized me": the word "sweat" was unacceptable in French. See Boileau, *Oeuvres complètes* (Paris: Gallimard, 1966), 356–58 and 416.

14. The cultivation of Empire is one of the messages imprinted on queens when they don the royal robe strewn with fleurs-de-lys, as was traditional at weddings; the antique legend about the origin of the lily is that it is drops of Juno's milk that fell to the ground. See Collette Beaune, *The Birth of Ideology, Myths and Symbols of Nation in Late-Medieval France*, trans. Susan Ross Uston (Berkeley: University of California Press, 1991), 204. Beaune underlines the combination of purity and fertility in the French national symbols, especially as related to notions of dynasty and empire.

15. For the state of medical thinking about women and procreation in the early modern period, see Evelyne Berriot-Salvadore's chapter "Le Discours de la Médecine et de la Science" in *L'Histoire des femmes*, vol. 3, ed. Georges Duby and Michelle Perrot (Paris: Plon, 1991); Thomas Laqueur's *Making Sex: Body and Gender from the Greeks to Freud* (Cambridge: Harvard University Press, 1990), 114–48; Jacques Gélis, *L'Arbre et le fruit: la naissance dans l'Occident moderne* (Paris: Fayard, 1984); and Ian Maclean, *The Renaissance Notion of Woman* (Cambridge: Cambridge University Press, 1980).

Having ascribed the queen's sweat to a semiotics of procreation, we must note that, in this particular case, the queen's physiological (i.e., mortal) body is not detrimental to, but rather constitutive of the display of monarchical power. This is quite different from the case of the monarch's dead body, which Ralph Giesey has shown to have unsettled rites of succession in the Renaissance, or that of Marie-Antoinette's sexual body, which Lynn Hunt has demonstrated played a role in the state-unbuilding of the Revolutionary tribunal.[16] Of course one might argue that if the depiction of a queen's biological-mortal body does not unsettle her own portrayal, it is for the simple reason that the queen did not have a divine dimension in the early-modern French monarchy since she could not inherit property and thus could not participate in the divine right of succession so fundamental to the political fiction of the king's two bodies as described by Kantorowicz. Even as I note this common assumption about French queens, however, I would step back from it as being too formulaic and not sufficiently nuanced. For, the interdiction against female succession to the throne was not operative outside France; Elizabeth I, for example, regularly invoked the dual status of her royal body in the rhetoric of her political propaganda.[17] Indeed one appeal to the French in making alliances with the Spanish Hapsburgs was the potential of the Spanish infanta to inherit the Hapsburg throne (to have a divine body, at least in Spain). This facet of the match was especially true in the case of Louis XIV's marriage, which did ultimately place a Bourbon on the Spanish Hapsburg throne, in part by means of the appeal to Marie-Thérèse's right to succession. It is thus that we should not concentrate our interpretation of Anne of Austria's "grosses gouttes" of libidinous desire around the divine-mortal distinction. Rather, we should focus on the fact that Anne's liquid adornment is produced in the service of buttressing political culture to legitimatize what might be a shaky political alliance between two adversarial nations (France and Spain). Indeed, a Foucauldian reading of this passage would underline the productive heterosociality of royal marriage in the service of state building in the Bourbon-Hapsburg alli-

16. Ralph Giesey, *The Royal Funerary Ceremony* and Lynn Hunt, "The Many Bodies of Marie-Antoinette: Political Pornography and the Problem of the Feminine in the French Revolution" in *Eroticism and the Body Politic*, ed. Lynn Hunt (Baltimore: Johns Hopkins University Press, 1991), 108–30.

17. See Marie Axton, *The Queen's Two Bodies: Drama and the Elizabethan Succession* (London: Royal Historical Society, 1977).

ance, a kind of coupling Foucault has contrasted to the gratuitous pleasure (*jouissance*) of nonreproductive sex.[18]

It appears, therefore, that by stressing the practical (procreative, heterosocial) dimensions of lawful alliance, Anne of Austria's sweat serves to drive home the permanent (reproducing) nature of the Bourbon dynasty. It seems that in royal marriage, making sweat is a necessary part of making the state. If the king does not make sweat in Garasse's text, that is probably because the queen's sweaty mortal body can stand in for that of the king. Kantorowicz and Giesey's work indeed suggests the necessity of such a displacement; within their paradigm, the king's libido and fertility can be displayed only at the expense of his sacred image. Note that such a reading maps gender difference onto the mortal-divine polarity by proposing the female body as mortal versus the male body as spiritual. This mapping of one opposition onto another is complicated, however, by the fact that it is difficult (although not impossible) to talk about a male versus a female body when discussing human reproduction as understood in the early seventeenth century. In this period, the knowledge of the role played by the male and female body in procreation was an issue of intense debate. For even if cultural notions of gender difference were fairly well entrenched in seventeenth-century Europe, the biological nature of male and female was not clearly differentiated; the reigning paradigm of sexual difference in early-modern Europe did not distinguish male from female as bodies whose essential natures were different, but rather as different forms of one essential body. In 1615, therefore, the dominant model of sexuality was what Thomas Laqueur has referred to as a one-sex model wherein gender difference was not polarized into a clear opposition between male and female, but organized as a hierarchy ranging from the most imperfect to the most perfect kind of body. In this model, the most imperfect body would be the most female, dominated by cold, dry humors, while the most perfect body would be the most male, dominated by the hot and moist (Laqueur, 4).

Given the indistinction between male and female physiology implied by such a model, it might be prudent to recast our consideration of the sweaty body of Anne of Austria by stepping back from the mortal-divine polarity to wonder how she is situated on the more fluid and slippery spectrum of gender. For, as Anne of Austria's wet heat

18. Michel Foucault, *The History of Sexuality*, vol. 1, trans. Robert Hurley (New York: Vintage Books, 1990).

shows her to be ripe, it also moves her toward the male realm. Such bi-
sexuality was not an unusual concept since it was generally accepted
that people would not fall squarely into either extreme of the spectrum, but would be situated around the middle of the gender scale. The
necessity of moist heat in procreation allied that activity with the
male, more perfect, end of the spectrum and involved suggesting a bit
of the male was necessary in the female for generation. Such notions
suggest that in 1615, the understanding of reproductive biology did not
provide clear distinctions between male and female, but rather re-
volved around a confusing and potentially collapsible hierarchy. Is it
possible, therefore, that just as the contemporary understanding of the
biology of procreation necessitated a balancing act between the nature
of male and female (fungible fluids), the construction of the sovereign's
image at the moment of marriage, another kind of birth or procreation,
might involve an equally delicate adjudication between male and female? For as Anne of Austria's sweat marks her ripeness, it defines her
as female while also sliding her imperceptibly toward moist male
humors. This confusing duality begins to suggest that the perpetuity of
the corporate body as represented in royal marriage may not depend
simply on adjudicating the mortal and divine dimensions of the sovereign body, but also its gender. In so far as gender is an undecidable
category, the perpetuity of the corporate body may also necessitate
working out tensions between the potential heterosociality and homosociality of the gendered body politic (and its political culture).

FINDING THE QUEEN IN THE KING'S TWO BODIES

In light of the way in which Anne of Austria's body can now be read as
both a ripe female and a perfect male body, it is interesting that it is not
the difference between male and female (Louis and Anne) that Garasse
emphasizes in the lines that lead to his description of Anne of Austria's
procreating (fe/male) body. Rather, those lines focus on the similarity
between the king and his new bride, as for example, in Garasse's description of the reaction of the crowd present in the cathedral for the
Marriage Mass:

> Some admired the grace of this young Princess, others the solemn
> majesty of the Queen Mother, or the extraordinary beauty of the king,
> but no one could get over the unbelievable resemblance of the couple:
> because two brothers would never have been more similar than these
> two in everything that can be alike [car deux freres n'eurent jamais plus

de rapport, qu'ils avoient par ensemble en tout ce qui peut estre semblable]. [107–108]

The description of the drops of sweat on Anne of Austria's face, a detail that, when read in isolation, seems to display heterosocial fertility, is actually preceded by an underlining not of the heterosociality of the alliance, but of the fantasy of its homosociality, when the crowd is described as amazed over the "unbelievable resemblance" between the young king and his new queen. For the crowd, this resemblance is not just any kind of resemblance, but that between two brothers alike in "*everything* [my emphasis] that can be alike [tout ce qui peut estre semblable]." With this general and widespread observation on the part of the crowd [*Tous*], the Mass seems to be less a sanctification of heterosocial union than a celebration of perfect male harmony and bonding. As such we might begin to focus less on the relation between one king's own two bodies or even on the relation between a king and a queen's body. Instead we must shift our gaze to consider the relations between sovereign bodies more generally, between male sovereign bodies, kings' bodies.

Since royal marriages are ultimately not made between men and women, but arranged among men (kings and diplomats), we might recall, at this point, the work of Claude Lévi-Strauss. In his study of the structures of kinship, Lévi-Strauss established that the exchange of women (which is what is occurring in the Bourbon-Hapsburg marriage) is a mode of establishing relations between male kin and thus of moving kinship groups (or nations) from discord to civil or symbolic relations.[19] In her critique of Lévi-Strauss, the French feminist critic Luce Irigaray describes such male-male bonding as "hom(m)o-sexualité," an interaction she argues founds civil society, "reigning everywhere, although prohibited in practice . . . played out through the bodies of women, matter, or sign." For Irigaray, the exchange of women or heterosociality is "an alibi for the smooth workings of man's relations with himself."[20] Following Irigaray's logic, we might consider that the sweet libidinous sweat adorning Anne of Austria's face is just an alibi for the fantasy of a marriage that does not simply participate in reproductive heterosociality but is also based on the pure and gratuitous (read nonreproductive) pleasure (*jouissance*) of political coupling.

19. Claude Lévi-Strauss, *The Elementary Structures of Kinship*, trans. James Harle Bell, John Richard von Sturmer, and Rodney Needham (Boston: Beacon Press, 1969).

20. Luce Irigaray, "Women on the Market" in *This Sex Which is Not One*, trans. Catherine Porter (Ithaca, New York: Cornell University Press, 1985), 172.

Irigaray, however, notes that if such a nonreproductive practice is the basis of the state, that fact is always suppressed. And indeed we might wonder if Anne's "grosses gouttes," in suggesting her female ripeness, serve to wash the traces of the "hom(m)o-sociality" (that they also suggest) from the face of the Bourbon-Hapsburg alliance. We might now begin to see two competing readings of marriage emerge, one stressing the female role and another effacing or eliding it.[21] Interestingly, as we read on in the material that precedes the description of Anne of Austria adorned by her "grosses gouttes," two other points of view about the couple are offered. In them, we find these two competing readings actually put forward.

The first alternative viewpoint offered in Garasse's text is that of a Spanish theologian, who balances the crowd's potentially untutored reaction:

> There was a Spanish theologian who gave a learned oration on the marvelous connections and similarities [convenances] of this marriage to the most excellent marriages that ever were, including, namely, that of Adam and Eve married by the hand of God himself in earthly paradise. [108]

Note how, in his oration, the theologian shifts the reader from the amazement of the crowd at the couple's homosociality (like two brothers) to refocus on marriage between man and woman by taking up the example of Adam and Eve. This example seems to return the viewer to the heterosociality of marriage, the reading in which Anne is a procreating female body. For the story of Adam and Eve is, at least on one level, the story of the first heterosexual couple, the story of the birth of sexual difference (Eve) out of Adam. It further resonates with the image of the sweating bride in recalling the sweaty trials and tribulations to which the couple was condemned, most particularly that of procreation after the Fall, the sentence that runs down Anne of Austria's smiling face during the Marriage Mass. Beyond this obvious parallel, the example may also serve to undercut the crowd's fantasy of male bonding by reminding the reader that brothers (Cain and Abel would naturally come to mind here) seldom live in harmony. On the

21. These readings, one which stresses heterosociality and the other homosociality, replay the debate with anthropological models of kinship exchange about the role played by the exchanged women in men's relations with each other raised by feminist critics such as Luce Irigaray in the essay mentioned above and by Gayle Rubin in "The Traffic in Women: Notes on the 'Political Economy' of Sex" in *Toward an Anthropology of Women*, ed. Rayna R. Reiter (New York: Monthly Review Press, 1975), 157-210.

contrary, such similarity ("two brothers would never have been more similar than these two in everything that can be alike") leads to sterility since it breeds only mimetic rivalry and fratricide.

But the Spanish theologian does not have the final word on Adam and Eve. The narrator, Garasse, offers a gloss on the foreigner's message:

> But he forgot this similarity of body & of humors [convenance de la semblance de corps, & d'humeurs], as it was in the first married couple: because the Rabbis Aben Esra and Simon Bercepha remarked in their secret writings that Adam & Eve were marvelously alike in their countenance, from which one of our Christian poets learned that they were called *Juvenes aetate pares & formâ geminos*, young men similar in body and age. The King looked at her often, laughing: she, although burdened by the weight of the robes and gems, sweating large drops. . . .
> [108–09]

When Garasse corrects the Theologian ("but he forgot"), he offers a revisionary reading that he had overlooked, "this similarity of body, and of humors, as it was in the first married couple." Returning to the naive observation of the crowd, Garasse anchors and authorizes it with another foreign tradition, the Rabbis' secret writings about the first creation story in which Adam was said to contain both male and female elements ("And God created man in His image, in the image of God He created him; male and female He created them"[22]). Indeed it is the interpretation of these lines from Genesis 1:27 that serve as the basis for various Kabbalistic (and Midrashic) traditions in which Adam was thought to have been, at least initially, a hermaphrodite, both male and female.[23] The tradition may also have had Gnostic origins.[24] Of course, Garasse would not have had direct access to the Gnostic tradition in 1615. He was much more likely to have gained access to the mythology via writers such as Leone Ebreo whose *Dialoghi d'Amore* were translated into French in 1551, or via Christian Hebraicists.[25] In

---

22. Genesis 1:27.

23. For the Judaic reading of Adam, see *Midrash Rabbah*, vol. 1, ed. Rabbi H. Freedman and Maurice Simon (London: The Soncino Press, 1961).

24. Elaine Pagels, *The Gnostic Gospels* (New York: Random House, 1979), 56 and "The Gnostic Vision: Varieties of Androgyny Illustrated by Texts from the Nag Hammadi Library," in *Parabola* 3/4 (1978): 6–9.

25. For information on the Christian Hebraicists, see the excellent article on that subject in *The Encyclopaedia Judaica* (Jerusalem: Keter Publishing House, 1971). For a discussion of hermaphroditism in Leone Ebreo, see Naomi Yavneh, "The Spiritual Eroti-

invoking this rich and complex tradition to counter the Spanish orator, Garasse seems to reverse the story of Adam and Eve. For, in falling from Grace, Adam and Eve were consigned to the postlapsarian world of heterosocial sweat and turmoil. But Garasse returns the story to a prelapsarian universe that erases the separateness of bodies (male and female, divine and mortal, French and Spanish), picking up on the neoplatonism common to the Kabbalah and the Christian Hebraicists from which Garasse would have been drawing his knowledge.[26] Thus, in Garasse's paradise (perhaps the Golden Age or *Siecle d'or* he invokes in the title of his text), Adam and Eve are fused into one body, a stronger and more complete body (nation) than that of either member of the pair after the Fall when male and female only join in heterosocial sweat and turmoil.

I would underline at this point that although he cites the Kabbalah, for Garasse, the Adam of Genesis 1:27 does not maintain the constitutive differences of male and female as does the Adam of the Judaic tradition alluded to. Rather, Garasse's Adam is a hermaphroditic body composed of double maleness, "young men similar in body and age." This twist on the myth becomes apparent in Garasse's reference to what the Christian poets took from the Kabbalistic tradition, the idea that Adam and Eve were like twins, "*Juvenes aetate pares & formâ [sic] geminos/youth* equal in age and *twin* in appearance [my emphasis]," a line Garasse mistranslates as "young *men* similar in body and age [my emphasis]." For Garasse, it seems, the Golden Age or prelapsarian paradise of the hermaphroditic Adam invokes a Pauline state of fusion, an ideal world in which "there is neither Jew nor Greek; there is neither slave nor free, there is neither male nor

cism of Leone's Hermaphrodite," in *Playing with Gender: A Renaissance Pursuit*, ed. Jean R. Brink, Maryanne C. Horowitz, and Allison P. Coudert (Urbana: The University of Illinois Press, 1991), 85–98.

26. See *Midrash Rabbah*, 54 to compare the Midrash to Plato (*Symposium* 189b). For discussions of the Platonic hermaphrodite in the Renaissance, see Carla Freccero, "The Other and the Same: The Image of the Hermaphrodite in Rabelais," in *Rewriting the Renaissance: The Discourses of Sexual Difference in Early Modern Europe*, ed. Margaret W. Ferguson, Maureen Quilligan, and Nancy J. Vickers (Chicago: University of Chicago Press, 1986), 145–58, Pierre Ronzeaud, *L'Utopie Hermaphrodite* (Marseilles: Publication du C.M.R.,17,1982), and Jerome Schwartz, "Aspects of Androgyny in the Renaissance," in *Human Sexuality in the Middle Ages and Renaissance*, ed. Douglas Radcliff-Umstead (Pittsburgh: Center for Medieval and Renaissance Studies, 1978), 121–31.

female; for you are all one in Jesus Christ."[27] For Garasse, the hermaphrodite is a bodily fusion that erases sexual difference, falling back on the default mode of two male bodies fused together (the body of Christ).[28]

In light of these resonances we might ask, finally, if the shift from a male-female hermaphrodite to a male-male hermaphrodite is linked to the fundamental tension in Garasse's text between the male and female position, a tension that founds the state of royal marriage, made among men, but necessitating women to reproduce (and assure the future of) such alliances. For no sooner does Garasse allude to the ultimate homosocial construct, a doubly male hermaphroditic Adam, than the fusion falls apart; when the doubly male king-couple looks at his bride, the bodies of the two young men are separated and the reader is reminded once more that Adam must couple with Eve and not himself. We might now say that the fantasy of the hermaphroditic Adam is, finally, a fantasy of one body's absolute sovereignty in being able to reproduce without the female. For it reminds us of an Adam who gave birth to Eve in a prelapsarian age that did not need gender difference (or women) to reproduce. But we must note as well how, in the face of such a fantasy of independence and usurpation (perhaps the Bourbon fantasy about the political coupling with Hapsburg Spain), the queen immediately appears to remind the reader of her role, of her ineluctable necessity for procreation (political, biological, symbolic). When the king looks at his new bride he faces that reality literally and figuratively as the sweat indicating her symbolic construction drips down her smiling face.[29]

27. Galatians 3:28.

28. Indeed, the Christian tradition was resistant to the Judaic idea of the hermaphrodite as a divine origin because if Adam was created in the image of God and he was at once male and female, God would also be male and female. The implication that the deity was both male and female would contradict the idea of the trinity as the greatest possible reflection of divinity. This contradiction would also unsettle the status of unification with Christ as a way of acceding to the divine. And, it would unsettle the image of the king as, like Christ, both mortal and divine, to shift him to being like Adam, male and female. On the Judaic tradition and the Christian response, see Maryanne Cline Horowitz, "The Image of God in Man—is Woman Included?" in *The Harvard Theological Review* 72 (1979): 175–206.

29. Indeed, Eve may actually be the ultimate example of the constructed woman since she is, literally, constructed out of Adam. Garasse's text seems to replay this construction of her body and sexuality, underlining as well the constructedness of the king's body. For an argument concerning the constructed and symbolic nature of the sexual body (and not just the gendered one), see Judith Butler, *Gender Trouble, Feminism and the Subversion of Identity* (London: Routledge, 1990).

SLIPPERY BODIES IN SLIPPERY TEXTS

Any restoration of a Golden (prelapsarian) Age alluded to in Garasse's text is, finally, only a fantasy; the alliances did not fuse France and Spain just as the hermaphrodite did not fuse two male bodies.Rather, Garasse's *Royal Reception* remains firmly rooted in the post-Edenic world of the laborious reproduction and cultivation of truths (genders, sexualities, and bodies). In this textuality, the queen's body (or the slippery truth about it) emerges as a sign not simply of fertility, but of the arduous task of repressing the truth, here about royal treaty-marriages, that they are only about men and women in so far as marriage occasions the pleasurable playing out of mimetic and other relations among competing males. It is thus that the scene of Anne of Austria's sweat is a scene of alternating fantasies about the hetero-sociality and homosociality of political coupling in royal marriage. As Garasse's text shifts back and forth between these two idealities, it leaves us, finally, with a queen who is both female (ripe) and male (hot and moist). Such a queen is a figure whose symbolic malleability mirrors the adjudication occurring in Garasse's own text, a vacillation that we saw leads to a hermaphroditic or fused political body in which the female position, necessary, but threatening to defuse the situation, is elided and usurped.[30] We might say, therefore, that Garasse's text does not vacillate between the mortal and divine body of the sovereigns it describes, but between notions of political coupling and thus between symbolic agendas linked to gender and generation, and not to death and decay. Such vacillation might be enough to make a Hapsburg princess sweat on her wedding day, although we should note it does not seem to affect the French king. That is because the sweat displayed on Anne of Austria's face is not the sign of anxiety, but of the laborious effort of the symbolic apparatus of the text to reinstate order in/on the face of the emerging male fantasy of national reproduction.

Of course, we should not be surprised by such textual labor. As noted above, Garasse makes it clear early on in his account that reporting on "celebrated acts" (like royal marriage) is slippery, sweaty work, because of "the nature of truth, which is itself slippery [*glissante*] and of itself vanishes and disperses" (59) in "la presse," crowd scenes (or publishing) of large-scale (state) events. I might note now that the

---

30. Freccero makes a similar argument about the effacement of the feminine in her reading of the hermaphrodite in Rabelais (156) and suggests that the figure of two men bonded "may be symptomatic of a more widespread Renaissance thematics" (150).

slipperiness or sweatiness of truth in print accounts of important state rituals is akin to the slipperiness of the sexuality of political coupling as we have seen it in *La Royalle Reception*.[31] And I would underline, once more, that it is not the tension between the physical/mortal body and the necessarily divine image of monarchy that unveils this slippery truth, but rather the emergence of the fantasy of the hermaphroditic king and the desire or nostalgia for the homosocial pleasure of alliance, a fantasy and desire out of which also emerges the necessity of the hot, moist queen to make such sterile, albeit "marvelous" unions stick (by producing future monarchs who can then recouple with each other in future kinship exchanges, as would happen 45 years later in 1660). The sweet libidinous sweat that emerges on the face of Anne of Austria may now be read as the symptom of the labor behind trying to adjudicate those "truths" even as the fixed binary logic of truth (be it the fiction of the king's two bodies or that of the simple heterosociality of political coupling) is dissolved.

In conclusion, I would state that my goal in this essay has not been to refute the paradigm of the "King's 'Two Bodies'" that has, for so long, productively oriented our discussion of the fictions of sovereignty and the representation of kingship in early-modern Europe. Rather, my aim has been to emphasize dimensions which easily slip out of sight in privileging that model. Indeed, a close reading of Kantorowicz reveals that he is much less dogmatic about the separation of the king's two bodies than are many of us who adopt his paradigm. This is especially true in his discussion of France, which he sees as offering contradictory evidence to the fictions he uncovers for England.[32] It is thus that reading the sweat that emerges on Anne of Austria's face as the semiotic symptom of the homosociality of state-building, a dimension of treaty alliances masked by the elaborate choreography of a

31. Garasse's text brings to mind the comments Foucault makes in the introduction to his edition of the memoirs of the nineteenth-century hermaphrodite Herculine Barbin about the diffused relation between truth and sexuality. *Herculine Barbin*, trans. Richard McDougall (New York: Pantheon Books, 1980).

32. Kantorowicz actually argues that it is only in England that there is a "consistent" articulation of the theory of the "King's Two Bodies." He states clearly that in France, while there was an awareness "of the different manifestations of individual king and immortal Dignity," under absolutism such distinctions were often "blurred or even eliminated" (446). In *Les Origines culturelles de la révolution française* (Paris: Seuil, 1991), Roger Chartier further underlines the collapse between the king's sacred and profane bodies in an interesting and convincing discussion. For more French examples that seem to contradict Kantorowicz's (supposed) dualism for the case of death rituals, see Alain Boureau's *Le simple corps du roi* (Paris: Les Editions de Paris, 1988).

ritual of heterosocial bonding, invites us to reconsider symbolic activities, "la presse des grandes assemblées," most particularly their restaging by print culture, "la Presse des Imprimeurs." In so doing, we begin to notice that gender may ultimately found and confound representations of sovereignty in ways the Kantorowicz and Giesey paradigm may not have been able to account for because the fictions of kingship may have more complexity or slipperiness than just the cut and dry duality between the divine and mortal body (or the male and female). And, we also may recognize that, if the "truth" about political coupling is repressed in the fictions of royal marriage, the textual symptom of it is irrepressible. For the sweat that emerges officially in 1615, reemerges in 1660, albeit, once again, only momentarily, in the margin, in one text published first in a provincial city, Toulouse, and then in Paris, before being erased by critical paradigms, evaporating, leaving barely a trace, barely a streak, in print culture's reproduction of its fairy tale fantasy of sovereign power.

Contributors

ALAIN BOUREAU, Directeur d'études at the Ecole des Hautes Etudes en Sciences Sociales (Paris), is the author of *La Papesse Jeanne* (1988), *Le simple corps du roi* (1988), *Histoire d'un historien: Kantorowicz* (1990), and *L'événement sans fin* (1993).

KEVIN BROWNLEE is Professor of Romance Languages at the University of Pennsylvania where he teaches medieval French and Italian literature. He has recently completed a book on autobiography and literary models in Christine de Pizan.

ALAIN CANTILLON is Professeur agrégé de lettres modernes and is currently completing a book on Pascal's wager at the Ecole des Hautes Études en Sciences Sociales (Paris).

BRIGITTE CAZELLES is Professor of French at Stanford University. Author of *La faiblesse chez Gautier de Coinci* (1968), *Le Vain Siecle Guerpir* (with P. A. Johnson, 1979), *Le corps de sainteté* (1982), and *The Lady as Saint* (1991), she is currently completing an analysis of Chrétien's last romance entitled *The Unholy Grail: A Social Reading of Chrétien de Troyes's* Conte du Graal.

THOMAS M. GREENE is Frederick Clifford Ford Professor of English and Comparative Literature at Yale University. His most recent book is *Poésie et magie* (1991).

NOAH GUYNN is a Ph.D. candidate in the department of French at Yale University and is the editorial assistant of YALE FRENCH STUDIES.

FRANÇOISE JAOUËN is Assistant Professor of French at Yale University. She has just completed a book on the rhetoric of pleasure in the

YFS 86, *Corps Mystique, Corps Sacré: Textual Transfigurations of the Body from the Middle Ages to the Seventeenth Century,* ed. Françoise Jaouën and Benjamin Semple, © 1994 by Yale University.

seventeenth century and is currently preparing a volume on Preciosity and the Republic of Letters.

SARAH KAY is Lecturer of French at Cambridge University, and a Fellow of Girton College, Cambridge.

FRANK LESTRINGANT is professor of French and Renaissance Studies at the Université Charles de Gaulle (Lille, France). He is the author of *Le Huguenot et le sauvage* (1990), *L'Atelier du cosmographe* (1991; translated in 1994 under the title *Mapping the Renaissance World*), *Le Cannibale, grandeur et décadence* (1994), and numerous articles on Marot, Rabelais, Montaigne, and sixteenth-century travelers and geographers. He is currently completing a new edition of d'Aubigné's *Les Tragiques.*

HÉLÈNE MERLIN, Maître de Conférences in French literature at the Université d'Artois (Arras, France), has just completed *Le Public dans les lettres. Histoire d'un transfert (XVIIe siècle)* which is forthcoming, and is preparing another volume in collaboration with Christian Jouhaud: *Littérature et politique. Les termes de l'échange (XVIIe siècle).*

TIMOTHY MURRAY is Professor of English at Cornell University. He is the author of *Theatrical Legitimation: Allegories of Genius in Seventeenth-Century England and France* (1987) and *Like a Film: Ideological Fantasy on Screen, Camera, and Canvas* (1993).

BENJAMIN SEMPLE is Assistant Professor of French at Yale University and a medievalist. He is preparing a study of dreams and visions in French medieval literature.

ALLISON TAIT is a Ph.D. candidate in the department of French at Yale University.

ABBY ZANGER is Assistant Professor of French at Harvard University. She is the author of numerous articles on French classical theater and is currently completing a book entitled *Exploded Symbols: Imagining the Queen in the Marriage of Louis XIV.*

The following issues are available through **Yale University Press,** Customer Service Department, P.O. Box 209040, New Haven, CT 06520-9040.

63 The Pedagogical Imperative: Teaching as a Literary Genre (1982) $17.00

64 Montaigne: Essays in Reading (1983) $17.00

65 The Language of Difference: Writing in QUEBEC(ois) (1983) $17.00

66 The Anxiety of Anticipation (1984) $17.00

67 Concepts of Closure (1984) $17.00

68 Sartre after Sartre (1985) $17.00

69 The Lesson of Paul de Man (1985) $17.00

70 Images of Power: Medieval History/Discourse/ Literature (1986) $17.00

71 Men/Women of Letters: Correspondence (1986) $17.00

72 Simone de Beauvoir: Witness to a Century (1987) $17.00

73 Everyday Life (1987) $17.00

74 Phantom Proxies (1988) $17.00

75 The Politics of Tradition: Placing Women in French Literature (1988) $17.00

Special Issue: After the Age of Suspicion: The French Novel Today (1989) $17.00

76 Autour de Racine: Studies in Intertextuality (1989) $17.00

77 Reading the Archive: On Texts and Institutions (1990) $17.00

78 On Bataille (1990) $17.00

79 Literature and the Ethical Question (1991) $17.00

Special Issue: Contexts: Style and Value in Medieval Art and Literature (1991) $17.00

80 Baroque Topographies: Literature/History/ Philosophy $17.00

81 On Leiris (1992) $17.00

82 Post/Colonial Conditions Vol. 1 (1993) $17.00

83 Post/Colonial Conditions Vol. 2 (1993) $17.00

84 Boundaries: Writing and Drawing (1993) $17.00

85 Discourses of Jewish Identity in 20th-Century France (1994) $17.00

Special subscription rates are available on a calendar year basis (2 issues per year):
Individual subscriptions $24.00   Institutional subscriptions $28.00

ORDER FORM   **Yale University Press,** P.O. Box 209040, New Haven, CT 06520-9040

I would like to purchase the following individual issues:

_____

_____

For individual issue, please add postage and handling:
Single issue, United States $2.75   Each additional issue $.50
Connecticut residents please add sales tax of 6%
Single issue, foreign countries $5.00   Each additional issue $1.00

Payment of $_____ is enclosed (including sales tax if applicable).

Mastercard no. _____

4-digit bank no._____Expiration date_____

VISA no._____Expiration date _____

Signature _____

SHIP TO _____

_____

_____

See the next page for ordering other back issues. Yale French Studies is also available through Xerox University Microfilms, 300 North Zeeb Road, Ann Arbor, MI 48106.

The following issues are still available through the **Yale French Studies Office,** 2504A Yale Station, New Haven, CT 06520.

19/20 Contemporary Art $6.00
33 Shakespeare $6.00
35 Sade $6.00
38 The Classical Line $6.00
39 Literature and Revolution $6.00
42 Zola $8.00
43 The Child's Part $8.00
44 Paul Valéry $8.00

45 Language as Action $8.00
46 From Stage to Street $6.00
47 Image & Symbol in the Renaissance $6.00
52 Graphesis $8.00
53 African Literature $6.00
54 Mallarmé $8.00
57 Locus in Modern French Fiction: Space, Landscape, Decor $9.00

58 In Memory of Jacques Ehrmann $9.00
59 Rethinking History $9.00
61 Toward a Theory of Description $9.00
62 Feminist Readings: French Texts/American Contexts $9.00

Add for postage & handling

One-Two Issues, United States $2.90 (Priority Mail)
Single issue, United States $1.75 (Third Class)   Each additional issue $.50
Single issue, foreign countries $2.50   Each additional issue $1.50

YALE FRENCH STUDIES, P.O. Box 20851, New Haven, Connecticut 06520-8251

A check made payable to YFS is enclosed. Please send me the following issue(s):

Issue no.   Title   Price

_____

_____

Postage & handling   _____

Total   _____

Name_____

Number/Street _____

City_____State _____Zip_____

The following issues are now available through Kraus Reprint Company, Route 100, Millwood, N. Y. 10546.

1 Critical Bibliography of Existentialism
2 Modern Poets
3 Criticism & Creation
4 Literature & Ideas
5 The Modern Theatre
6 France and World Literature
7 André Gide
8 What's Novel in the Novel
9 Symbolism
10 French-American Literature Relationships
11 Eros, Variations...
12 God & the Writer
13 Romanticism Revisited
14 Motley: Today's French Theater
15 Social & Political France
16 Foray through Existentialism

17 The Art of the Cinema
18 Passion & the Intellect, or Malraux
21 Poetry Since the Liberation
22 French Education
24 Midnight Novelists
25 Albert Camus
26 The Myth of Napoleon
27 Women Writers
28 Rousseau
29 The New Dramatists
30 Sartre
31 Surrealism
32 Paris in Literature
34 Proust
48 French Freud
51 Approaches to Medieval Romance

36/37 Structuralism has been reprinted by Doubleday as an Anchor Book.
55/56 Literature and Psychoanalysis has been reprinted by Johns Hopkins University Press, and can be ordered through Customer Service, Johns Hopkins University Press, Baltimore, MD 21218.

The Popular Culture of Modern Art

Picasso, Duchamp, and Avant-Gardism, 1909-1917

Jeffrey Weiss

This provocative book explores the deeply ambiguous relation between modern art and popular culture, focusing on the work of Picasso and Duchamp in France in the first two decades of this century. 151 illus. $45.00

Atget's Seven Albums

Molly Nesbit

This first complete reproduction of Eugène Atget's seven photographic albums of Paris at the height of the city's belle époque.

"At once art criticism, social history, biography and cultural theory [this book]...is a rich and provocative study."—Richard Locke, *The Wall Street Journal*

577 illus. $30.00 **paper**

Selected as a Notable Book of the Year (1993) by The New York Times Book Review

Imagining Paris

Exile, Writing, and American Identity

J. Gerald Kennedy

This book explores the imaginative process of five expatriate Americans—Gertrude Stein, Ernest Hemingway, Henry Miller, F. Scott Fitzgerald, and Djuna Barnes—by showing how the experience of living in Paris shaped their careers and literary works.

17 illus. $15.00 **paper**

Louis XVI

John Hardman

"Thorough research into primary sources enables [Hardman] to give us a clear picture of what Louis thought and felt and why he tried to rule as he did. The result is not just sound scholarship but a book that reads like a first-rate murder mystery."—Olivier Bernier, *The Wall Street Journal* 24 illus. $16.00 **paper**

The Fabrication of Louis XIV

Peter Burke

This engrossing book gives an account of contemporary representations of Louis XIV—in paintings and engravings, medals and sculptures, plays, ballets, and operas—to show how the making of a royal image illuminates the relationship between art and power.

"[A] lucid study of art and power in the *ancien régime*."—Marina Warner, *The Independent on Sunday* 90 illus. $15.00 **paper**

To order call 1-800-YUP-READ

Yale University Press

P.O. Box 209040, New Haven, CT 06520